The One Show

The One Show: Advertising's Best Print, Radio, TV

Volume 3

A Presentation of
The One Club for Art and Copy

Published by
American Showcase, Inc.
New York

The One Club
for Art and Copy

Norman Tanen
PRESIDENT

Peter Hirsch
CHAIRMAN, PUBLICATION COMMITTEE

Beverley Daniels
DIRECTOR

American Showcase

Tennyson Schad
CHAIRMAN & CO–PUBLISHER

Ira Shapiro
PRESIDENT & CO–PUBLISHER

Christopher Curtis
DIRECTOR OF SPECIAL PROJECTS

Seymour Chwast and Richard Mantel
Push Pin Studios, New York
DESIGNERS

Terry Berkowitz and Peter Ross
Push Pin Studios
LAYOUT AND DESIGN PRODUCTION

Mechanical Marvel, New York
MECHANICALS

Elise Sachs and Beverley Daniels
EDITORIAL COORDINATION

Sunlight Graphics, New York
TYPESETTING

Dai Nippon Printing Co., Ltd., Tokyo, Japan
COLOR SEPARATIONS, PRINTING AND BINDING

PUBLISHED BY
American Showcase, Inc.
724 Fifth Avenue
New York, New York 10019
(212) 245-0981

IN ASSOCIATION WITH
The One Club for Art and Copy, Inc.
251 East 50th Street
New York, New York 10022
(212) 935-0121

U.S. AND CANADIAN BOOK DISTRIBUTION:
Robert Silver Associates
95 Madison Avenue
New York, New York 10016
(212) 686-5630

OVERSEAS BOOK DISTRIBUTION:
American Showcase, Inc.
724 Fifth Avenue
New York, New York 10019
(212) 245-0981

First Printing.
ISBN 0-960-2628-3-0
ISSN 0273-2033

Contents

President's Message

I've been around long enough to remember the "non-team" concept.

For those of you who haven't been around that long, the way it worked then was that "copy" would mysteriously appear in the "artist's" office (me) complete with visual suggestions. Of course I knew there was a Copy Writer someplace in the agency as well as an Account Executive who was supposed to "sell" the ad.

Only I never met them.

When I discovered Doyle Dane Bernbach and the "team concept" in 1960, I felt like I had journeyed to Mecca.

It's been an incredible 21 years now. Twenty-one years of experiencing the comforting feeling of support from working with an assortment of wonderful copy counterparts.

It seems to me, with all of us having worked so well together, teaching each other, that we are starting to learn each other's jobs.

Art Directors are writing copy. And Copy Writers are art directing.

Is there a message here?

You bet!

I see over the next ten years the acceptance of The Art Director/Writer or The Writer/Art Director.

If you've been a closet team of one—come out, come out whoever you are.

And if you've been shyly "thinking about" it, stop thinking and just do it.

And to all you young Bill Bernbachs, David Ogilvys, and Mary Lawrences, whether you be a potential Writer/Art Director or an Art Director/Writer, study this book as if your life depended on it.

At the very least, your future livelihood does.

Norman Tanen

1981 Gold & Silver Awards

Crunchy on the outside, hard in the middle.

Polo.

Prices from £3,115. Brochures from Sales Enquiries, Volkswagen (GB) Ltd., Yeomans Drive, Blakelands, Milton Keynes, MK14 5AN. Tel. (0908) 679121. Export Sales: 95 Baker Street, London, W1M 1FB. Tel. 01-486 8411.

1 GOLD

WHEN YOU BUILD THE RIGHT KIND OF CAR YOU DON'T HAVE TO PAY PEOPLE TO BUY IT.

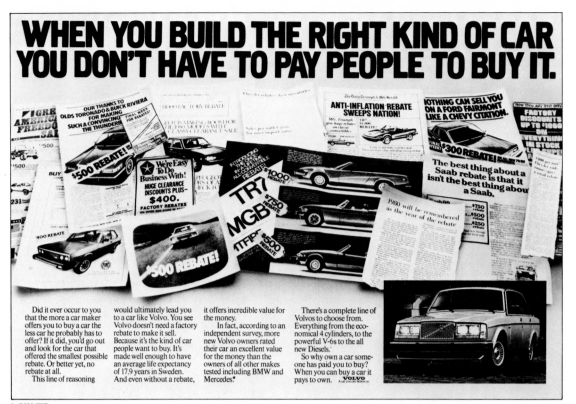

Did it ever occur to you that the more a car maker offers you to buy a car the less car he probably has to offer? If it did, you'd go out and look for the car that offered the smallest possible rebate. Or better yet, no rebate at all.

This line of reasoning would ultimately lead you to a car like Volvo. You see Volvo doesn't need a factory rebate to make it sell. Because it's the kind of car people want to buy. It's made well enough to have an average life expectancy of 17.9 years in Sweden. And even without a rebate, it offers incredible value for the money.

In fact, according to an independent survey, more new Volvo owners rated their car an excellent value for the money than the owners of all other makes tested including BMW and Mercedes.*

There's a complete line of Volvos to choose from. Everything from the economical 4 cylinders, to the powerful V-6s to the all new Diesels.†

So why own a car someone has paid you to buy? When you can buy a car it pays to own.

VOLVO
A car you can believe in.

Consumer Newspaper
Over 600 Lines
Campaign

3 GOLD
Art Director:
Jim Perretti
Writers:
Frank Fleizach
Larry Cadman
Designer:
Jim Perretti
Photographer:
Phil Mazzurco
Client:
Volvo
Agency:
Scali, McCabe, Sloves

4 SILVER
Art Directors:
Mark Yustein
Bob Phillips
Ron Arnold
Writers:
Neil Drossman
John Russo
Photographers:
Phil Mazzurco
Photographic House
Client:
Einstein Moomjy
Agency:
Drossman Yustein Clowes

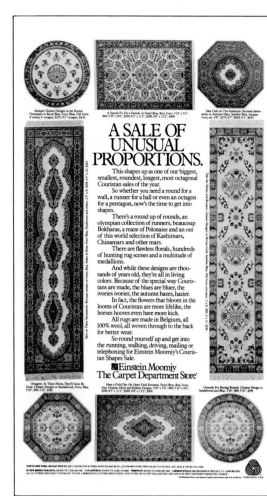

**Consumer Newspaper
600 Lines or Less
Single**

5 GOLD
Art Director:
Gordon Trembath
Writer:
Lionel Hunt
Photographer:
Stock-Austral
Client:
Woman's Day
Agency:
The Campaign Palace/Australia

6 SILVER
Art Director:
George White
Writer:
Marc Deschenes
Designer:
George White
Photographer:
Jim Wood
Client:
Joseph Herman Shoe
Agency:
**Humphrey Browning MacDougall
Boston**

How to kill a baby.

It's easy. All you do is walk up to it. It won't run away.

Then, as it looks up at you trustingly, mistaking you for its mother, you smash in its skull with a baseball bat.

That's what happens to baby seals in Canada every year in a bloody ritual that lasts six weeks.

In Japan they do it a different way. They herd dolphins into the shallows, wait for the tide to leave them stranded, then go through the same grisly process.

Then there's the whales. You know what happens to them.

Doing it is dead easy if your mind is warped enough. Stopping it is a whole lot harder, but there is something you can do.

In this week's Woman's Day we're running a thought provoking article on what's happening to these beautiful creatures.

We're also running a simple competition that you and your children can enter. All you have to do is tell us in less than twenty words what the seals, the dolphins or the whales would say to us if they could speak.

There are cash prizes, but far more importantly, for every entry in the competition Woman's Day will donate 10 cents to Greenpeace to help their work in bringing this ghastly business to a halt.

Look for this week's Woman's Day. It's the one with the baby seal on the cover, seconds before it dies.

Woman's Day.

9 YEARS WITHOUT TAKING A LEAK.

John Stout of Monroe, Michigan has had a pair of waterproof Survivors® for 7 years. Ernest Krieger of Boston, Massachusetts has had a pair for 16 years. And they haven't had a damp toe yet.

How can boots last so long and still keep your feet warm and dry? Well, we don't take any short cuts making them for one thing. Haven't for over 100 years. And never will. So if you knock the dirt off and waterproof your Survivors every now and then, they'll keep your feet cozy and perfectly dry for a long, long time.

How long? We don't really know. But you just might set a new record.

HERMAN SURVIVORS
BOOTS THAT NEVER SAY DIE.™

STORE NAME

6 SILVER

**Consumer Newspaper
600 Lines or Less
Campaign**

7 GOLD
Art Director:
Roy Grace
Writer:
Tom Yobbagy
Designer:
Roy Grace
Photographer:
David Pruitt
Client:
IBM Office Products Division
Agency:
Doyle Dane Bernbach

8 SILVER
Art Director:
George White
Writer:
Marc Deschenes
Designer:
George White
Photographer:
Jim Wood
Client:
Joseph Herman Shoe
Agency:
**Humphrey Browning MacDougall
Boston**

Make no mistake.

To correct just a single typing error on an original document—using correction paper takes 8 seconds.

Using an eraser, 10 seconds.

Correction fluid, as much as 25 seconds.

But using an IBM Correcting Selectric, Typewriter takes only 3.6 seconds.

Compared to correction paper, that's a time-saving of 55%. Compared to an eraser, a time-saving of 64%. Correction fluid, as much as 86%.

When you consider the number of errors made each year, the IBM Correcting Selectric produces real savings.

It also produces error-free work—because it actually lifts errors clean off the page.

Get an IBM Correcting Selectric.

To order, call your local IBM Office Products Division Representative at 901-529-6276. Or call IBM *Direct* toll-free at 800-631-5582, Ext. 12.

(If you own an IBM electric typewriter, be sure to ask about IBM's attractive trade-in allowance.)

The IBM Correcting Selectric: With the cost of everything else going up, it's nice to know you can bring the cost of mistakes down.

IBM.
**Correcting Selectric, Typewriter
901-529-6276**

The three most common mistakes in typing.

The eraser. Correction paper. Correction fluid.

It's not just that they leave tell-tale signs. They take extra time. And time is money.

To correct just a single typing error on an original document—correction paper takes 8 seconds.

The eraser, 10 seconds.

Correction fluid, as much as 25 seconds.

But an IBM Correcting Selectric, Typewriter takes only 3.6 seconds.

That's twice as fast as correction paper. About 3 times faster than the eraser. And as much as 7 times faster than correction fluid.

When you consider the number of errors made each year, the IBM Correcting Selectric produces real savings.

It also produces error-free work—because it actually lifts errors clean off the page.

To order, call your local IBM Office Products Division Representative at 405-272-1432. Or call IBM *Direct* toll-free at 800-631-5582, Ext. 11.

(If you own an IBM electric typewriter, be sure to ask about IBM's attractive trade-in allowance.)

Get an IBM Correcting Selectric. And correct the error of your ways.

IBM.
**Correcting Selectric, Typewriter
405-272-1432**

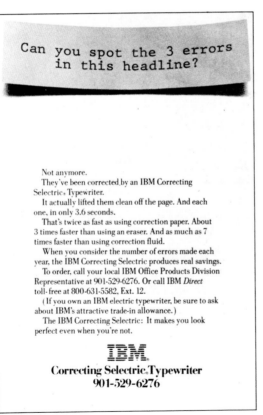

Can you spot the 3 errors in this headline?

Not anymore.

They've been corrected by an IBM Correcting Selectric, Typewriter.

It actually lifted them clean off the page. And each one, in only 3.6 seconds.

That's twice as fast as using correction paper. About 3 times faster than using an eraser. And as much as 7 times faster than using correction fluid.

When you consider the number of errors made each year, the IBM Correcting Selectric produces real savings.

To order, call your local IBM Office Products Division Representative at 901-529-6276. Or call IBM *Direct* toll-free at 800-631-5582, Ext. 12.

(If you own an IBM electric typewriter, be sure to ask about IBM's attractive trade-in allowance.)

The IBM Correcting Selectric: It makes you look perfect even when you're not.

IBM.
**Correcting Selectric, Typewriter
901-529-6276**

7 GOLD

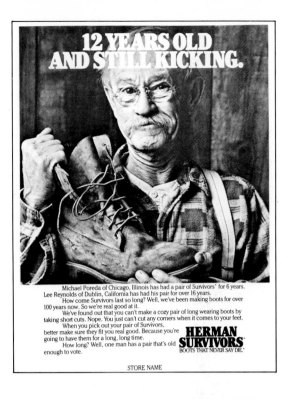

12 YEARS OLD AND STILL KICKING.

Michael Poreda of Chicago, Illinois has had a pair of Survivors® for 6 years. Lee Reynolds of Dublin, California has had his pair for over 16 years.

How come Survivors last so long? Well, we've been making boots for over 100 years now. So we're real good at it.

We've found out that you can't make a cozy pair of long wearing boots by taking short cuts. Nope. You just can't cut any corners when it comes to your feet.

When you pick out your pair of Survivors, better make sure they fit you real good. Because you're going to have them for a long, long time.

How long? Well, one man has a pair that's old enough to vote.

HERMAN SURVIVORS
BOOTS THAT NEVER SAY DIE.®

STORE NAME

AFTER 7 YEARS, THE TONGUE STARTS TO CURL.

Alan Mokrzycki of Northampton, Massachusetts has had a pair of Survivors® for 9 years. Mario Vitale of Springfield, Illinois has had his pair for almost 12 years. Survivors seem to last forever.

But we don't want you to think that nothing ever goes wrong with them. About every four years the laces break. And after 10 years or so you got to expect a few stitches to come a little loose.

But if you take good care of your Survivors, they'll stay cozy and take real good care of your feet. For how long? Heaven only knows.

HERMAN SURVIVORS
BOOTS THAT NEVER SAY DIE.®

STORE NAME

9 YEARS WITHOUT TAKING A LEAK.

John Stout of Monroe, Michigan has had a pair of waterproof Survivors® for 7 years. Ernest Krieger of Boston, Massachusetts has had a pair for 16 years. And they haven't had a damp toe yet.

How can boots last so long and still keep your feet warm and dry? Well, we don't take any short cuts making them for one thing. Haven't for over 100 years. And never will. So if you knock the dirt off and waterproof your Survivors every now and then, they'll keep your feet cozy and perfectly dry for a long, long time.

How long? We don't really know. But you just might set a new record.

HERMAN SURVIVORS
BOOTS THAT NEVER SAY DIE.®

STORE NAME

8 SILVER

9 GOLD

10 SILVER

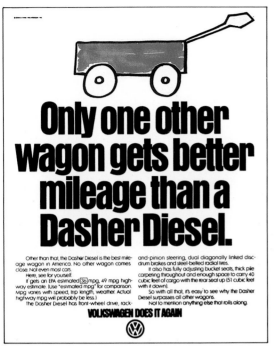

Only one other wagon gets better mileage than a Dasher Diesel.

Other than that, the Dasher Diesel is the best mileage wagon in America. No other wagon comes close. Not even most cars.

Here, see for yourself.

It gets an EPA estimated [36] mpg, 49 mpg highway estimate. (Use "estimated mpg" for comparison. Mpg varies with speed, trip length, weather. Actual highway mpg will probably be less.)

The Dasher Diesel has front-wheel drive, rack-and-pinion steering, dual diagonally linked disc-drum brakes and steel-belted radial tires.

It also has fully adjusting bucket seats, thick pile carpeting throughout and enough space to carry 40 cubic feet of cargo with the rear seat up (51 cubic feet with it down).

So with all that, it's easy to see why the Dasher Diesel surpasses all other wagons.

Not to mention anything else that rolls along.

VOLKSWAGEN DOES IT AGAIN

11 GOLD

18.7 YEARS CITY.

18.7 YEARS HIGHWAY.

A lot of car makers today are trying to sell you economy with EPA figures. But at Volvo, we believe true economy isn't just more miles per gallon. It's more years per car.

So if you just want to buy less gas and save a little money, look at EPA figures. But if you like the idea of buying fewer cars and saving a lot, consider Volvo's figures.

Average life expectancy of a Volvo in Sweden. Driving conditions in the U.S. may differ. So your Volvo may not last as long. Then again, it may last longer. **VOLVO** A car you can believe in.

12 SILVER

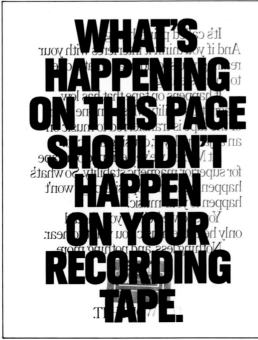

13 GOLD

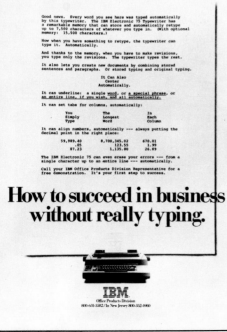

"WE'D NEVER PUT OUR BROWNIES IN A LITTLE TIN BOX."

Carole Levine, Brownie Troop Leader.

As you can see, the leaders of Brownie Troop #1900 in Los Angeles have a lot of responsibility. So when it came to choosing troop transportation, they were very tough cookies.

As one of them puts it, "I must have frustrated half the car salesmen in southern California looking for the right station wagon. The ones I looked at were so small and tinny. No way would I ever feel safe driving a bunch of girls around in any of them."

One by one, each of these Brownie leaders ended up at a Volvo dealer. And today, Troop #1900

travels around in a Volvo wagon train.

According to one of the other leaders, "I was sold on the Volvo wagon the minute I saw it. I knew the girls would fit very comfortably inside and there would be plenty of room left for their gear. When I drove the Volvo, it wasn't all over the road like other wagons I'd driven. It offered great visibility. And it just plain felt solid and safe."

If you're looking for a station wagon you can feel good about putting your kids in, join Troop #1900. Buy a Volvo. **VOLVO** A car you can believe in.

"ANYONE WHO'S THINKING OF SPENDING $24,000 FOR A LUXURY CAR SHOULD TALK TO A PSYCHIATRIST."

—Dr. John Boston, psychiatrist and Volvo owner, Austin, Texas

John Boston, a Texas psychiatrist, owns a '73 Volvo. He bought that Volvo because, as he puts it: "I had admired what Volvo had done in the area of safety. The car seemed well-built. It offered solid European craftsmanship without the inflated price."

We wanted Dr. Boston's opinion of the new Volvo GLE, which has a full assortment of luxury features as standard equipment—and a price tag thousands of dollars below that of the well-known German luxury sedan.

"It's an excellent value. In my opinion, the individual buying this car would have a strong, unsuppressed need

to get his or her money's worth. He or she would probably also have a strong enough self-image not to need a blatant status symbol."

When we told him that some people were actually paying five to ten thousand dollars more for a luxury car, Dr. Boston's response was characteristically succinct.

"That's not using your head."

Finally, we asked Dr. Boston if, when he was ready for a new car, he'd consider the Volvo GLE for himself.

"I'd be crazy if I didn't." **VOLVO** A car you can believe in.

18.7 YEARS CITY.

18.7 YEARS HIGHWAY.

A lot of car makers today are trying to sell you economy with EPA figures. But at Volvo, we believe true economy isn't just more miles per gallon. It's more years per car.

So if you just want to buy less gas and save a little money, look at EPA figures. But if you like the idea of buying fewer cars and saving a lot, consider Volvo's figures. *Average life expectancy of a Volvo in Sweden. Driving conditions in the U.S. may differ. So your Volvo may not last as long. Then again, it may last longer. **VOLVO** A car you can believe in.

15 GOLD

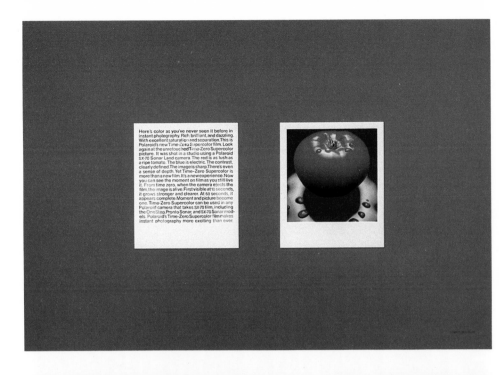

Here's color as you've never seen it before in instant photography. Rich, brilliant, and dazzling. With excellent saturation and separation. This is Polaroid's new Time-Zero Supercolor film. Look again at the unretouched Time-Zero Supercolor picture. It was shot in a studio using a Polaroid SX-70 Sonar Land camera. The red is as lush as a ripe tomato. The blue is electric. The contrast, clearly defined. The image is sharp. There's even a sense of depth. Yet Time-Zero Supercolor is more than a new film. It's a new experience. Now you can see the moment on film as you still live it. From time zero, when the camera ejects the film, the image is alive. First visible at 10 seconds, it grows stronger and clearer. At 60 seconds, it appears complete. Moment and picture become one. Time-Zero Supercolor can be used in any Polaroid camera that takes SX-70 film, including the OneStep, Pronto Sonar, and SX-70 Sonar models. Polaroid's Time-Zero Supercolor film makes instant photography more exciting than ever.

Look closely. This is Polaroid's new Time-Zero Supercolor film. It develops twice as fast as any other instant color film. Now you can see the moment on film as you still live it. Beginning at time zero, when the camera ejects the film, the image is alive. You first see it at 10 seconds. At 30 seconds, it's getting stronger, clearer. And at 60 seconds, it appears complete. Moment and picture become one. Look again at the unretouched Time-Zero Supercolor picture. It was shot in a studio with a Polaroid SX-70 Sonar Land camera. The image is sharp. The colors are brilliant and dazzling. With excellent saturation, superb separation. Colors that once seemed impossible to obtain in instant photography are now possible. Colors that once seemed to melt together are now pure and distinct. Time-Zero Supercolor can be used in any Polaroid camera that takes SX-70 film, including the OneStep, Pronto Sonar and SX-70 Sonar models. Polaroid's Time-Zero Supercolor film makes instant photography more exciting than ever.

At last, the time difference between taking a picture and seeing a picture has been reduced to merely seconds. This is Polaroid's new Time-Zero Supercolor film, the world's fastest-developing color film. From the instant this new film leaves the camera, the image is alive. You first see it at 10 seconds. At 30 seconds, it's growing stronger, clearer. And at 60 seconds, it appears complete. Suddenly, the moment and picture become one. Look closely at the Time-Zero Supercolor picture. It's unretouched. The image is sharp. The colors are rich and bright. With superb saturation and separation. It was shot by a professional using a Polaroid SX-70 Sonar Land camera. Now you can get the same dazzling color and clarity because new Time-Zero Supercolor can be used with any Polaroid camera that takes SX-70 film, including the OneStep, Pronto Sonar and SX-70 Sonar models. Time-Zero Supercolor is a new experience. Its color, sharpness, and developing speed make instant photography more exciting than ever.

**Consumer Magazine
Less than One Page
B/W or Color
Single**

17 GOLD
Art Director:
Dennis D'Amico
Writer:
Tom Messner
Photographer:
Hunter Freeman
Client:
Pentax
Agency:
Ally & Gargano

18 SILVER
Art Director:
George White
Writer:
Marc Deschenes
Designer:
George White
Photographer:
Jim Wood
Client:
Joseph Herman Shoe
Agency:
**Humphrey Browning MacDougall
Boston**

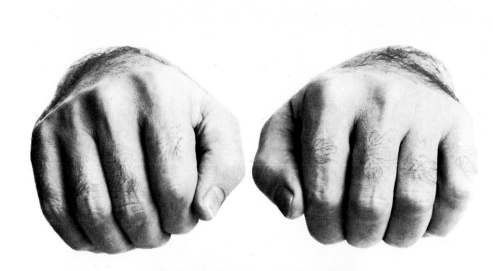

WHICH HAND HAS THE PENTAX CAMERA?

The one on the right holds the Pentax Auto 110, the only 110 SLR camera with interchangeable lenses.

But, if you guessed the one on the left, you weren't far off. It holds the optional wide-angle and telephoto lenses.

The purpose of this demonstration? To show how small and convenient a high quality, SLR camera system can be.

If you've ever missed a great photograph because you didn't feel like lugging a big camera around, you now know what to do: Just get your hands on an Auto 110. **THE PENTAX AUTO 110.**

17 GOLD

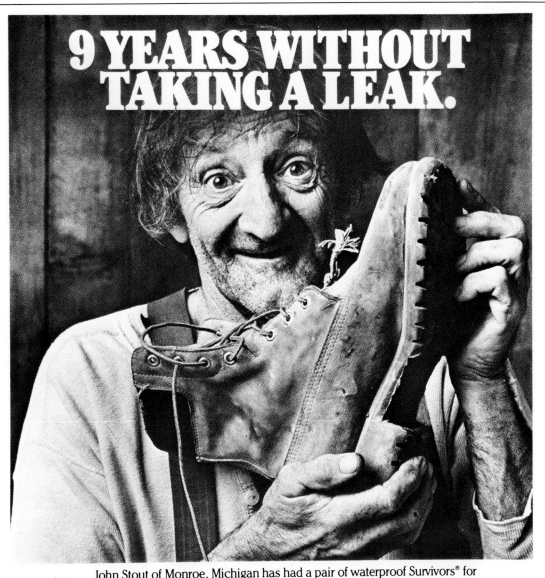

9 YEARS WITHOUT TAKING A LEAK.

John Stout of Monroe, Michigan has had a pair of waterproof Survivors® for 7 years. Ernest Krieger of Boston, Massachusetts has had a pair for 16 years. And they haven't had a damp toe yet.

How can boots last so long and still keep your feet warm and dry? Well, we don't take any short cuts making them for one thing. Haven't for over 100 years. And never will. So if you knock the dirt off and waterproof your Survivors every now and then, they'll keep your feet cozy and perfectly dry for a long, long time.

How long? We don't really know. But you just might set a new record.

HERMAN SURVIVORS®
BOOTS THAT NEVER SAY DIE.™

STORE NAME

19 GOLD
Art Director:
Phil Silvestri
Writers:
**Jay Taub
Harold Karp**
Designer:
Phil Silvestri
Photographer:
James Moore
Client:
Alexandra de Markoff
Agency:
**Della Femina, Travisano
& Partners**

20 SILVER
Art Director:
Simon Kentish
Writer:
Tony Bodinetz
Photographer:
Simon Kentish
Client:
The Kirkwood Company
Agency:
The Kirkwood Company/London

de MARKOFF.
FOR THE WOMAN WHO PLAYS HARD TO FORGET.

It's an attitude.
A certain unpredictability.
A style that dares, even these days, to be elegant. A style that no one can second guess. Or forget.
It comes easy to you. With Countess Isserlyn Makeup.
A precision-blended foundation that's as weightless as your own skin. With a radiant finish that gets things started.
And like you, it just won't quit. It actually looks better as the day goes on. Countess Isserlyn by Alexandra de Markoff. In liquid and creme.
They'll all want to know you. By heart.

"In 1970 I started an advertising agency. I liked it so much, I think I'll do it again."

Ten years ago, two ambitions led me to create the Kirkwood Company.

The first was to make money.

(As you can see, this advertisement is going to be honest, as well as decent, legal and truthful.)

The second was to build an agency that would consistently command respect, from its clients and its competitors, above all for the quality of its work.

I'm still working at ambition number one. But I have finally created the kind of agency I always wanted.

Which is just as well.

Because the three chaps who can (and do) claim a good deal of the credit for the work we've been producing and the business we've been winning recently, and who have for some time shared with me the management of the agency, are now ready, as I was ten years ago, to do their own thing.

(I believe that's the current argot.)

So, on the principle of 'If you can't stop 'em, back 'em', I've decided to set them up in a new agency of their own.

The two gentlemen to my left in the picture will be Joint Managing Directors.

John Horner, who joined me from Leo Burnett five years ago, is next to me; next to him is Jonathan White, who learned his trade at CDP and has been with Kirkwood's since 1976.

On my right is Tony Bodinetz. He's been an outstanding Creative Director for me. Despite the fact that Jonathan and John have saddled him with the additional title of Vice Chairman, I'm sure he'll do a great job for them, too.

By the way, John and Jonathan and Tony have kindly asked me to join them in their new agency as Executive Chairman.

An offer I was delighted to accept.

On two conditions.

The first was that my clients and my agency should know about, and approve of, the new arrangement. (They do.)

The second was that the new agency should not make the mistake others have found so tempting (no names, no pack drill) of inventing a new name in order to immortalise the new management team.

(Horner, Kirkwood and White sounds reasonable enough, but Bodinetz? Most people can't even pronounce it, let alone spell it.)

They generously agreed to my conditions. So, on June 30th, after ten exciting years, the old Kirkwood Company closes its doors. To be replaced, on July 1st, with the new Kirkwood Company.

I look forward to enjoying my next ten years in the business as much as I have enjoyed my last.

Ronnie Kirkwood

The Kirkwood Company, 23 Buckingham Gate, London SW1. Telephone 01 828 8010.

21 GOLD

The most famous German word in the English language.

Beck's. The number one imported German beer.

22 SILVER

**Trade
Less than One Page
B/W or Color
Single**

23 GOLD
Art Director:
Ed Albrecht
Writer:
Ken Rabasca
Client:
WE'RE Associates
Agency:
Greenstone & Rabasca

24 SILVER
Art Director:
Felix Burgos
Writer:
Kathleen Angotti
Client:
Einstein Moomjy
Agency:
Drossman Yustein Clowes

23 GOLD

EINSTEIN MOOMJY NEEDS A LIVE WIRE WITH WALL TO WALL CONNECTIONS.

Einstein Moomjy, the Carpet Department Store, is looking to sign a Contract Salesperson on the dotted line.

A special someone who combines the meticulous ability of an engineer with a personality that could sell ice to an Eskimo.

Someone well installed in the carpeting industry. Someone with a great following. But someone with a great follow through.

Here's an opportunity to go from door to door with the best and widest assortment of floor to floors.

Working for a company with a growing number of store to stores.

For Einstein Moomjy, with its four stores in New Jersey, is opening a new Moom over Manhattan.

So if you're a company man looking for a new company, give Jim Allan a call at (201) 575-0895 and get your foot in the right door.

**Einstein Moomjy
The Carpet Department Store**

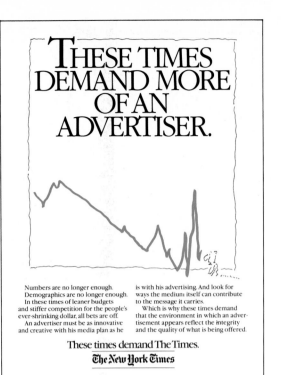

25 GOLD

FOLLOW YOUNG CASSIUS TO HIS FALL AT CAESARS PALACE.

We've known him for a long time. In fact we first met him during Dwight Eisenhower's last term. And since then he's taken us down so many emotionally winding roads that we don't even bother to ask where we're going anymore—we just follow.

There are some who want to believe he's nothing more than a balloon. There are others who want to believe he was born in a manger in Louisville, Ky.

But the one thing we all believe, is that it the ring he was the consummate artist...and out of the ring the consummate con artist.

This then is Cassius Clay, a.k.a. Muhammad Ali, Boxer, Crusader, Entertainer.

And this November, Inside Sports examines the many sides of this man by asking some famous people to go deep inside themselves. People like Alex Haley, Jesse Jackson, Hunter Thompson, Dave Anderson, Peter Bonventre and Reggie Jackson, to name a few. Not one of them takes his typewriter to a neutral corner.

This then is Inside Sports, which in this same November issue features a candid interview with Wilt Chamberlain. In the article Wilt talks about Bill Russell (though he hasn't spoken to him in 11 years). And Kareem Abdul-Jabbar (of whom Wilt says, "In my sleep I could out-rebound Abdul-Jabbar").

We also list baseball's 10 smartest free agent deals. And the 10 dumbest. And there's an article on the NFL's strongest man (who believes that a gorilla would not make a good offensive lineman because it takes more than brawn.) Plus, you'll find reports on the Denver Broncos, the Hot Stove League, LSU, Gordie Howe and California quarterbacks.

Of course, what you won't find in Inside Sports are articles on short shooting, fang gliding or bird watching in the Baffin Islands. That's because we cover the basics. And that's why in only 7 months we've managed to attract over 3,000,000 readers.

You see, other sports magazines might talk about giving you in-depth coverage of the major sports, but every month at Inside Sports... we make an issue out of it.

INSIDE SPORTS

WE COVER A SIDE OF SPORTS NOBODY ELSE IS COVERING. THE INSIDE.

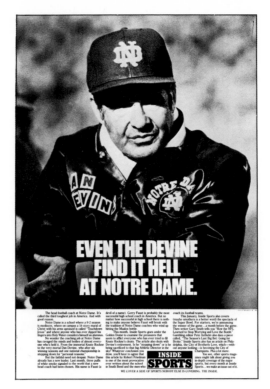

EVEN THE DEVINE FIND IT HELL AT NOTRE DAME.

The head football coach at Notre Dame. It's called the third toughest job in America. And with good reason.

Notre Dame is a school where a 9-2 season is mediocre, where on campus a 14-story mural of Christ with his arms upraised is called "Touchdown Jesus" and where anyone who has ever dipped his fingers into Holy Water considers himself an alumnus.

No wonder the coaching job at Notre Dame has ravaged the minds and bodies of almost everyone who's held it. From the immortal Knute Rockne to the very mortal Dan Devine, who after six winning seasons and one national championship is stepping down for "personal reasons."

But the faithful need not despair. Notre Dame already has a new leader. Last month, three puffs of white smoke signaled to the world that a new head coach had been chosen. His name is Faust (a devil of a name). Gerry Faust is probably the most successful high school coach in America. But no matter how successful in high school there is nothing to make anyone believe Faust will break with the tradition of Notre Dame coaches who wind up hitting the Maalox bottle.

This month, Inside Sports goes under the Golden Dome to examine the pressures that seem to affect everyone who has ever tried to fill Knute Rockne's cleats. The article also deals with Devine's settlement. Is he "stepping down" or is he being sacrificed so that big Athletic Director in the sky? Whatever conclusion you draw, you'll have to agree that this article by Robert Friedman is one of the most provocative ever written about the school in South Bend and the men who coach its football teams.

This January, Inside Sports also covers (maybe smothers is a better word) the spectacle of the Super Bowl. For starters, we're announcing the winner of the game...a month before the game. Then writer Gary Smith tells you "How the NFL Learned to Stop Worrying and Love the Bomb." Gambling editor Pete Axthelm also does a piece called, "The Season's Last Big Bet: Going for Broke." Inside Sports also has an article on Philadelphia, the City of Brotherly Love, which—without anyone looking—is becoming the City of Champions. Plus a lot more.

You see, other sports magazines might talk about giving you in-depth coverage of the major sports, but every month at Inside Sports...we make an issue out of it.

INSIDE SPORTS

WE COVER A SIDE OF SPORTS NOBODY ELSE IS COVERING. THE INSIDE.

WHY VINCE FERRAGAMO SAYS HIS AGENT AND THE RAMS ARE ROUGHING THE PASSER.

Vincent Anthony Ferragamo—with an arm like a bullwhip, statistics as shiny as any passer in the league and a face hijacked from a schoolgirl's dream—is the quarterback of the '80s. Trouble is, the Los Angeles Rams are paying him like a quarterback of the '60s.

Ferragamo is disgusted with his treatment by the Rams, confused by a whirlpool of advice and concerned that one humming pull or two interceptions and the job is Pat Haden's again. He could be the only $52,000 a year worker in America who has had two contract attorneys, an entertainment agent, an acting agent and an accountant in the last year.

This month in Inside Sports, writer Gary Smith investigates the frustrations, confusions and suspicions that plague Vince Ferragamo—from his tense relationship with teammate Pat Haden to the controversial negotiations between his attorney, his team and himself.

One NFL team executive has termed these dealings unethical, while the Rams say "other teams in the league have done it." The lawyer must be offered to take his negotiation fee from the Rams to sane Vince money. While Vince's wife says the collapsed three-year contract was a "three-year gross sentence."

Any way you look at it, the whole thing is enough to make ol' J.R. Ewing chuckle.

Also in December's Inside Sports, there's an article on Dallas original first family. The Cowboys. And two of its proudest sons: quarterback Danny White, who's finally at the helm after waiting four long years for the Jolly Roger to be put in moth balls, and Ed "Too Tall" Jones, who's much more at home running rings around offensive linemen than he was a boxer in the ring.

Then Al McGuire, former coach and current announcer, picks what he believes will be this year's batch of Birds, Magics and Dunkensteins. Looking into his crystal basketball, Stormin McGuire even tells us who's going to go all the way in the NCAA crown this March in Philly.

Inside Sports also offers its version of the Boswell Chronicles. Baseball's Thomas Boswell, that is. What he's chronicled are the 1980 baseball playoffs and World Series—three of the most bizarre weeks in baseball history. Plus, you'll find a whole lot more. No wonder, 3,000,000 sports addicts can't wait to get their hands on the December issue.

You see, other sports magazines talk about giving you in-depth coverage of the major sports, but every month at Inside Sports...we make an issue out of it.

INSIDE SPORTS

WE COVER A SIDE OF SPORTS NOBODY ELSE IS COVERING. THE INSIDE.

Collateral
Brochures
Other than by mail

27 GOLD
Art Director:
Mark Greitzer
Writer:
Wendy Jackson
Designers:
Mark Greitzer
Elana Foundos
Photographer:
Catharine Leuthold
Client:
Martex
Agency:
Millennium Design

28 SILVER
Art Director:
Tim Girvin
Writer:
Stephen Darland
Designers:
Chris Spivey
Tim Girvin
Rick Lindberg
Artists:
Chris Spivey
Tim Girvin
Photographer:
David Watanabe
Client:
Kaplan Paper
Agency:
Tim Girvin Design/Wash.

Collateral
Sales Kits

29 GOLD
Art Director:
James Sebastian
Designers:
James Sebastian
Michael Lauretano
Rita Muncie
Photographer:
Joe Standart
Client:
West Point Pepperell
Agency:
Designframe

30 SILVER
Art Director:
Rene Vidmer
Writer:
Ken Baron
Designer:
Rene Vidmer
Client:
Champion Papers
Agency:
Vidmer, Phin

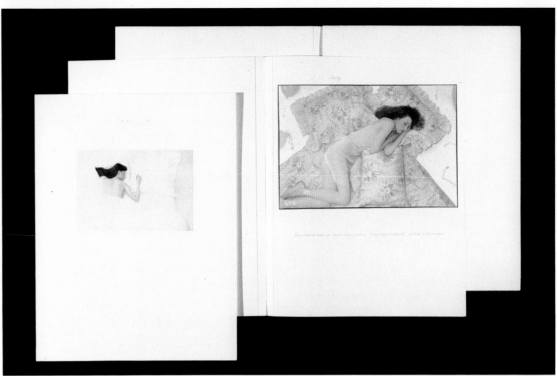

27 GOLD

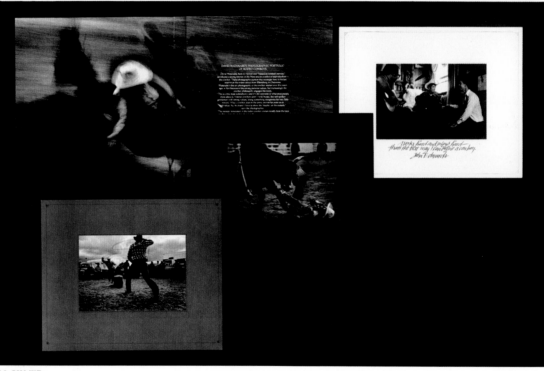

28 SILVER

29 GOLD

30 SILVER

Collateral
Direct Mail

31 GOLD
Art Director:
Glyn Powell
Writer:
Arthur Eisenberg
Designer:
Glyn Powell
Client:
**Dallas Society of
Visual Communications**
Agency:
Eisenberg Inc./Dallas

32 SILVER
Art Directors:
**June Robinson
Lupe Garcia**
Writers:
**Becky Benavides
Bev Coiner**
Photographer:
Rick Kroninger
Client:
Ed Yardang & Associates
Agency:
**Ed Yardang & Associates
San Antonio**

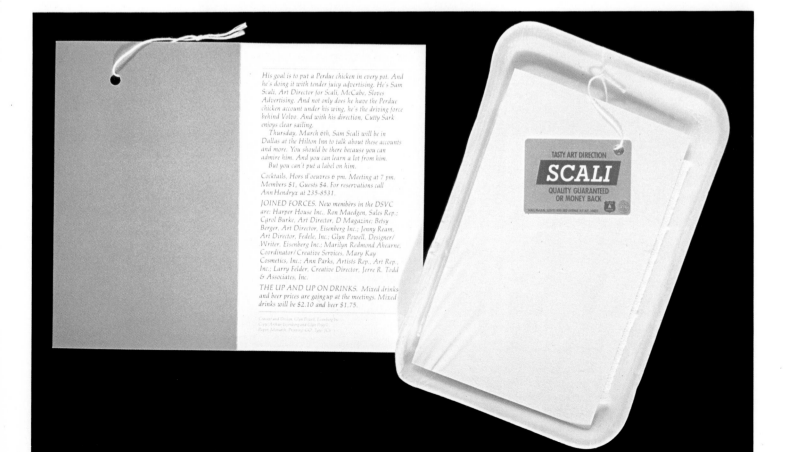

31 GOLD

ED YARDANG & ASSOCIATES PRESENT

THE · AD

AS · ART

The 59th Annual New York Art Directors Show
The first showing outside of NYC.
Witte Museum, San Antonio
November 15 - 22, 1980

32 SILVER

33 GOLD

34 SILVER

35 GOLD

36 SILVER

37 GOLD
Art Director:
Rod Fenol
Writer:
Dennis L. Sullivan
Designer:
Dennis L. Sullivan
Agency:
Jan Grey
Client:
Western Insecticide
Agency:
Corker Sullivan/Wash.

38 SILVER
Art Director:
Ira Madris
Writer:
Bruce Nelson
Artist:
R.O. Blechman
Client:
New York Times
Agency:
McCann-Erickson

MAY YOU LIVE IN THE MOST INTERESTING OF TIMES.
—Chinese Proverb

These times demand The Times.
The New York Times
Home Delivery Call 800-631-2500

It was the best of times,
it was the worst of times,
it was the age of wisdom,
it was the age of foolishness,
it was the epoch of belief,
it was the epoch of incredulity,
it was the season of light,
it was the season of darkness,
it was the spring of hope,
it was the winter of despair.
—Charles Dickens
"A Tale of Two Cities," 1859

These times demand The Times.
The New York Times
Home Delivery Call 800-631-2500

THESE TIMES DEMAND THE TIMES.

The New York Times

38 SILVER

**Public Service
Newspaper or Magazine
Single**

39 GOLD
Art Director:
Keith Lane
Writer:
Seumas McGuire
Designer:
Keith Lane
Artist:
Ed Parker
Client:
City of Boston
Agency:
**Hill, Holliday, Connors,
Cosmopulos/Boston**

40 SILVER
Art Director:
Stan Kovics
Writer:
Larry Plapler
Photographer:
Onofrio Paccione
Client:
**Planned Parenthood
of New York City**
Agency:
**Levine, Huntley, Schmidt,
Plapler & Beaver**

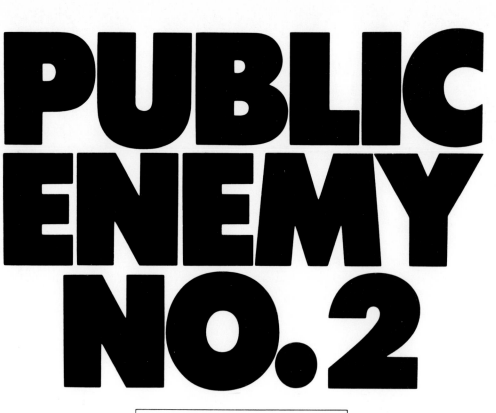

The streets of Boston have always been rich in tradition, but unfortunately they've also been covered by a certain substance which is something less than a tourist attraction. So, as of April 1st, everyone walking a dog must carry the means to pick up after him, and must clean up the dog's waste and deposit it in a proper receptacle.

WHAT DOGS DO IN BOSTON CAN BE A CRIME.

CLEAN UP AFTER YOUR DOG OR FACE A $50 FINE.

City of Boston Department of Health and Hospitals.

ABORTION SHOULD BE BETWEEN YOU AND A DOCTOR. NOT A POLITICIAN.

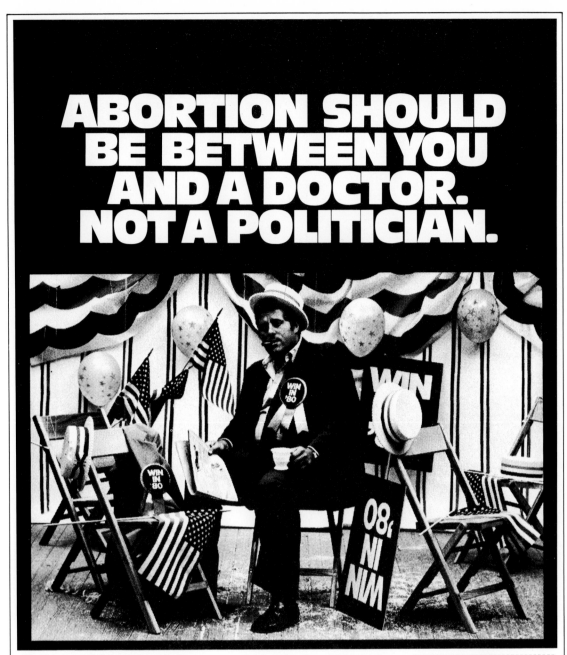

The "right to life" movement feels your right to have an abortion isn't a personal issue...it's a political issue.

They believe, despite medical advice, you should not be allowed the choice of abortion. By law.

Even if your doctor feels your pregnancy could disable you.

Even if your pregnancy results from rape.

Even if you're only a child yourself.

And many of your other rights are being challenged: The right to have any number of children. When you want them. Or none at all. And the right to use contraceptives.

Don't stand by silently and let outrage become law. Fight back.

Take pen in hand and fill out the Planned Parenthood coupon. Give generously of your time and money.

Your most important possession is being threatened: your freedom.

THE TIME HAS COME AGAIN WHEN AMERICANS MUST FIGHT FOR THEIR FREEDOM.

Public Service Newspaper or Magazine Campaign

41 GOLD
Art Director:
Mike Vitiello
Writer:
Larry Vine
Artist:
Myers & Noftsinger
Client:
Anti-Defamation League of B'nai B'rith
Agency:
Smith/Greenland

42 SILVER
Art Director:
Stan Kovics
Writers:
Lee Garfinkel
Larry Plapler
Photographer:
Onofrio Paccione
Client:
Planned Parenthood of New York City
Agency:
Levine, Huntley, Schmidt, Plapler & Beaver

DON'T LET THE GLITTER OF GOLD BLIND YOU TO THE TRUTH ABOUT THE 1980 OLYMPICS IN MOSCOW.

There's going to be much more at stake than winning gold medals.

Human rights are going to be on the line.

And based on some of the events the Russians have planned there's a good chance human rights will be set back 44 years — to when the Olympics were held in Nazi Germany.

One event is called "Rounding-Up Jews." In this event, the entrants win a free trip to jail, prison, a rest home or a sanitarium for the summer. The idea is to keep the so-called activists as far away from the media as possible. And all you have to do to qualify is be a Jew who has applied for emigration.

Entrants, or Prisoners of Conscience as they call themselves, will also be entitled to a daily food ration of 900 calories of rotten, worm infested food, denial of family visits and medical attention, and a windowless 6' X 9' cell.

Of course there are other ways to qualify, in addition to applying for a visa.

If you should be found teaching Hebrew, owning Hebrew Bibles or writing letters to Soviet officials, there's an excellent chance that you'll find yourself in exile in Siberia with Ida Nudel. She is serving four years for hanging a banner outside her apartment that said: "KGB, GIVE ME MY VISA."

Another event the Russians are planning is called "Find the Children of Moscow." It's going to be tough. Because the Russians are sending as many Moscow children as they can away to camp. Away from TV cameras. And away from the thousands of Westerners who could poison their minds with thoughts about freedom and democracy.

The children are already being taught in school that Westerners will try to poison their bodies by offering them chewing gum laced with bacteria.

And, to make sure that the Olympics are a very uneventful time for the newspeople, the Russians have built a central press center. It contains every facility necessary for instant coverage. It also makes it unnecessary for the press people to leave the premises. The Russians hope that a controlled environment will make it easier to control the media.

The Russians have thought of everything. They're determined to present Russia as an ideal society unmatched anywhere in the world.

In fact, the only thing that the Russians have forgotten in preparation for the Olympics is the meaning of the Games.

And that's what we shouldn't forget.

We all have to remember to write the International Olympic Committee stressing the importance of maintaining the Olympic Games in the spirit of international brotherhood, good sportsmanship and, above all, freedom.

Otherwise, it's human rights that stand to lose the most at the 1980 Summer Olympics in Moscow.

PROVIDED AS A PUBLIC SERVICE BY THE ANTI-DEFAMATION LEAGUE OF B'NAI B'RITH AND THE NATIONAL CONFERENCE ON SOVIET JEWRY.

The Message Prepared by Smith/Greenland Inc., Advertising, 1414 Ave. of America, New York, New York 10019

THE 1980 OLYMPICS IN MOSCOW WILL HAVE THE LARGEST CAPTIVE AUDIENCE IN HISTORY.

You won't hear them cheering. In fact, if everything goes as the Russians plan, you won't even see them.

A large part of the Jewish population may be out of town when the Olympics are in Moscow.

And it won't be a staggering case of coincidence. It will be another flagrant example of the Russians violating human rights. A perfect follow up to their invasion of Afghanistan.

The Soviets are determined to present Russia as an ideal society unmatched anywhere in the world. And if that means keeping the people they've branded "undesirables" away from the free world's media, they'll do it.

All a person has to do to qualify as undesirable is be a Jew who has applied for emigration. That entitles the applicant to a free summer away from Moscow. Jails, prisons, rest homes and sanitariums throughout the U.S.S.R. are already being prepared for their arrival.

Applicants, or Prisoners of Conscience as they call themselves, will also be entitled to a daily food ration of 900 calories of rotten, worm infested food, denial of family visits and medical attention, and a windowless 6' X 9' cell.

There are other ways to qualify, in addition to applying for a visa.

If a person should be found teaching Hebrew, owning Hebrew Bibles or writing letters to Soviet officials, there's an excellent chance he will find himself in exile in Siberia with Ida Nudel. She is serving four years for hanging a banner outside her apartment that said: "KGB, GIVE ME MY VISA."

Of course, there's no fear of the Russians losing their audience once the Olympics are over. Life will simply go back to normal.

The Jewish community will still be prohibited from establishing schools to pass on Jewish history.

The publishing of prayer books, or any Jewish books, newspapers and magazines will still be forbidden.

And, it will become even more difficult for a Jew to emigrate. Recently, 50 Jewish families from Kiev were denied visas after first being granted them. After they had already sold all their belongings.

Yes, the Russians have thought of everything. It seems the only thing they have forgotten is the meaning of the Games.

And that's what we shouldn't forget.

We all have to remember to write the International Olympic Committee stressing the importance of maintaining the Olympic Games in the spirit of international brotherhood, good sportsmanship and, above all, freedom.

And none of us can afford to forget that the 1980 Summer Olympics are going to be held in the country with the worst track record for human rights.

PROVIDED AS A PUBLIC SERVICE BY THE ANTI-DEFAMATION LEAGUE OF B'NAI B'RITH AND THE NATIONAL CONFERENCE ON SOVIET JEWRY.

THE 1980 SUMMER OLYMPICS ARE BEING HELD IN THE COUNTRY WITH THE WORST TRACK RECORD FOR HUMAN RIGHTS.

The games that represent brotherhood and equality of opportunity are being held in the country that denies human rights to millions of its citizens. Russia.

The awarding of host city status to Moscow becomes even more of a travesty when you consider recent events in Afghanistan.

And based on some of the events the Russians have planned for the Summer Olympics, it looks like no other country will even come close to their record.

One event is called "Rounding-Up Jews." In this event, the entrants win a free trip to jail, prison, a rest home or a sanitarium for the summer. The idea is to keep the so-called activists as far away from the media as possible. And all you have to do to qualify is be a Jew who has applied for emigration.

Entrants, or Prisoners of Conscience as they call themselves, will also be entitled to a daily food ration of 900 calories of rotten, worm infested food, denial of family visits and medical attention, and a windowless 6' X 9' cell.

Of course there are other ways to qualify, in addition to applying for a visa.

If you should be found teaching Hebrew, owning Hebrew Bibles or writing letters to Soviet officials, there's an excellent chance that you'll find yourself in exile in Siberia with Ida Nudel. She is serving four years for hanging a banner outside her apartment that said: "KGB, GIVE ME MY VISA."

Another event the Russians are planning is called "Find the Children of Moscow." It's going to be tough. Because the Russians are sending as many Moscow children as they can away to camp. Away from TV cameras. And away from thousands of Westerners who could poison their minds with thoughts about freedom and democracy.

The children are already being taught in school that Westerners will try to poison their bodies by offering them chewing gum laced with bacteria.

And, to make sure that the Olympics are a very uneventful time for the newspeople, the Russians have built a central press center. It contains every facility necessary for instant coverage. It also makes it unnecessary for the press people to leave the premises. The Russians hope that a controlled environment will make it easier to control the media.

The Russians have thought of everything. They're determined to present Russia as an ideal society unmatched anywhere in the world.

In fact, the only thing that the Russians have forgotten in preparation for the Olympics is the meaning of the Games.

And that's what we shouldn't forget.

We all have to remember to write the International Olympic Committee stressing the importance of maintaining the Olympic Games in the spirit of international brotherhood, good sportsmanship and, above all, freedom.

Otherwise, it's human rights that will come in last at the 1980 Summer Olympics in Moscow.

PROVIDED AS A PUBLIC SERVICE BY THE ANTI-DEFAMATION LEAGUE OF B'NAI B'RITH AND THE NATIONAL CONFERENCE ON SOVIET JEWRY.

41 GOLD

We, the people who make and sell distilled spirits, urge you to use our products with common sense.

Knowing when you've had your fill, instead of asking for a refill, isn't square. It's smart.

Because when you get right down to it, you know something that no one else knows. You know when you've had enough.

You're not a square if you don't have another round.

DISTILLED SPIRITS COUNCIL OF THE U.S.
1300 Pennsylvania Building, Washington, D.C. 20004

43 GOLD

Nobody ever had to be deprogrammed from The Episcopal Church.

44 SILVER

Corporate
Newspaper or Magazine
Single

45 GOLD
Art Director:
Sam Scali
Writer:
Mike Drazen
Designer:
Sam Scali
Photographer:
Dwayne Michaels
Client:
Sperry Corporation
Agency:
Scali, McCabe, Sloves

46 SILVER
Art Director:
Ron Travisano
Writer:
Jerry Della Femina
Designer:
Ron Travisano
Photographer:
Ralph Morse
Client:
New York Mets
Agency:
**Della Femina, Travisano
& Partners**

"WHAT'S THE POINT OF TALKING, YOU DON'T LISTEN TO ME, ANYWAY."

It starts out innocently enough.

A man tunes in a football game and tunes out his wife's attempts to be heard.

A woman gets so wrapped up in her problems she barely listens as her husband talks about his own.

And before long, without even realizing how it came about, a deadly silence starts to grow between them.

The fact is, listening, like marriage, is a partnership; a shared responsibility between the person speaking and the person listening. And if the listener doesn't show genuine interest and sensitivity to what's being said, the speaker will stop talking. And the communication will fail.

Which is why we at Sperry feel it's so critical that we all become better listeners. In our homes. And in our businesses.

We've recently set up special listening programs that Sperry personnel worldwide can attend. And what we're discovering is that when people really know how to listen (and believe us, there's a lot to know) they can actually encourage the speakers to share more of their thoughts and feelings, bringing everyone closer together.

Which is of great value to us when we do business.

And perhaps even greater value when we go home.

✦SPERRY

We understand how important it is to listen.

Sperry is Sperry Univac computers, Sperry New Holland farm equipment, Sperry Vickers fluid power systems, and guidance and control equipment from Sperry division and Sperry Flight Systems.

This is dedicated to the guys who grew up watching Jackie Robinson torturing a pitcher just by leading off third base

He was beautiful to watch.

He would come roaring around second and slide into third base like he was going to carry any third baseman who dared get in his way right up into the Ebbets Field stands.

Then he would get up, dust himself off, stand on the base and ignore the pitcher for the first few seconds.

But the pitcher, the pitcher couldn't take his eyes off him. And if you were a young kid sitting in the bleachers, you couldn't take your eyes off him either.

Then Jackie took his lead, one step...two steps...three steps...four.

Now his eyes were fixed on the pitcher. Both his arms reaching out. Then the pitcher would go into his stretch and their eyes would meet and

everyone in the ball park would hold their breath. And the pitcher would lose the battle of the eyes. His attention would go to the batter and he would make his pitch.

Suddenly there was number 42. Getting up to full speed in 3 strides. There would be a cloud of dust, an angry catcher, a frustrated pitcher, another run on the scoreboard for the Dodgers. And you coming out of your seat screaming with joy.

Jackie Robinson was a hero.

A hero who taught us more than baseball. He was the handsome, ebony giant of our youth who taught us determination, taught us perseverance and finally he taught us justice.

The new owners of the New York

Mets feel that you and your kids should get as much out of baseball now as you did then. We feel that there is something very special about sharing a baseball game with your kids. With your family and friends.

The new Mets are a young team and that means they may not win every day. But they're a proud team and they'll be trying every day.

And baseball, when it's played by proud young people who try, is beautiful, win or lose.

Come see Steve Henderson, Lee Mazzilli, Doug Flynn, Elliott Maddox, Joel Youngblood, Craig Swan, Alex Trevino and all the Mets take on Dick Williams and his tough Montreal Expos with Larry Parrish, Andrè Dawson, Ron LeFlore and Ellis Valentine this Tuesday and Wednesday.

The New Mets. The Magic is back.

47 GOLD

48 SILVER

ANOTHER QUALITY CHICKEN PART FROM PERDUE

With the introduction of Perdue eggs, you'll now be able to enjoy Perdue quality from beginning to end. You'll find the same excellent quality in our eggs that you've found in our chickens because Perdue eggs come from those same chickens you enjoy on your dinner table. The eggs you buy now come from chickens raised to lay as many eggs as possible. Perdue chickens are raised for their edible quality. Our chickens lay fewer eggs but as a result the eggs are larger, more consistent in color and size, and have a thicker shell. And if one of our chickens has a bad day, Perdue eggs have a money back guarantee. So next time you pick up eggs, pick up Perdue.

49 GOLD

Pick the three month old egg.

50 SILVER

Consumer Television
60 Seconds Single

51 GOLD
Art Director:
Graham Watson
Writer:
Mike Cozens
Client:
Lego (U.K.)
Director:
Ken Turner
Production Co.:
Clearwater Films/London
Agency Producer:
Jane Bearman
Agency:
TBWA/London

52 SILVER
Art Director:
Nicholas Gisonde
Writer:
Jeane Bice
Client:
Miller Brewing
Director:
Bob Giraldi
Production Co.:
Bob Giraldi Productions
Agency Producer:
Marc Mayhew
Agency:
Backer & Spielvogel

51 GOLD

MVO: You see I was standing outside my mousehole the other day...

When all of a sudden along comes this cat.

So quick as a flash, I turned into a dog. (Ruff, Ruff)

But the cat turned into a dragon.

So I turned into a fire engine. How's that. (Chuckle)

And then, and then he turned into a submarine.

So I became a submarine-eating kipper. I said a kipper not a slipper. Thank you very much. (Chuckle)

But he turned into an anti-kipper ballistic missile.

So I turned into a missile cruncher. Crunch, crunch, crunch, crunch, crunch.

Just in time to see him change into a very, very big elephant. So do you know what I did then?...

I turned back into a mouse and gave him the fright of his life.

MVO: Lego. It's a new toy every day.

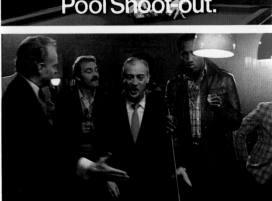

The Great Lite Beer Pool Shoot-out.

52 SILVER

MIZERAK: I make one trick shot in a Lite Beer commercial, and everybody thinks they know how to shoot pool. So these guys decided to take me on, to shoot a little pool, and drink a little Lite Beer from Miller. Because it's less filling.

GROUP: Tastes great!

MIZERAK: Less filling!

JONES: Let's quit talking and start chalking.

BUTKUS: You break, Bubba.

SMITH: Sure, I haven't broken anything all day.

GRESHAM: Hey Mickey, what happened?

SPILLANE: It's a mystery to me.

MEREDITH: Laughter.

HORNUNG: You show 'em, Rodney.

DANGERFIELD: (Sigh)

MIZERAK: You guys got me all wrong. I think Lite tastes great too. But when you're shooting pool, the only thing you want to get filled up is the pockets.

HORNUNG: Steve, how do you do that?

MIZERAK: Practice, Practice, Practice.

ANNCR(VO): Lite Beer from Miller. Everything you always wanted in a beer. And less.

Consumer Television 60 Seconds Campaign

53 GOLD

Art Directors:
Roger Mosconi
Franco Moretti
Paul Frahm
Tim Short

Writers:
Scott Miller
Roger Mosconi
J.C. Kaufmann
Penny Hawkey
Carl Casselman

Client:
Coca-Cola

Directors:
Joe Pytka
Neil Tardio
Adrian Lyne

Production Cos.:
Levine/Pytka
Lovinger/Tardio/Melsky
Jennie & Company

Agency Producers:
J.C. Kaufmann
Paul Frahm

Agency:
McCann-Erickson

53 GOLD

MAN: Hey, Slim? Tell it again.

SLIM: Ahhh...O.K.
I'm walking into the kitchen see.
This little breeze is easin' through the curtains.
I open up the refrigerator door...
It's like January in there.
And I look way in the back, back behind
  the mayonnaise.
I spy me an icy bottle of Coke. And I reach in...
it's cold to the touch—almost frozen.
And I pop the top.
And when that ice-cold Coke...
hits the back of my throat...

SINGERS: *A Coke and a Smile—two of a kind.*
So refreshing,
Makes me feel nice,
Have a Coke and a Smile.
Coca-Cola adds life
Have a Coke and a...

SLIM: Now that's the real thing.

SINGERS: Smile!

ALL: gibberish.

GIRL: (yelling broken English-Swedish) Hello!
(says a few words in Swedish)

BOY: Looks like you need some help...huh? Do you
speak any English?

GIRL: No... (Swedish)

BOY: No English?

GIRL: No.

BOY: I think I'm in love. Hmm...would you marry me?

GIRL: Mary.

BOY: Yeah!

GIRL: Yah! Mary Swenson Klauser.

BOY: Hello, Mary Swenson Klau... (stumbles over last
name.) How about a Coke?

GIRL: Coke?

BOY: Coke!...Drink!...Hmmm.

GIRL: Ahh...Coca-Cola!

BOY: Yeah! Whoaw!

SONG: *A Coke and a Smile...*
...makes me feel good...
...makes me feel nice...
Have a Coke and a Smile.

(MUSIC UP AND UNDER)

SONG: *Coca-Cola adds life.*

(MUSIC UNDER)

BOY: Well Mary Swenson Klauser...where to?

GIRL: (in perfect English) Oh, just down to the next
gas station.

SONG: *Have a Coke and a Smile.*

(SFX: TRAIN AND WHISTLE)

GUY: Hi everybody.

(VOICE UNDER CALLS LITTLE GIRL: "NICOLE")

(SFX: TRAIN CONTINUES THROUGHOUT)

GUY: Do you speak English? Parlez vous Francais?

SHE MUMBLES: Parlez vous francais

GUY: Sprechenze Deutsche?

(SFX: GUY'S LAUGHTER)

(SFX: MUSIC UNDER BEGINS)

VENDOR: Coca-Cola (German)
("Ice Cold" German translation) Coca-Cola

GUY: Coca-Cola

GIRL: Coca-Cola?

GUY: Yeh, Coca-Cola!

GIRL: Coca-Cola

SINGERS: *A Coke and a Smile*

GUY: Coca-Cola

LITTLE GIRL: Coca-Cola

SINGERS: *Makes me feel good.*

OLD LADY: Coca-Cola

SINGERS: *That's the way it . . .*

VENDOR: Coca-Cola

SINGERS: *. . . should be . . . And I'd like to see . . .*

GUY: Coca-Cola

SINGERS: *The whole world . . .*

MAN: Coca-Cola Bitte

SINGERS: *Smiling with me . . . Coca-Cola adds life, have a Coke and a . . .*

GUY: You don't speak English?

SINGERS: *Smile.*

**Consumer Television
60 Seconds Campaign**

54 SILVER
Art Director:
Arnie Blum
Writers:
**Arnie Blum
Phil Dusenberry
Elin Jacobson**
Client:
Pepsi Cola
Director:
Rick Levine
Production Co.:
Levine/Pytka
Agency Producer:
Arnie Blum
Agency:
BBDO

54 SILVER

SINGERS:
Catch that Pepsi Spirit.

(MUSIC)

Catch that Pepsi Spirit.

(MUSIC)

Catch that Pepsi Spirit.

(MUSIC)

*Catch that Pepsi Spirit. Catch that Pepsi Spirit.
Drink it in. Drink it in.
Drink it in.
Catch that Pepsi Spirit.
Drink it in. Drink it in. Drink it in.
It's the love and the laughter.
The taste of life
the world is after.*

(MUSIC)

*Catch
that Pepsi Spirit.
Drink it in. Drink it in. Drink it in.*

SINGERS:

*It's the smilin' shinin' feelin' the light of a brand
new day.
And you're the Pepsi generation
you're the spirit of today.
There's a feeling deep inside you, a spirit you just
can't hide.
And with every taste of life that's new
Well that Pepsi spirit shines right through.
Catch that Pepsi Spirit.
Drink it in. Drink it in. Drink it in.
Catch that Pepsi Spirit. Drink it in.
Drink it in. Drink it in.
Now your spirits are risen
You're headin' for a new horizon.
Catch that Pepsi Spirit. Drink it in.
Drink it in. Drink it in.*

SINGERS:

*There's a feeling deep inside you,
a spirit you just can't hide.
And with every taste of life that's new
Well, that Pepsi spirit
shines right through.
Catch that Pepsi Spirit. Drink it in.
Drink it in. Drink it in.
Catch that Pepsi Spirit.
Drink it in. Drink it in. Drink it in.
It's the love and the laughter.
The taste of life the world is after.
Catch that Pepsi Spirit.
Drink it in.
Drink it in. Drink it in.*

Consumer Television
30 Seconds Single

55 GOLD
Art Director:
Michael Tesch
Writer:
Patrick Kelly
Client:
Federal Express
Director:
Joe Sedelmaier
Production Co.:
Sedelmaier Films/Chicago
Agency Producer:
Maureen Kearns
Agency:
Ally & Gargano

56 SILVER
Art Director:
Roy Grace
Writer:
John Noble
Client:
Mobil Oil
Director:
William Helburn
Production Co.:
Wiliam Helburn Productions
Agency Producer:
Susan Calhoun
Agency:
Doyle Dane Bernbach

55 GOLD

BOSS: Read it back.

CRATCHET: That package must be here by Spring of '76, or the proposition is terminated.

BOSS: That is telling them!

(SFX: TELEGRAPH)

BUSINESSMAN: Tell them I gotta have the package in three months or forget the whole thing.

(SFX: BANGING)

GARMENT CENTER GUY: I need it in two weeks, you got it, two weeks?

BUSINESSMAN: I need it tomorrow.

ANNCR(VO): Just when the need for Federal Express came along, along came Federal Express.

(SFX: JET)

ANNCR(VO): When it absolutely, positively has to be there overnight.

56 SILVER

VO: This is the oil that saves you gas. But it does more.
It can take you . . .

NEW YORKER: From New York . . .

ENGLISHMAN: to London . . .

FRENCHMAN: to Paris . . .

SWEDISH GIRL: to Sweden . . .

JAPANESE MAN: to Tokyo . . .

MOVIE STAR: to Hollywood . . .

NEW YORKER: . . . and back to New York.

VO: 25,000 miles without an oil change.
Mobil 1.
The oil that saves you gas.
And more.

Consumer Television
30 Seconds Campaign

57 GOLD
Art Director:
Nicholas Gisonde
Writer:
Jeane Bice
Client:
Miller Brewing
Director:
Bob Giraldi
Production Co.:
Bob Giraldi Productions
Agency Producer:
Marc Mayhew
Agency:
Backer & Spielvogel

57 GOLD

(SFX: BAR NOISES)

MADDEN: Excuse me. I'm not the same crazy coach who used to storm around the sidelines yelling at the officials. I've learned to relax, and I drink Lite Beer from Miller.

Do you know that Lite's got a third less calories than their regular beer? And listen to this. Lite doesn't fill me up.

Besides that, Lite tastes fantastic. Oh sure, there are a lot of other beers around and you can drink any one you want.

But let me tell you this:
For my money...

ANNCR(VO): Lite Beer from Miller. Everything you always wanted in a beer. And less.

MADDEN: I say why drink anything else. As I was saying, I don't care what anybody thinks...

Mickey Spillane
Famous Mystery Writer

Everything you always wanted
in a beer.

Carlos Palomino
Ex-welterweight champ

(SFX: TYPING)

MICKEY VO: Chapter 9. I kicked in the door and shouted "freeze" to the lone figure in the room. Even in the darkness I could see she was the most beautiful woman I ever met.

Suddenly I saw the Lite Beer from Miller.

"It's got a third less calories than their regular beer. And it's less filling," she whispered. "But the best thing is it tastes so great." Suddenly all the pieces fell into place. And I knew I had come to the end of a long, long road.

She poured, we drank. To be continued.

ANNCR(VO): Everything you always wanted in a beer. And less.

CARLOS: Y'know, one of the best things about coming to America was that I got to try American beers. I tried them all. And the one I like best is Lite Beer from Miller. It's got a third less calories than their regular beer. It's less filling. And it really tastes great. That is why I tell my friends from Mexico, "When you come to America, drink Lite Beer. But don't drink the water."

Consumer Television
30 Seconds Campaign

58 SILVER
Art Director:
Roy Grace
Writer:
John Noble
Client:
Mobil Oil
Directors:
Phil Kellison
William Helburn
Production Cos.:
Coast Productions
William Helburn Productions
Agency Producer:
Susan Calhoun
Agency:
Doyle Dane Bernbach

58 SILVER

VO: This is a can of Mobil 1. What's in it for you?

LADY: Gas.

MAN: Lots of gas.

VO: Lots and lots of gas. If you drive 25,000 miles a year and get about 15 miles per gallon... you can save up to 80 gallons of gas a year by changing to Mobil 1. The oil that saves you gas. And more.

ANNCR(VO): At about $4.50 a quart . . . this is one of the most expensive motor oils in the world.

ANNCR(VO): Or is it?

If you drive 25,000 miles a year

the money you save on gas, oil changes and oil filters alone . . .

can add up to $83.00. Up to $83.00 by switching from conventional 10W40 motor oil . . . to synthetic Mobil 1.

Mobil 1. The oil that saves you gas.

And more.

VO: This is the oil that saves you gas. But it does more. It can take you . . .

NEW YORKER: From New York . . .

ENGLISHMAN: to London . . .

FRENCHMAN: to Paris . . .

SWEDISH GIRL: to Sweden . . .

JAPANESE MAN: to Tokyo . . .

MOVIE STAR: to Hollywood . . .

NEW YORKER: . . . and back to New York.

VO: 25,000 miles without an oil change.
Mobil 1.
The oil that saves you gas.
And more.

Consumer Television
10 Seconds Single

59 GOLD
Art Director:
Michael Tesch
Writer:
Patrick Kelly
Client:
Federal Express
Director:
Joe Sedelmaier
Production Co.:
Sedelmaier Films/Chicago
Agency Producer:
Maureen Kearns
Agency:
Ally & Gargano

60 SILVER
Art Director:
Lars Anderson
Writer:
Peter Levathes
Client:
Maxell
Director:
Henry Sandbank
Production Co.:
Sandbank Films
Agency Producer:
Dane Johnson
Agency:
Scali, McCabe, Sloves

59 GOLD

ANNCR(VO): Federal Express will come to your office, pick up the package, and deliver it clear across the country overnight. You don't even have to move an inch.

(SILENT)

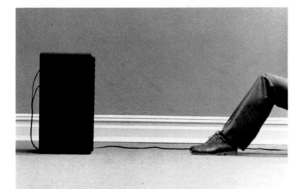

60 SILVER

VO: Even after 500 plays,
(SFX: MUSIC EXPLODES)
our high fidelity tape still delivers high fidelity.
Maxell. it's worth it.

Consumer Television
10 Seconds Campaign

61 GOLD
Art Director:
Michael Tesch
Writer:
Patrick Kelly
Client:
Federal Express
Director:
Joe Sedelmaier
Production Co.:
Sedelmaier Films/Chicago
Agency Producer:
Maureen Kearns
Agency:
Ally & Gargano

61 GOLD

(SFX: SNORING)

ANNCR(VO): Federal Express is so easy to use, you can do it in your sleep.

GUY (OC): Hellooooooooo Federal.

BOSS (OC): Fortunately, Bingham here

VO: sent the blueprints to Birmingham for the big meeting tomorrow.

ANNCR(VO): Next time you blow it, remember, there's always Federal Express.

ANNCR(VO): Federal Express will come to your office, pick up the package, and deliver it clear across the country overnight. You don't even have to move an inch.

(SILENT)

Consumer Television
10 Seconds Campaign

62 SILVER
Art Director:
Priscilla Croft
Writer:
Debby Mattison
Client:
Frigidaire
Director:
Mark Story
Production Co.:
Bean/Kahn Films
Agency Producer:
Peter Cascone
Agency:
Needham, Harper & Steers

62 SILVER

(SFX: MUSIC)

WOMAN: (Muffled) In the past 15 years we've had
32 blizzards, 5 snowblowers... and one refrigerator.
A Frigidaire.

VO: Frigidaire.
Here today, here tomorrow.

(SFX: MUSIC)

MAN: In the past 15 years, I've had 7 sports cars, 14 sports car mechanics... and one refrigerator. A Frigidaire.

VO: Frigidaire. Here today, here tomorrow.

(SFX: MUSIC)

MAN: In the past 15 years, we've had ten mailmen.

WOMAN: Five new rugs...

DOG: Rrrrruff!

WOMAN: And one refrigerator. A Frigidaire.

VO: Frigidaire. Here today, here tomorrow.

Public Service Television 60 Seconds Single

63 GOLD
Art Director:
Peter Jones
Writer:
Dianne Allen
Client:
The Parkinson Foundation of Canada
Director:
Chris Sanderson
Production Co.:
T.D.F. Productions/Canada
Agency Producer:
June Whibley
Agency:
Ogilvy & Mather/Canada

64 SILVER
Art Director:
Ross Richins
Writers:
James Gartner
Ron Anderson
Client:
The Church of Jesus Christ of Latter-day Saints
Director:
Norman Griner
Production Co.:
Myers & Griner/Cuesta
Agency Producer:
James Gartner
Agency:
Bonneville Productions/Utah

Public Service Television 30 Seconds Single

65 GOLD
Art Directors:
Ron Travisano
Ron Devito
Writers:
Ron Travisano
Ron Devito
Neal Rogin
Client:
World Hunger Project
Director:
Nick Samardge
Production Co.:
Nick Samardge
Agency Producers:
Dominique Bigar
Peter Yahr
Agency:
Della Femina, Travisano & Partners

66 SILVER
Art Director:
Dick Hane
Writer:
Ron Newman
Client:
Hennepin County/Minn.
Director:
Jim Hinton
Production Co.:
Wilson-Griak
Agency Producers:
Dick Hane
Ron Newman
Agency:
Stevenson & Associates/Minn.

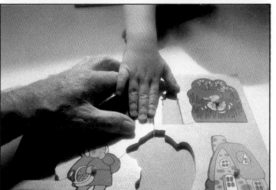
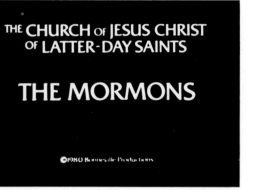

63 GOLD

(SFX: MUSIC UNDER)

(SFX: SOUND OF THE WOODEN PUZZLE PART BEING PUT INTO PLACE.)

(SFX: ELECTRONIC PUNCTUATION)

MVO: Tremor in the hand, stiffness of the muscles, lack of coordination can make an adult more helpless than a child.

One in every 200 Canadians over the age of 40 is hit with Parkinson's Disease.

If you think it could be you or someone in your family, contact the Parkinson Foundation for help.

Because there is help.

(SFX: ELECTRONIC PUNCTUATION)

64 SILVER

FIRST VO: I'm sad. I'm lonely. I'm afraid. I want to belong to someone.

(LYRICS UP)

I won't be left behind.
My heart must find the will to move on.
Even though it seems happiness is just a dream in my mind—
I won't be left behind.

SECOND VO: I don't like coming home. I don't like to be here. When I open the door, I'll be alone. I'll eat alone. The phone won't ring.

ANNCR(VO): Being alone. it's hard, and sometimes it hurts. But I know that I have a lot to offer. I have a lot to give... It's not what life does to you... It's what you do with life.

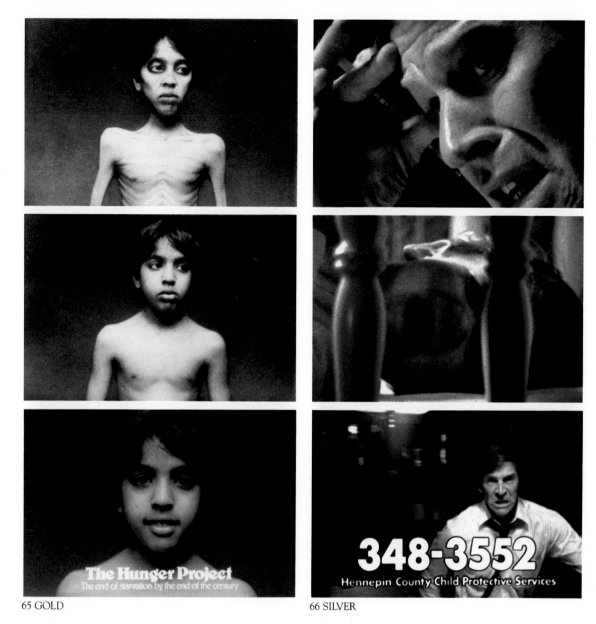

65 GOLD

66 SILVER

VO: The time has come on our planet for hunger and starvation to end. Not just merely dealt with, not just handled more effectively . . . but to be ended. Finally, once and for all, forever. Starvation will end on this planet by the end of this century. It's an idea whose time has come. The Hunger Project. The end of starvation by the end of the century.

(SFX: BABY CRYING, INCREASING IN INTENSITY, BECOMING MORE AND MORE PIERCING)

DAD: Please Jeff. Please.

(SFX: CRYING REACHES MAXIMUM, MADDENING)

DAD: Shut up!

(SFX: CRYING, COMBINED WITH MOOG, HEIGHTENS EFFECT)

DAD: Shut up!

ANNCR(VO): If you're a parent who has trouble coping, call for help.

Corporate Television
60 Seconds Single

67 GOLD
Art Director:
Rebecca Cooney
Writer:
Art Tuohy
Client:
Texaco
Production Co.:
Paisley Productions/Calif.
Agency Producer:
Paul McDonough
Agency:
Benton & Bowles

68 SILVER
Art Director:
Michael Leon
Writer:
Kathy Cantwell
Client:
IBM Corporate
Director:
Dick Loew
Production Co.:
Gomes Loew
Agency Producer:
Ellyn Epstein
Agency:
Doyle Dane Bernbach

Corporate Television
30 Seconds Single

69 GOLD
Art Directors
& Writers:
Chris Perry
Dennis Okerbloom
Ed Ward
Client:
**Blue Cross & Blue Shield
of N.E. Ohio**
Director:
Reuben Shapiro
Production Co.:
Centipede Productions
Agency Producer:
Chris Dieck
Agency:
Meldrum & Fewsmith/Ohio

70 SILVER
Art Directors:
Richard Paynter
John Clapps
Writers:
Leland Rosemond
Sueanne Peacock
Client:
First National State Bank
Director:
R.O. Blechman
Production Co.:
The Ink Tank
Agency Producer:
Knight Russell
Agency:
Bozell & Jacobs/New Jersey

67 GOLD

ANNCR(VO): This year marks the Fortieth Anniversary of... the longest running... sponsored program in radio history. Texaco's Metropolitan Opera radio broadcasts bringing the opera... to millions of people who can't get to the opera.

(SINGING)

(SFX: CLAPPING)

HOPE: Can you drive that well?

ANNCR(VO): Texaco is privileged to have been your ticket to the opera for forty years.

Sing on!

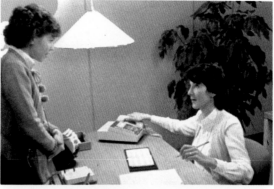

68 SILVER

RECEPTIONIST (VO): Betty Turner?

RECEPTIONIST: First day, huh?... Through this door turn left past the water cooler, turn right, you're looking for Miss Hunter.

MISS HUNTER: Betty? Olive Hunter.

MISS HUNTER: This is Miriam...

MIRIAM: Hi!

MISS HUNTER: and Doug...

DOUG: Hi!

MISS HUNTER: ... and this is you. That's really something, isn't it Betty?... Betty?

ANNCR(VO): The IBM Displaywriter. It's easy for people to adjust to because it adjusts to people. It practically teaches you itself.

It gives you step by step instructions... A dictionary of about 50,000-words that helps you check your spelling.

There's even a way to check your math. It almost makes errors obsolete.

You can type, edit, correct and zip out page after page. Some people worry about a machine making them feel uneasy.

The IBM Displaywriter makes them feel they can handle just about anything.

MOTHER: How'd it go?

BETTY: Piece of cake!

ANNCR(VO): IBM. Helping put information to work for people.

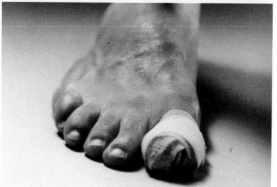

69 GOLD

70 SILVER

VO: You're looking at...

...the world's most sophisticated machine...

(SFX: AUTO WIND ON CAMERA) The human body.

(SFX: CAMERA SOUND SEGUES TO MACHINE SOUND IN SYNC WITH HEAD MOVEMENT)

(SFX: SEGUE TO MACHINE SOUND IN SYNC WITH ARM MOVEMENT)

(SFX: SEGUE TO MACHINE SOUND IN SNYC WITH TORSO)

(SFX: SEGUE TO MACHINE SOUND IN SYNC WITH KNEE MOVEMENT)

(SFX: FADE UNDER)

Of course, sometimes...

even the most sophisticated machine

(SFX: WRENCH STRIKING PIPE WITH A "CLUNK")

needs repair.

Blue Cross and Blue Shield

(SFX: SNAP OF CARD)

The world's most popular health club.

VO: Big New York banks used to overshadow banks in New Jersey. Until First National State Bank did something about it.

We supported development of Newark International Airport and helped New Jersey business grow.

We helped build the Meadowlands and helped New Jersey sports grow.

We helped rejuvenate Atlantic City, and helped New Jersey tourism grow.

Helping New Jersey people and business also helped First National State grow.

Our first concern is New Jersey. And those who do business here.

Yamaha
Agency Producer:
Richard O'Neill
Agency:
Chiat/Day-Los Angeles

72 SILVER
Writer:
Gary LaMaster
Client:
Marquette Hotel
Agency Producers:
Gary LaMaster
Candace Carruthers
Agency:
Martin/Williams-Mpls.

Consumer Radio Campaign

73 GOLD
Writers:
Mike Nichols
Elaine May
Client:
American Express
Agency Producers:
Nancy Perez
Tom Rost
Agency:
Ogilvy & Mather

71 GOLD

(SFX: MUSIC, YAMAHA THEME UP.)

ANNCR: If you're in the market for a high-performance sports car, you can probably get one almost like the one you want, in a color you sort of like, for about $21,000 and a three-month wait. Of course, if you think that's a bit much to ask, just to have fun going around corners, there is an alternative. A high-performance motor-cycle... from Yamaha. You'll get plenty of room for you and a really good friend. Terrific mileage. A price tag that won't choke the average horse. And twice the performance of a sports car... with half the wheels. A Yamaha will also give you the satisfaction of knowing that while other guys are off following the crowd... you're not.

(SFX: MUSIC & SINGERS HOLD TO END.)

72 SILVER

(SFX: RESTAURANT SOUNDS)

WOMAN: Gee, the Orion Room sure has a big selection of fresh seafood dinners. Lobster, swordfish, shark, abalone.

MAN: I think I'll have steak.

WOMAN: Honey, you're always saying you should be more adventurous. Try the seafood.

MAN: You're right. Waiter, I'll try the shark.

WAITER: The Orion Room's Shark Montpellier? Very good, sir.

(SFX: PAUSE, THEN THEME MUSIC FROM JAWS)

MAN: Sandy, did you hear something?

WOMAN: What?

MAN: Never mind. It's probably just my imagination.

(SFX: MUSIC AGAIN)

MAN: Waiter, is the shark fresh?

WAITER: Very. The Orion Room's seafood is flown in daily.

(SFX: MUSIC AGAIN, LOUDER THIS TIME)

WOMAN: Bill, what's wrong? You look petrified. (Pause) Oh, good, here comes the food.

(SFX: MUSIC GETS MORE INTENSE.)

MAN: I can't look.

WAITER: Your shark, sir.

MAN: Huh? (Relieved) Gee, it doesn't seem so scary with a wedge of lemon on it.

ANNCR: Enjoy fresh seafood now in the Orion Room at the top of the IDS Center, followed by live entertainment in The Orion Room Lounge. There's even a free seafood sampler table. So, if you aren't sure you like seafood, you don't have to be afraid to try it.

ANNCR: Mike Nichols and Elaine May for the American Express Card.

NICHOLS: Honey.

MAY: Yes?

NICHOLS: When you were in Rome did you, uh, go out much?

MAY: No, hardly at all.

NICHOLS: Really, just sort of quiet?

MAY: No, not much doing in Rome.

NICHOLS: Mm Hmm.

MAY: Sort of disappointing.

NICHOLS: I was just going over some of the bills from your American Express Card. You know they have a very interesting service; they send me a copy of the signed receipt when you go out somewhere. So for instance, let's say you take fourteen or sixteen people to Porcolinos for the evening and spend $18,000.00—I get a copy of your signed receipt.

MAY: Really?

NICHOLS: Isn't that an interesting service?

MAY: Yes! I had no idea they had that service.

NICHOLS: Hmmm.

MAY: Hmmm.

NICHOLS: Want to change your story?

ANNCR: To apply for an American Express Card look for the application display wherever the Card is welcomed.

The American Express Card. Don't leave home without it.

ANNCR: Mike Nichols and Elaine May for the American Express Card.

NICHOLS: Oh, I love this new cuisine monsieur.

MAY: Oh yes, the canard was delicious.

NICHOLS: Delicious canard, but still it was all so light. That's your monsieur.

MAY: Well, because I think really good French food is light.

NICHOLS: It is now.

MAY: Yeah, yeah.

NICHOLS: It's nouvelle. That's why they call it nouvelle cuisine monsieur...just hand me the check here. What would eighty-seven million francs be?

MAY: Eighty-seven million francs in American dollars, let's see. (They are figuring out amount) Eighty seven million francs is, uh, a hundred and seventy-five thousand dollars, now wait a minute, that can't be right.

NICHOLS: That sounds a little stiff. We had wine, though.

MAY: One hundred and seventy-five thousand dollars and that's with the wine.

NICHOLS: Let me just ask him. Monsieur, garcon, s'il vous plait, plait, uh, acceptez-vous American Express? Oh, thank heavens!

MAY: Yeah, now let's figure out the tip.

ANNCR: To apply for an American Express Card, call 800-528-8000. The American Express Card. Don't leave home without it.

ANNCR: Mike Nichols and Elaine May for the American Express Card.

NICHOLS: (Speaking German)

MAY: Huh?

NICHOLS: (Speaking German)

MAY: I'm an American. I'm told that everyone in the American Express offices speaks American.

NICHOLS: Bitte?

MAY: Uh, Uh, speak American to me! I'm an American!

NICHOLS: Yah, Gud.

MAY: Look, I've lost my American Express Card and I'd like another one in twenty-four hours. Because I'd like to do some shopping here.

NICHOLS: (Speaking German)

MAY: What?

NICHOLS: (Speaking German)

MAY: You're supposed to speak English, I mean everyone in American Express offices is supposed to speak English. I can't understand a word you're saying.

NICHOLS: (Speaking German)

MAY: Uh, look Ish lost mine American Express Card, gone. And I'm supposed to be able to get another one in twenty-four hours, of course, you're supposed to speak English. So, can I get one? Is there any way...

NICHOLS: Yes, Hernzie. American Express is ta eenext a teur.

MAY: Pardon?

NICHOLS: Is next door!

ANNCR: To apply for an American Express Card, call 800-528-8000. The American Express Card. Don't leave home without it.

Consumer Radio Campaign

74 SILVER
Writers:
Bert Berdis
Dick Orkin
Client:
Astoria Federal Savings & Loan
Agency Producer:
Ken Rabasca
Agency:
Greenstone & Rabasca

BERT: So, Mr. Bagely, you're applying for a job as one of Astoria's friendly tellers?

DICK: (Loud) That's right, buster!

BERT: Ahuh... Well, let's suppose I'm one of Astoria's loyal customers. I walk up to the window and you say...?

DICK: Next window.

BERT: No.

DICK: Get in line.

BERT: No, no.

DICK: I'm out to lunch (No) supper (No) late night snack? (No)

BERT: Mr. Bagely, with all of our branches, Astoria Federal is known as a neighborhood bank. So we say...

DICK: Turn down that stereo.

BERT: No.

DICK: Get your dog off my lawn.

BERT: No...

DICK: Who swiped my newspaper?

BERT: Look, we provide service with a smile, recognize our customers and say things like...

DICK: Hi, Baldy, wanna cash a check?

BERT: Mr. Bagely, you're just not right for Astoria Federal. I'm sorry.

DICK: You're sorry. Boy, I'll never get my old job back.

BERT: What was that?

DICK: Librarian.

BERT: Librarian?

DICK: I don't know why they fired me. One day they...

ANNCR: Astoria Federal Savings. We've got lots of convenient branches filled with lots of friendly folks to help you. No wonder so many people save with Astoria. We're right on the money.

BERT:	My family and the movers are waiting out there.
DICK:	I know.
BERT:	We're supposed to move into your house!
DICK:	I know that.
BERT:	Cuz you're moving out to, uh...
DICK:	Fargo, North Dakota.
BERT:	Yeah.
DICK:	Okay, try and take this in the spirit in which I intend it, okay?
BERT:	Yes?
DICK:	We're not moving!
BERT:	(Shocked Sound)
DICK:	That's the spirit. See, we all just found out something very serious... about Fargo.
BERT:	What??
DICK:	May I be frank with you?
BERT:	What?
DICK:	Astoria Federal doesn't have a branch there.
BERT:	Astoria...
DICK:	Astoria Federal Savings has branches all over the place and they're easy to get to. Here's a branch... there's a branch... But nothing in Fargo.
BERT:	So what?
DICK:	Well, we all just decided without Astoria it's NO GO Fargo.
BERT:	You're kidding.
DICK:	You see, my family has always been loyal to Astoria... my Mom & Dad, Grandma... Grandpa...
BERT:	I don't believe it.
DICK:	Oh yeah... see, Astoria makes you feel your money is safe... earns the highest interest allowed by law (they are friendly, helpful neighborhood folks).
BERT:	Mr. Simmons!
DICK:	Call me Mel.
BERT:	What am I gonna do with my family and... a truck full of furniture out there...
DICK:	Wanta take a quick look at a nice 3 bedroom Cape Cod?
BERT:	Okay.
DICK:	Go down that street... make a left.
BERT:	Where is this house?
DICK:	It's in Fargo. Then go three thousand miles til you come to a stop sign, then turn left...
BERT:	(Shocked sound)
ANNCR:	Astoria Federal Savings. Ask any of our over 100,000 loyal customers who save with us. They'll tell you. We're right on the money.

MIR:	Herb, wake up!
DICK:	I'm up. I'm up.
MIR:	We're at Astoria Federal Savings.
BERT:	Hi, welcome to Astoria.
MIR:	Oh, hello, my husband and I would like to open... now where did he go?
BERT:	Is he wearing a blue windbreaker?
MIR:	Yes.
BERT:	He's sleeping on our loan officer's desk.
MIR:	Herb!
DICK:	I'm up, I'm up. I was just resting my eyes.
MIR:	You see, Herb hasn't slept for 12 years.
BERT:	12 years?
MIR:	Well, he just lies awake at night worrying about his money.
BERT:	Well, there's no risk for Astoria savers. All the savings are insured and earn the maximum allowable interest, too.
MIR:	Well, that's why we came to Astoria.
BERT:	Oh, good.
MIR:	Herb!
DICK:	I'm up. I'm up.
MIR:	That is not a pillow! That's a potted palm!
DICK:	I wasn't sleeping, hon. I was just checking for aphids.
MIR:	Oh, the poor thing.
BERT:	Well, he can rest easy now. Astoria offers all the savings and loan services such as Money Market Accounts, Savings Certificates, IRA Accounts and they're all safe, no risk.
MIR:	Great. Herb! Herb!
BERT:	He is sleeping on the copy machine.
MIR:	Herb!
DICK:	I'm up. I'm up. I was just checking for aphids.
ANNCR:	You can rest while your savings work at Astoria. We're right on the money.
BERT:	Do you want a hundred copies of Herb's face...
MIR:	I don't think so, do you Herb?
DICK:	I'm up, I'm up...

Public Service
Radio Single

75 GOLD
Writers:
Marshall W. Karp
Andrew J. Langer
Client:
The City of New York
Agency Producer:
Diane Jeremias
Agency:
The Marshalk Company

76 SILVER
Writer:
Geoffrey Frost
Client:
Greater New York Conference
on Soviet Jewry
Agency Producer:
Gary Grossman
Agency:
Scali, McCabe, Sloves

Public Service
Radio Campaign

77 GOLD
Writers:
Kevin Kelly
Khaliel Kelly
Client:
The Church of Jesus Christ
of Latter-day Saints
Agency:
Bonneville Productions
Utah

75 GOLD

MAYOR KOCH: John Harris always thought he was a perfectly normal law abiding New Yorker. Until the day he shot and killed his 8-year-old son Michael.

He didn't actually pull the trigger himself. All he did was leave a handgun hidden in a closet at home. Michael, being curious, found the gun, found the bullets and lost his life.

This is Mayor Ed Koch and while the names have been changed the story is all too true. In fact, if you have a handgun in the house, chances are it will wind up shooting someone you were trying to protect, not someone you were protecting them from.

I urge you to get your illegal handguns out of the house now. You have until August 11 to turn them into any police station, The New York Post, El Diario or the Amsterdam News.

Please, turn in your handgun today. And tonight, do what John Harris still can't do. Sleep.

ANNCR: Handgun Amnesty. Now through August 11. We don't want your name. We just want your gun.

76 SILVER

(MUSIC)

ANNCR: Last year 4,000 Jews were allowed to leave the Soviet Union every month. This year, that number's been cut nearly in half.

April 27th is Solidarity Sunday for Soviet Jewry. If you didn't march last year because things were getting better, march this year, before things get any worse.

March on Solidarity Sunday, April 27th. Sponsored by the Greater New York Conference on Soviet Jewry.

MAN: Last fall when I was looking for a job, it took five months from the first interview until I was hired. And as I came home each day, I don't think I've ever been so discouraged. My wife had a job and was working, and I didn't. I don't ever recall her criticizing me. She knew what I wanted, and she knew I wouldn't be happy unless I got it. And she was the one that told me that.

ANNCR: Love isn't something you fall into . . . it's something you grow. From the Mormons, The Church of Jesus Christ of Latter-day Saints.

WOMAN: One day my husband came home and it had been one of *those* days. You know, everything was just horrible. There was laundry all over the front room. I saw him walk in, and I was just ready for him to say, "What have you been doing around here?" And he said, "I wouldn't have your job for anything." And I almost started to cry, because he understood what I was going through.

ANNCR: Love isn't something you fall into . . . it's something you grow. From the Mormons, The Church of Jesus Christ of Latter-day Saints.

WOMAN: I need your touch.
MAN: Oh, what a day.
WOMAN: I need to hold your hand.
MAN: I'm beat.
WOMAN: We need to talk.
MAN: I know I'm late.
WOMAN: You need to understand.
MAN: Let's eat.
WOMAN: So much to say.
MAN: More bills to pay.
WOMAN: So much to share.
MAN: It isn't fair.
WOMAN: You seem so distant there. I need to know you really care.
MAN: You always work.
WOMAN: Oh, what a day.
MAN: Sometimes I wish you'd stop.
WOMAN: No space.
MAN: I'm home at last.
WOMAN: There's just no way.
MAN: Why can't we really talk.
WOMAN: This place.
MAN: Oh, look at me.
WOMAN: Smile at me.
MAN: Don't turn away.
WOMAN: That special way.
BOTH: I have so much to share.
MAN: You need to know I really care.
ANNCR: (Spoken) Love isn't something you fall into . . . it's something you grow. From the Mormons, The Church of Jesus Christ of Latter-day Saints.

Public Service
Radio Campaign

78 SILVER
Writers:
James Gartner
Ron Anderson
Client:
The Church of Jesus Christ
of Latter-day Saints
Agency:
Bonneville Productions
Utah

Corporate Radio
Single

79 GOLD
Writer:
Steve Kasloff
Client:
Sperry Corporation
Agency Producer:
Richard Berke
Agency:
Scali, McCabe, Sloves

80 SILVER
Writer:
Art Novak
Client:
3M Company/
Commercial Chemicals
Agency Producer:
Art Novak
Agency:
Campbell-Mithun/Mpls.

78 SILVER

WOMAN: Why am I the one to get divorced and why can't I have a happy marriage. I struggle, but I'm a better person for it. If life was always easy there would be no accomplishment.

ANNCR: It isn't fair. It's life. And sometimes it hurts. But it's not what life does to you. It's what you do with life.

WOMAN: It hurts but I can make it.

ANNCR: From the Mormons, The Church of Jesus Christ of Latter-day Saints.

ANNCR: It isn't fair.

GIRL: You're ugly. You're fat. And that's what I think in bed at night and I hate myself. That's when I'm loneliest. And being single, I really want to belong to someone. Sometimes I just whisper, "I love you" when there's no one there to say it to. But sometimes I just pretend there's someone else saying it to me too.

ANNCR: It just isn't fair.

GIRL: But being lonely doesn't make me bad. Being lonely doesn't mean I have to hate myself. I'm learning to like myself more and more all the time. And I like me. I really do. But maybe that's why I feel lonely. Because I am important.

ANNCR: It isn't fair. It's life. And sometimes it hurts. But it's not what life does to you, it's what you do with life. From the Mormons. The Church of Jesus Christ of Latter-day Saints.

ANNCR: It isn't fair.

MAN: There isn't a day that goes by that I'm not acutely aware of the fact that I don't have my wife. When you go to bed at night, you're alone. And you wake up in the morning and you're alone again. That's the roughest part of the whole thing.

ANNCR: It just isn't fair.

MAN: In the beginning, it's important to suffer and let the grief come out. But after a while you've just got to put the grief aside. You can't make it a life of grief. You've got to recover, you've got to overcome.

ANNCR: It isn't fair. It's life. And sometimes it hurts. But it's not what life does to you, it's what you do with life. From the Mormons. The Church of Jesus Christ of Latter-day Saints.

JOYCE: What a day I had. Harvey, put down the paper and listen. First I drive the kids to the 8:05 bus at 8:00. But it comes 5 to 8.

HARVEY: Uh-huh.

JOYCE: Then Philip gets his thumb stuck in a fingerpaint jar.

HARVEY: Uh-huh.

JOYCE: Harvey, you're not listening.

HARVEY: Uh-huh.

ANNCR: It's a simple fact that people spend half their waking hours listening. Yet retain only 25% of what they listen to.

JOYCE: So I couldn't get his thumb out.

HARVEY: Uh-huh.

JOYCE: (Pause) It's still in there.

HARVEY: Uh-huh.

JOYCE: For the rest of his life Harvey, our little boy will wear a fingerpaint jar on his thumb.

HARVEY: Uh-huh.

JOYCE: I'm running off with the mailman.

HARVEY: Uh-huh.

ANNCR: At Sperry Corporation, we're concerned about this listening problem. So we've set up listening programs that Sperry employees worldwide can attend. We know these programs are making us a lot better at listening to the people we do business with. And, we like to think the people we live with.

JOYCE: Just the two of us Harvey. The mailman and me and a nice little bungalow in the Poconos.

HARVEY: That's nice. (Pause)

ANNCR: Sperry. We understand how important it is to listen.

(SFX: STREET SOUNDS)

HIM: Excuse me, ma'am... do you know any brand names famous for carpet protection?

HER: (Irritated) What?... Look, I've been handed lines before, but this—

HIM: I'm taking a survey.

HER: Right, and I'm Annie Oakley. Seriously, I'm happily married, so bug off.

HIM: If you could just give me a leading carpet protection brand name...

HER: Sure, Scotchgard, OK? Now, I'm gonna level with you. I'm not married, but I do have a boyfriend. Comprende?

HIM: Can you name any brands besides Scotchgard?

HER: (Softening up) OK, OK, he's not exactly my boyfriend. But we do have a date tonight and—

HIM: Can you?...

HER: Break my date?!!

HIM: No...

HER: (Disappointed) Oh...

HIM: Can you name any brands besides Scotchgard?

HER: Hey, come off it... Scotchgard is the *only* well-known name in carpet protection. Now, about tonight, I did have a bowling engagement with my Uncle Max...

HIM: Uh, I'll need to know your name, age, and occupation.

HER: Hey, I'll go out with you. But don't start getting serious on me.

ANNCR: Scotchgard Carpet Protector. The name that needs no introduction.

The Gold Award Winners on the Gold Award Winners

The Gold Award Winners on the Gold Award Winners

Consumer Newspaper
Over 600 Lines
Campaign

Agency: Scali, McCabe, Sloves
Client: Volvo

It's always exciting when you're at a disadvantage. Or at least what appears to be a disadvantage. Because then the challenge is so much greater.

Last year people were visiting automobile showrooms for two reasons; cash rebates and great gas mileage. Volvo offered neither. What it did offer was a car made well enough to last an average of 18.7 years in Sweden.

Still, it seemed that the only logical way to generate traffic for Volvo dealers was to address the issues of rebates and gas mileage.

During the creation of the campaign, Jim would pay close attention to competitive advertising. He'd often come into the office, slam a newspaper on the desk and say something like, "Look at this, Frank! Every day they're offering you more money to buy one of these heaps. It's unbelievable." It started to look as if car makers were stepping over each other to see who could promise the highest rebate. Then suddenly it just hit us. The more money someone offered you to buy a car, the less desirable that car obviously has to be. We just followed that line of reasoning to its logical conclusion. The headline and visual came simultaneously. Then we started clipping rebate ads like coupons for the photograph.

Next we needed an ad that touted highway and city mileages. Again, studying the competitive ads we noticed that the most impressive figures seem to have been achieved by sacrificing the quality of the car construction. The logic of trying to save money with an economy car that would fall apart in a few years escaped us. "Figures, figures," Jim kept saying. "What *we* need is *a* figure." "We've got a figure," I said. "18.7 years." That's all I remember. The 18.7 Year Highway/City ad was just there. As if it had always been there. In the three years Jim and I worked together I don't think we ever knew as instantly an ad was right as we knew this one was.

The psychiatrist ad came to us one day when we were comparing the cost of a high-end Volvo with the cost of a low-end Mercedes. Considering what you got with each car, it occurred to us that anyone who bought the Mercedes was crazy.

"Maybe we can get a psychiatrist to attest to that fact," one of us suggested.

After a lot of searching, we found a psychiatrist who owned a Volvo and loved it. He totally understood the idea behind the ad, and was willing to do it on two conditions. First, that all his proceeds from the ad be donated to a local hospital. And, second, that the idea of his doing an ad be approved by a group of doctors on the local medical ethics committee.

We waited for two weeks for a decision from the doctors.

The ad lived.

Frank Fleizach, Jim Perretti, Larry Cadman

Consumer Newspaper
600 Lines or Less
Campaign

Agency: Doyle Dane Bernbach
Client: IBM Office Products Division

The problem was the same as it's always been: to find the most important thing you could say about the product. And then find a new, fresh, imaginative, highly-memorable way of attracting the reader's attention and making him believe and buy.

With the IBM Correcting Selectric Typewriter, we were lucky. It has a correcting feature that can actually lift a typing error clean off the page in less than 4 seconds.

Without it, you have to use correction paper (8 seconds). Or an eraser (10 seconds) Or correction fluid (as much at 25 seconds).

Fortunately, once again, nobody's perfect. Making a typing error is a very human experience nearly everyone has had. Even the best typists make occasional errors.

So our product has interest: First, it saves you time. And time is money. Second, it makes you look perfect—even when you're not.

We chose newspaper advertising for its immediacy. And we chose small space for the extra frequency it gave us. Less is more.

Roy Grace, Tom Yobbagy

Make no mistake.

To correct just a single typing error on an original document—using correction paper takes 8 seconds.
Using an eraser, 10 seconds.
Correction fluid, as much as 25 seconds.
But using an IBM Correcting Selectric Typewriter takes only 3.6 seconds.
Compared to correction paper, that's a time-saving of 55%. Compared to an eraser, a time-saving of 64%. Correction fluid, as much as 86%.
When you consider the number of errors made each year, the IBM Correcting Selectric produces real savings.
It also produces error-free work—because it actually lifts errors clean off the page.
Get an IBM Correcting Selectric.
To order, call your local IBM Office Products Division Representative at 901-529-6276. Or call IBM *Direct* toll-free at 800-631-5582, Ext. 12.
(If you own an IBM electric typewriter, be sure to ask about IBM's attractive trade-in allowance.)
The IBM Correcting Selectric: With the cost of everything else going up, it's nice to know you can bring the cost of mistakes down.

IBM
Correcting Selectric Typewriter
901-529-6276

18.7 YEARS CITY. **18.7 YEARS HIGHWAY.**

**Consumer Magazine
Color Page or Spread
Including
Magazine Supplements**

Agency: Doyle Dane Bernbach
Client: Volkswagen

Only one other wagon gets better mileage than a Dasher Diesel.

The subject of the ad was not new: reiterate the fact that Volkswagen's Dasher Diesel Wagon was the best mileage wagon in America. As an out-and-out statement by itself, it was a powerful piece of advertising; but we felt it had already been done to death.

So to explore a slightly different approach to the message, we wondered if there was possibly a wagon lurking somewhere that the EPA might have overlooked. And we found one.

Peter Bregman, Joseph Del Vecchio

11

**Consumer Magazine
Color Campaign
Including
Magazine Supplements**

Agency: Scali, McCabe, Sloves
Client: Volvo

The "Brownie" ad is interesting. After you work on Volvo for a few years you learn some things. One of them is that station wagon ads, as a rule, are the hardest ads to do. I don't know why. They just are.

This one, however, was a pleasant exception. It came about as a result of a letter sent to us by three Brownie leaders from California who trooped everywhere in Volvos. And considering our objectives, it was an ideal solution.

We always try to talk about the safety afforded by the quality of construction in a Volvo wagon. Simply because wagons are purchased, for the most part, by people with small children. Over the years we've had many discussions about parents' concern for the safety of their children. One issue that frequently came up was that the concern was even more intense when they were responsible for someone else's kids. We were struck by the realization that these women were responsible for someone else's kids every day. That seemed to make their choice of Volvo wagons even more meaningful.

The headline was actually inspired by the photograph that accompanied their letter. Looking at it we were saying things like, "What great little kids. But what a responsibility." I think I said, "You wouldn't want to pack *them* into a piece of tin." It didn't take long to hammer that into the final headline.

Frank Fleizach, Jim Perretti, Larry Cadman

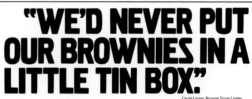

15

Consumer Magazine
Less than One Page
B/W or Color Single

Agency: Ally & Gargano
Client: Pentax

If there was any creative act here, it happened years ago in Japan when an anonymous industrial designer looked at the junk euphemistically called "pocket cameras" and drew up the initial plans for a 110 camera that would be an SLR, have interchangeable fine glass lenses, and would fit in the palm of your hand.

The ad simply demonstrated the guy's camera.

As for the media, the ad ran on consecutive right hand pages.

Which added to its effectiveness for all those readers who don't skim a magazine from the back to the front.

Dennis D'Amico, Tom Messner

**WHICH HAND
HAS THE PENTAX CAMERA?**

The one on the right holds the Pentax Auto 110, the only 110 SLR camera with interchangeable lenses.
But, if you guessed the one on the left, you weren't far off. It holds the optional wide-angle and telephoto lenses.
The purpose of this demonstration? To show how small and convenient a high quality, SLR camera system can be.
If you've ever missed a great photograph because you didn't feel like lugging a big camera around, you now know what **THE PENTAX AUTO 110.**
to do: Just get your hands on an Auto 110.

17

Trade
Black and White
Page or Spread

Agency: Della Femina, Travisano & Partners
Client: Alexandra de Markoff

Creating this ad was perhaps the single most difficult assignment any one of us had ever had.

I remember how it all started like it was yesterday. Our creative director was pacing up and down the halls, patting the perspiration off his brow and screaming, "Great Caesar's ghost."

The three of us (all being college graduates) knew something was up.

"What's the matter chief?" Harold asked.

"Look," he said, "we're on the verge of losing de Markoff and you three guys are the only ones who can save it. Will you help?"

"Sure," we all answered in unison. And after three or four days of going through old award annuals and pleading with friends for their help, we finally came up with what many consider the most provocative piece of cosmetic advertising ever done.

In fact, it was so well received, three months after this award winning work started running, we lost the account.

Jay Taub—Former Associate Creative Director, now sells shoes through the mail.
Harold Karp—Former Associate Creative Director, now owns his own Carvel franchise.
Phil Silvestri—Former Art Director, now teaches at the School of Visual Arts.

de MARKOFF.
FOR THE WOMAN WHO PLAYS HARD TO FORGET.

It's an attitude.
A certain unpredictability.
A style that dares, even these days, to be elegant. A style that no one can second guess. Or forget.
It comes easy to you. With Countess Isserlyn Makeup.
A precision-blended foundation that's as weightless as your

own skin. With a radiant finish that gets things started.
And like you, it just won't quit. It actually looks better as the day goes on. Countess Isserlyn by Alexandra de Markoff. In liquid and creme.
They'll all want to know you. By heart.

19

Trade
Color Page or Spread

Agency: Della Femina, Travisano & Partners
Client: Simac Appliances

October 25, 1980—Stan and I receive work requisition for a 4/C introductory ad for PastaMatic. Due in one month. No problem.
November 24, 1980—Stan and I receive reminder ad is due tomorrow. We ask account group for extension. "Impossible." Stan and I sit down to work.
June 2, 1981—One Show requests that we write about creation of Gold Award Winner for PastaMatic. Due in three weeks. No problem.
June 22, 1981—Stan and I receive reminder that article is due tomorrow. We ask One Show for extension. "Impossible." Stan and I sit down to work.

Frank DiGiacomo, Stan Block

21

Trade
Less than One Page
B/W or Color Single

Agency: Greenstone & Rabasca
Client: WE'RE Associates

It's no secret that the inner city is becoming less and less desirable to big business, and that moving corporate offices, or at least support services, computers, accounting, etc., to the suburbs is more prevalent than ever. Thus, developers and builders in areas surrounding New York City (New Jersey, Westchester, Rockland County, Southern Connecticut and Long Island) are fiercely fighting for a share of the market. Anyone who has ever taken a look at the commercial real estate sections of *The Wall Street Journal* or *The New York Times* knows the clutter; a hodgepodge of tombstone and picture-of-the building ads.

The assignment was simple (he says with tongue in cheek). Create a small space ad that will stand out. The client wants a headline telling prospects his space is one-half the cost. We came up with dozens of ways to say that—but when put together with a number of visual approaches, they all seemed to lack impact.

Back to the target prospect. What's this person like—background, etc. Well, he's dealing with blueprints all the time—dimensions—often expressed in lines with arrowheads. A square foot of space expressed in these terms would stand out we thought. The client loved it. But a square foot of space in *The New York Times* was more than the budget could bear. So would you believe ½ square foot? Even at one half the size it was originally intended to be, this ad has proven to be very effective—in getting prospects to call our client—and in winning awards.

Ken Rabasca

23

Trade
Any Size
B/W or Color Campaign

Agency: McCann-Erickson
Client: The New York Times

When you carry the weight of the world on your shoulders campaigns like this are a cinch.

Ira Madris, Bruce Nelson

THESE TIMES DEMAND THE TIMES.

The New York Times

25

Collateral
Sales Kits

Agency: Designframe
Client: West Point Pepperell

The task put to us by our client, Martex, was to develop a product book that would be given to buyers at the opening of Spring Market Week season. Martex wanted the end result of this project to be a creative presentation of their equally creative products, and to show how the various sheet patterns looked when placed in a complete environment.

Martex had already come up with the concept of featuring their products in an all-white setting. Their stylists also found all of the locations and designed the interiors in which the products would appear. This tremendous undertaking on their part made the project a wonderful joint effort between client and designer. It was a unique situation in which we could work closely with their stylists and the photographer to art-direct the images of product and environment.

We were encouraged by Martex to feel our way through the project; they didn't ask to approve the layouts or designs, but let us follow our instincts. We knew we wanted the classical look of a hard-bound book in a slipcase. We then searched for a certain typographic look, and began developing a visual theme. With our first priority being product detail, we went back to our studio to develop the story that unfolds in "White Rooms."

We wanted to develop a strong graphic theme by beginning each new pattern with a soft black and white photograph of an architectural detail found in the room. The first spread for each pattern is composed of this same detail and a selected element of the pattern. In the following two spreads more is learned about the rooms; the features of the pattern are revealed, eventually encompassing the entire environment and the product's relationship to it. Like a novel that begins by giving the reader a taste of what will come in future chapters, "White Rooms" begins with detail to entice the reader into looking further and learning more about the rooms.

The joint effort that culminated in "White Rooms" began in Martex's beautifully designed rooms and continued through the final production. Ideas were further developed in our work with the printers and binders, until the desired effects of color and mood were achieved. The result of the gradual unfolding of interior relationships was an elegant volume to be enjoyed long after its initial purpose is over. We could not have done this without the unusual amount of support and freedom given us by our client, or without the input of those who gave us the elements with which to work.

James A. Sebastian

29

Collateral
Direct Mail

Agency: Eisenberg Inc./Dallas
Client: Dallas Society of Visual Communications

The Dallas Society of Visual Communications has always offered the greatest creative opportunities for invitations and announcements to its meetings and seminars. Unfortunately, budget is limited. So, cleverness aside, the real creativity comes with what you can squeeze out of $300 and still attract creative people to a meeting after work.

Because we were talking to a market that was familiar with Sam Scali's relationship with Perdue Chicken, creating the invitation to hear him speak about the Perdue campaign was a cinch. The concept felt right from the start. And from there everything just fell into place.

The design consisted of elements of a regular package of Perdue Chicken: the Styrofoam trays we got from a supermarket chain: the two-color cards were printed at cost, and the shrink wrap was sealed one morning by meat packers at the local grocery. As for the copy, Scali's string of successful campaigns made writing about him easy. So there it is. Despite some late evenings and early Saturdays, Scali's Perdue Chicken invitation was duck soup.

Glyn Powell

31

Collateral
P.O.P.

Agency: Ed Yardang & Associates/San Antonio
Client: Ed Yardang & Associates

Looking back, the concept seems so obvious it's amazing:

A museum poster featuring the New York Art Director's Show in a museum. To show the public that good advertising is an art form.

How simple can you get? But anyone who's ever had to do a piece for their own agency knows it's usually the toughest assignment. Because there are no restrictions. No marketing plan. No client no-no's. Only a budget (nebulous) and a deadline (tight, of course). Plus the pressure you put on yourself and each other to come up with a great solution.

Around here, it turns into a sort of spontaneous combustion of ideas, arguments, compromise and compliments. Like other agencies, we call it the team concept, for lack of a precise term.

It's like having fun and being miserable at the same time.

And when you win a Gold, and are asked to write about the creative experience, it's tougher than having to come up with the idea in the first place.

June Robinson, Becky Benavides, Lupe Garcia, Bev Coiner

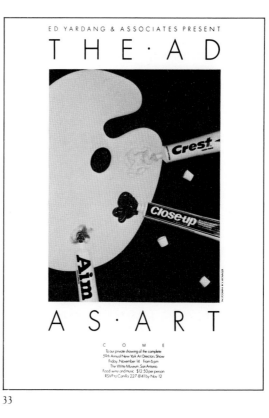

33

Outdoor Campaign

Agency: Corker Sullivan/Washington
Client: Western Insecticide

Ask any realtor..."you don't have to worry about termites in this area." This was the stigma Western Insecticide wanted to change when they hired Corker Sullivan.

In most regions, real estate market is synonymous with termite inspection volume. Western Insecticide was operating with limited funds and no annually allocated budget. This had a direct effect on the type of media to utilize. Rather than just inform people there were termites in Spokane, we wanted to show them. That eliminated radio. Television cost was prohibitive. Newspaper was the same with the additional problem of one-day shelf life, thus making it an unfeasible media buy.

Outdoor was the survivor, with a four-month exposure and low cost per impression. With a total expenditure of $5,000, we felt we could visually present our case with enough impact to get those darn critters (not the realtors, the termites!). Also, the initial impact, or greatest impact, of outdoor occurs within the first ten days after posting. We wanted and needed the board to work just as hard every day, month after month. It did! The client received 10-14 calls per day for four months, while his real estate-related temite-inspection business increased 85%. Today, more than a year after the board expired, Western Insecticide is still receiving calls related to this specific advertisement.

We are very proud to have won this award, (it's the first one ever sent to Spokane you know). We all felt it would win, since it was the first time anything like it has ever been done in the outdoor industry. The important thing, however, is to keep coming up with firsts. I mean anybody can come up with *a* first, but over the years it's how *many* firsts you create that counts. Just look at the Wright Brothers. Sure, they taught man to fly, but what have they done since? Look for us next year!

Dennis Sullivan

37

Public Service
Outdoor Single

Agency: Warwick, Welsh & Miller
Client: Distilled Spirits Council of the United States

At Warwick, Welsh & Miller, moderation in the use and enjoyment of distilled spirits is second nature to us. Given the fact that we handle a great deal of Seagram's business, it should certainly come as no surprise that we are keenly aware of our responsibilities in this area. In fact, many of the advertisements we produce for Seagram's brands carry their own moderation message within the body copy. So much for the preface.

The assignment that we received from the Distilled Spirits Council of the United States, was to create a poster that would simply and powerfully communicate a message of moderation when drinking. Given the media selection (TDI on trains and buses) we knew that we had to be short and sweet. No diatribes. It's just a fact of life that people who are "sardine-canned" into public transportation aren't inclined to want to spend time reading a message about moderation. They're probably wishing for a cool drink because they're undoubtedly suffering from perspiration.

Anyhow, Jerry and I sat down together and spent two days on the job. We came up with seven ideas that we felt were really terrific. Two posters were finally bought: one, which talked about drinking at business lunches, was headlined, "Staggering Lunch Hours"; the other was "Square."

Did we think we had done work that would win some awards? We'd honestly have to answer "yes." Besides taking the "Gold" in the One Show, "Square" and "Staggering" were print finalists for Public Service in this year's Clios.

The funny part about the whole thing is that we felt we had stronger stuff in the presentation.

Sounds kind of familiar, doesn't it?

Wait'll next year.

Alan Barcus, Jerry Prestomburgo

43

Corporate
Outdoor Single

Agency: Doyle Dane Bernbach
Client: American Airlines

Creating this ad was a lot like creating this explanation for creating this ad. It began with the phone call—"I know we aren't giving you much time and I'm sorry we're calling so late, but we need it."

So we sat down, looked at each other, looked at the floor, looked at the walls, looked at the ceiling, and finally one of us said, "I got it! Let's work on this tomorrow."

Next day, we're working. An hour, an hour and a half. The writer's throwing out visuals, the art director's throwing out headlines, finally the art director throws out the writer.

Next day, phone rings again. "So???" "So, what?" "Got anything yet?" "Not yet." "Client's all over me." "We're working on it." "Okay, thanks." (With this inspiration we go out for Sushi.)

The above continues for a few more days. Finally, after coming up with some of the worst ideas ever to grace a billboard, it comes. It's on paper. We look at it one more time before presentation and in one voice say: "They'll never buy it."

They buy it.
End of ad.
End of explanation.

Hal Kaufman, Joseph Del Vecchio

47

Student Competition

Student: Joseph Perz
Product: Perdue Egg

The 7:07 AM LIRR to Penn Station: egg thoughts
The introduction of branded eggs
branded chickens. Perdue
I wonder why Perdue doesn't introduce branded eggs?
eggs: money back guarantee
    larger
    harder shell
    more consistent in color and size
hatched, shell, broken, yoke, white, Easter, Easter Bunny,
basket, fresh, farm, scrambled, sunnyside, etc. carton
chicken little. The sky is falling. Ouch.
which came first, the chicken or the egg?
"egg" essential.
L.I. housewife finds snake in egg. 1980.
our eggs don't come in different sizes (positive?) maybe
different sizes, shapes, colors. That's a horse of...
chicken. Oakland Raiders (no)
that chicken on channel 5 cartoons w/the dog (that's a
    rooster)
Paramount. Cookin' Good. "Oh, Frank."
Perdue means quality. money back guarantee
"We feed our chickens better than you feed yourself."
Perdue eggs: "Now you can eat better than
    our chickens" (?)
Egg is beginning. Chicken is end.
Subway ads: "The quality of parts equal to whole."
each chicken part is labeled.
Ah! Perdue branded eggs: "Another Quality Chicken Part
    from Perdue."
(That's it)
8:00: "There's a train stuck ahead of us..."

Joe Perz

49

Consumer Television
60 Seconds Single

Agency: TBWA/London
Client: Lego (U.K.)

There were two satisfying aspects about writing this commercial.

The first that it has won many awards.

The second that it didn't require a cast of thousands or umpteen helicopter shots to do so.

It also proved that you don't have to resort to a presenter commercial if you're on a limited budget. Commercials which at best are dull, at worst invisible.

Like other winning commercials in The One Show, Kipper was a single, simple idea.

Probably like the others, it was far from simple getting there. We burned a lot of midnight oil to get the concept, and the account team wore out a lot of shoe leather (and no doubt credit cards) to get script approval.

The actual shooting time was seventeen days. This involved building each model in stages, shooting a few frames of film and building a little more. To give you some idea of what a mammoth task this is, the dragon model contained 20,000 Lego bricks.

Ken Turner and his team at Clearwater did a painstaking job; apart from having to work out the building sequences, they had to work out zooms and pans. No easy task, because they had to be worked out in stages to correspond with the building sequences.

Our decision to shoot the whole thing in one take didn't make life easier, either.

Finally, we must add three more names to the list of credits. David Lyall, model maker extraordinaire of Lego.

And Lego fans David Cozens age 9 and Jamie Watson age 8, both of whom were involved in an advisory capacity.

Mike Cozens, Graham Watson

Consumer Television
60 Seconds Campaign

Agency: McCann-Erickson
Client: Coca-Cola

We won our award for a television campaign, so there were a lot of people involved in the effort, and a variety of feelings and reflections resulting from it.

Generally, I can say that working on Coca-Cola is about as much fun as you can have in this business. It is one company that understands and believes in advertising. It is also one company that believes in leadership. And, in this very competitive market, that also makes it about as much of a challenge as you can have in this business.

Every commercial for Coca-Cola tries to be something special: it tries to be what Coca-Cola is.

Coca-Cola is the highest quality a soft drink can be: its advertising must reflect that quality in every detail. Coca-Cola has a unique and distinctive taste and refreshment, and its advertising must be distinctive from all other soft drinks. Coca-Cola has a legacy of over 90 years of imagery, and that imagery must be taken into account—must be considered a product ingredient. Coca-Cola is a leader, the most imitated product in the world, in fact. And one thing a leader can never do is imitate the imitators.

So every commercial for Coca-Cola must do what Coca-Cola does; it must make you feel refreshed, make you feel good, give you a lift, and it must say "only Coke is the real thing."

If you accomplish all that in a commercial for Coca-Cola, you can win an award, you can drive a huge business, you can energize thousands of Coca-Cola people around the country, and, for one brief moment, you can make the whole world smile.

Scott Miller

51

53

**Consumer Television
30 Seconds Single
10 Seconds Single
10 Seconds Campaign**

Agency: Ally & Gargano
Client: Federal Express

I'd like to take this opportunity to say hello and to thank a nice, kind, warm and wonderful woman who has sort of settled down and who now lives in Miami Beach on 94th Street and Collins Avenue.

My Mother.

My Mother, who just the other day called me to tell me that she saw one of my Federal Express commercials on television... and said it was art... and that I was so clever... and went on to recreate every possible frame she could remember... and told me the casting was great ... and the words were very witty... and she laughed a lot ... and went into *utter silence,* I mean silence, when I, in a very, very soft voice said:

"Mom, that was an Emery commercial."

Mike Tesch

55

59 and 61

**Consumer Television
30 Seconds Campaign**

Agency: Backer & Spielvogel
Client: Miller Brewing

There are two reasons why we are especially pleased to have won a Gold Medal in this category this year.

First, because competition in Television Campaigns is extremely stiff since most of the money is spent in media and production.

And second, because doing outstanding commercials for Lite Beer from Miller after 7 years and 70 previous commercials is a tough act to follow.

Giving credit where credit is due, we are in the rare position of being able to say that we have an unusually enlightened client.

Nicholas Gisonde, Jeane Bice

57

Public Service Television
60 Seconds Single

Agency: Ogilvy & Mather/Canada
Client: The Parkinson Foundation of Canada

The Parkinson Puzzle spot actually resulted from a lot of different elements coming together perfectly. First the client, who was open minded and gave Peter and me free rein. Then the disease itself, which had an intrinsic visual idea... the shaking hand which is the most obvious Parkinson symptom. The client had shown us a documentary and there was one scene of a woman's hand shaking that lasted for about two minutes. The amazing thing was that it wasn't boring, in fact it was hypnotizing. So we knew it would have to be the main visual.

The idea behind the spot was to *inform* people about the disease and the Foundation, not to get money. So there was an opportunity to show the cold facts. We wanted to make people feel what it was like to have the disease. That's why we decided to use a lot of point-of-view camera work.

The idea of the puzzle came from my three-year-old daughter Stephanie. I thought we should show how the disease made simple manual tasks really difficult for the patient. What could be more simple than a children's puzzle? And Stephanie had one at home. So Peter and I went out and bought a new one just like it to show the client. They loved the idea.

We were lucky enough after that to get some of the best production house talent in Toronto to shoot the spot, to find a real Parkinson patient who loved to act, and to have a director (Chris Sanderson) who got a great performance out of a really reticent three-year-old boy. And the white limbo ambience of the spot we owe totally to that great straight-jacket scene Tony Curtis did in the "Boston Strangler."

When we came to New York to pick up the award we went to the Underground disco and actually saw Curtis there. I wanted to thank him, but didn't think he'd be able to hear over all that loud music. He sure has aged since the "Boston Strangler."

Dianne Allen, Peter Jones

Public Service Television
30 Seconds Single

Agency: Della Femina, Travisano & Partners
Client: World Hunger Project

Someone was sharing his personal experience of watching a child die of starvation and he said, "If people could actually witness this, it would make them want to reverse this horrible process."

The idea for the commercial came within an instant of his making that comment. If I could do a commercial that showed the process of starvation in reverse, i.e., actually show a starving child getting healthy in front of their eyes, it might motivate people to do something about the fact that 15 million people die of starvation every year.

The end of *death by starvation* is an idea whose time has come and all the considerations that get in the way of doing something about it will be ground up in that context.

Ron Travisano

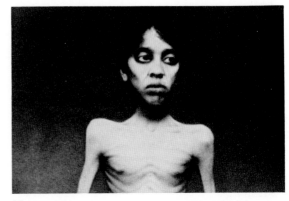

65

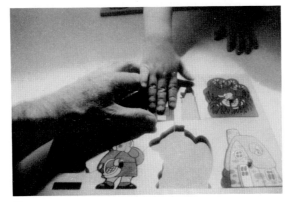

63

**Corporate Television
30 Seconds Single**

Agency: Meldrum & Fewsmith/Ohio
Client: Blue Cross & Blue Shield of Northeast Ohio

This commercial began on a gray morning in Cleveland. Of course, many of our commercials begin on gray mornings in Cleveland, but this one happened to be particularly gray.

You see, we had just been informed by our client, Blue Cross and Blue Shield of Northeast Ohio, that the theme line we recommended for our major multi-media campaign had been used by some other Blue Cross group, in some other market. If memory serves me, Paducah.

Needless to say, we were creatively devastated. I mean, how would you feel if an idea you had developed had already been done by some copywriter in Paducah. We had no choice but to change our theme. If, for no other reason, than to save face.

Lo and behold, the new line we created—"The world's most popuplar health club" meshed beautifully with nearly all the pieces that comprised our original Blue Cross campaign.

It meshed with the newspaper ads. The magazine ads. The direct mail. The outdoor posters. And *three* out of four T.V. spots.

That's right, only one T.V. spot did not work with our new line. Naturally, we replaced it with a new spot.

The new commercial (you guessed it) turned out to be our One Show Gold Medal winner "The Body."

So, at this time, I'd like to thank the judging committee for recognizing "The Body" in the 1981 One Show.

And I'd also like to thank an unknown copywriter in Paducah.

Chris Perry

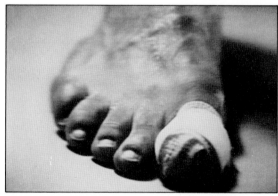

69

**Consumer Radio
Single**

Agency: Chiat/Day – Los Angeles
Client: Yamaha

Unfortunately for many creative people, the development of a radio campaign seems to flow from a basic three-step process.

Step One is to confront yet again the frightening reality that there are no pictures. The feeling of panic starts about the mid-calf, gradually moving up the body and terminating in the chest with symptoms not unlike those of a mild heart attack. I, myself, have seen creative people carted off to the Emergency Coronary Unit suffering from nothing more serious than "fear of radio."

Step Two is concerned mainly with fighting down an almost uncontrollable desire to change careers.

Step Three, of course, is to simply sit down and do the damn thing.

At Chiat/Day, we find it saves time to start with step three.

Now, if there was anything we'd learned about the prospective motorcycle buyer in three years of working on the Yamaha Motorcycle account, it was this: while logical considerations like engine size, handling characteristics, technology, price and economy are important to the purchase process, the final decision often has as much to do with emotion as it does with logic.

It was entirely logical, therefore, that our radio campaign of 13 (count 'em) commercials should deal with both of these realities in as memorable a way as possible.

We developed a theme line (or, if you insist, a slogan): YAMAHA THE WAY IT SHOULD BE. This seemed to sum up everything anyone ever felt about what it means to ride a motorcycle—freedom, escape, fun, technology, individuality, machismo—and thereby ascribed all those things to Yamaha.

With the help of John Bahlor, an excellent composer/arranger in Hollywood, we created not a jingle, but a song—music and lyrics in both ballad and rock form—to convey the imagery and emotion we were after.

And we developed an understated, self-assured, somewhat tongue-in-cheek narrative style which we felt would leap forth from the welter of hardsell boasting, claims and counter-claims which still seem to dominate the airwaves.

Directed at a combined audience of "owners" and "interested non-owners," all these elements worked together to communicate not only what it means to ride a motorcycle, but what it means to ride a Yamaha.

The commercial that won the One Show Gold Award talks specifically to that second audience, the "interested non-owners"—those people who rode a long time ago and are ready to get back on, as well as to folks who've never ridden and figure that maybe they've waited long enough.

The results of the campaign in the marketplace, if you're interested, (if you're not, you're in the wrong business) were very satisfying.

Brand awareness is up.

Ad awareness is up.

And sales are up.

Thank God for that.

And thank you for the award.

Dave Butler

SEE GOLD AWARD WINNER 71

Consumer Radio Campaign

Agency: Ogilvy & Mather
Client: American Express

How were these commercials written?

They weren't.

They are pure Nichols and May. Well, almost pure. Mike Nichols and Elaine May worked "live" and improvised. Nancy Perez and I edited. And laughed a lot.

It began with an assignment from the American Express Card people to do some radio commercials to reach people we weren't reaching in our television campaign. "Do You Know Me?" has been done on radio, mostly with restaurant owners and theatre producers, but famous or not, we wanted to try something different.

The original idea was to have a bunch of the best radio teams—Mike & Elaine, Bob and Ray, Dick and Bert, Stiller & Meara—but that fabulous idea was fabulously expensive. So leading off the list were Mike & Elaine— they hadn't teamed up in a while and we were happy to get together with them getting together.

Anyway, with some ads, brochures, a lunch or two as a briefing, we went to work. Or, they went to work.

It was fun to watch and listen to. Improvisation at its best; all guiding somehow to lead to a selling point for the American Express Card.

Along with all the funny lines went some work in cutting and splicing—not all the situations stopped with a punch line at sixty seconds: some sixty-seven, some forty-nine.

As Gold Award winners, the spots obviously pleased somebody. Including those of us at Ogilvy & Mather and at American Express.

But as they say, it sure is a joy to work with great material. And nice, smart and very funny people.

Thanks, Mike & Elaine.

Tom Rost

SEE GOLD AWARD WINNER 73

Public Service Radio Single

Agency: The Marschalk Company
Client: The City of New York

Before we did any advertising for Gun Control, we talked to three groups of people.

First came the politicians. People from the Mayor's office, the Police Commissioner's office and the District Attorney's office who had helped get the law written and passed, and who wanted to see it work.

Then came the cops. The guys who deal with the dope addicts, youth gangs and hard core criminals every day. The guys who know that some day one of those illegal handguns may be pointed at them.

Finally, we talked to the street kids. They ranged in age from 14 to 18 and any one of them (girl or boy) could have gotten us an illegal handgun before the close of business.

No three groups had less in common. Though their lives were linked by a single common thread—illegal handguns—their views on the subject were light-years apart.

Yet each group told us an identical story. They each told of young children finding guns in the house and accidentally killing themselves.

The politicians used the story as an example of the staggering incidence of guns in New York City. The cops told of fighting back tears when you see a six-year-old, gun at his side, lying in a pool of blood. The teenagers talked about "knowing someone in the neighborhood who lost a kid brother that way."

We created a number of radio commercials. They were packed with information about the toughness of the new gun law, and the logistics of getting rid of a handgun during the amnesty period. It all added up to a solid, strong campaign. Yet somehow, we felt something was missing. The emotional tug that we had felt from our group discussions wasn't there. So we went back to the one story that cut across all lines.

As the saying goes, the commercial wrote itself. We have learned over the years that the truth, unembellished, can sometimes be the most effective creative of all.

Mayor Koch recorded the spot for us. He got it on the third take. Hal Douglas generously volunteered his services for the tag. Trackworks donated the studio time.

No one knows how many lives were saved by the new gun law and the advertising that brought it to the public's attention.

We can, however, substantiate one case. While our commercial was playing during the awards presentation at The One Show, an absolutely flaming idiot stood up and screamed "No politics!"

Fortunately for him we had turned in our guns.

Marshall W. Karp, Andrew J. Langer

SEE GOLD AWARD WINNER 75

Public Service
Radio Campaign

Agency: Bonneville Productions/Utah
Client: The Church of Jesus Christ of Latter-day Saints

KEVIN: (His Version) I was working on some ideas for a Mother's Day Campaign. Our client, the Public Communications Department of the Mormon Church, had asked me to come up with something to give mothers a shot in the arm. This was my first time up to bat, as I had just come to Bonneville, and the legacy of nine years of award winning public service spots was staring me in the face. It was a bit terrifying.

I read a lot of books about family life, married life, and mother's lives, and after reading Dr. James Dobson's *What Wives Wish Their Husbands Knew About Women,* I realized that if I could give any mother a gift for Mother's Day it would say: Husband, be good to your wife —the mother of your children.

Driving to work one morning the idea for "Duet" came to me—a wife singing her deepest thoughts; her husband answering her with the surface things of the day—two people in two different worlds, yet in the same room, in the same home, in the same marriage. The tune and lyrics just came at the same time. When I got to the office I called my wife Khaliel. She was at home with our three kids. If anyone knew if it communicated, she would.

Khaliel liked the idea, and she's one of the best writers I know. She started refining the lyrics, helping with how a woman feels. It was a campaign that a married couple should work on together.

The Church liked the idea, but not for Mother's Day. And that was initially disappointing, but ultimately a blessing in disguise because later I was able to develop the concept into a full-blown radio and T.V. campaign.

Khaliel wrote the incredible tag, "Love isn't something you fall into . . . it's something you grow," and is the voice talent on the "Hers" spot. She's a gifted writer, a talented actress, and (best of all for me) a wonderful mate. The campaign brought us very close.

KHALIEL: (Her Version) These spots are essentially my husband's creation. I helped hone the lyrics and give the housewife's point of view. I remember staying up late one night after the kids were in bed and working and working and reworking the lyrics. It's the kind of creativity that, as Edison said, is 10% inspiration and 90% perspiration.

My other contribution was the tag. I enjoy writing the tags for these spots because what you do is encapsulate the message of the entire spot into one brief phrase. The tag has to be catchy. And I've learned something about the creative process that might be of interest here. It is this: you have to keep your focus *off* trying to be clever, catchy, creative, etc., and keep it *on* what you are trying to communicate. The cleverness will come if you give it room. When cleverness is your main objective, you just go stale. I wrote the tag, incidentally, while the family was eating breakfast.

I'm lucky to be married to a person who is secure enough to be able to include me in his creative work. And he is fortunate to be in a position where he is able to "advertise" things he believes in—in this case, marriage.

Khaliel and Kevin Kelly

SEE GOLD AWARD WINNER 77

Corporate Radio
Single

Agency: Scali, McCabe, Sloves
Client: Sperry Corporation

You asked for a short statement describing the creative process behind this commercial. As far as I can remember here's how it went.

RIGHT BRAIN HALF: Okay, so we have to write this Sperry "We understand how important it is to listen" spot. Think of it as a chance to do something terrific.

LEFT BRAIN HALF: Who are you kidding? It's radio, not TV.

RIGHT BRAIN HALF: Yeah, but it's for Sperry. They buy great work.

LEFT BRAIN HALF: It's also due tomorrow.

RIGHT BRAIN HALF: Look at how good we'll look if we come through.

LEFT BRAIN HALF: Look at how crummy we'll look after staying up all night.

RIGHT BRAIN HALF: If you don't be quiet I'm going to ignore your side and do it without you.

LEFT BRAIN HALF: You can't. We're right-handed. Without me your copy looks like Swahili.

RIGHT BRAIN HALF: Okay, how's this sound? Wife talking to husband over breakfast. He's glued to paper, not listening. She acts ridiculous to get his attention. Hey, we could even get Louise Lasser to do the wife. What do you think?

LEFT BRAIN HALF: I hate it. Borrowed interest. No big idea. Pedestrian. It doesn't go for the jugular. Off strategy.

RIGHT BRAIN HALF: Okay, you're right. We'll just have to stay up all night and really think this thing through.

LEFT BRAIN HALF: I love it.

Steve Kasloff

SEE GOLD AWARD WINNER 79

1981 Print Finalists

1981 Print Finalists

Consumer Newspaper Over 600 Lines Single

81

Art Director:
Peter Maisey

Writers:
Barry Sugondo
Paul Nuttall

Designer:
Peter Maisey

Artists:
Peter Maisey
Barry Sugondo

Client:
Walt Disney Prods.

Agency:
First City Advertising & Marketing/London

82

Art Director:
Paul Hanson

Writer:
Peter Little

Designer:
Paul Hanson

Photographer:
Paul Windsor

Client:
The Observer

Agency:
Davidson Pearce/London

83

Art Director:
Max Henry

Writer:
Stuart Blake

Designer:
Max Henry

Photographer:
Ian Giles

Client:
Volkswagen

Agency:
Doyle Dane Bernbach/London

84

Art Director:
Curvin O'Rielly

Writer:
Curvin O'Rielly

Designer:
Curvin O'Rielly

Photographer:
Cardio Fitness Center Files

Client:
Cardio Fitness Center

Agency:
O'Rielly & Partners/Conn.

85

Art Director:
Max Henry

Writer:
Stuart Blake

Designer & Artist:
Max Henry

Client:
Volkswagen

Agency:
Doyle Dane Bernbach/London

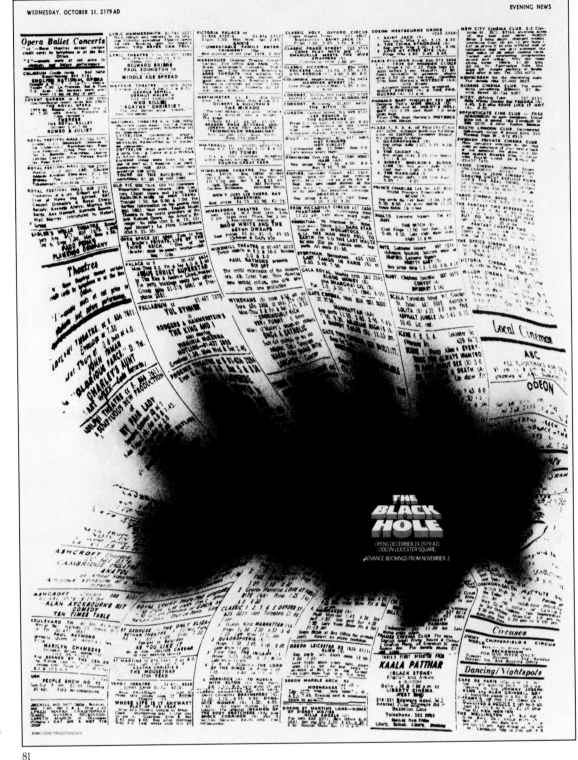

81

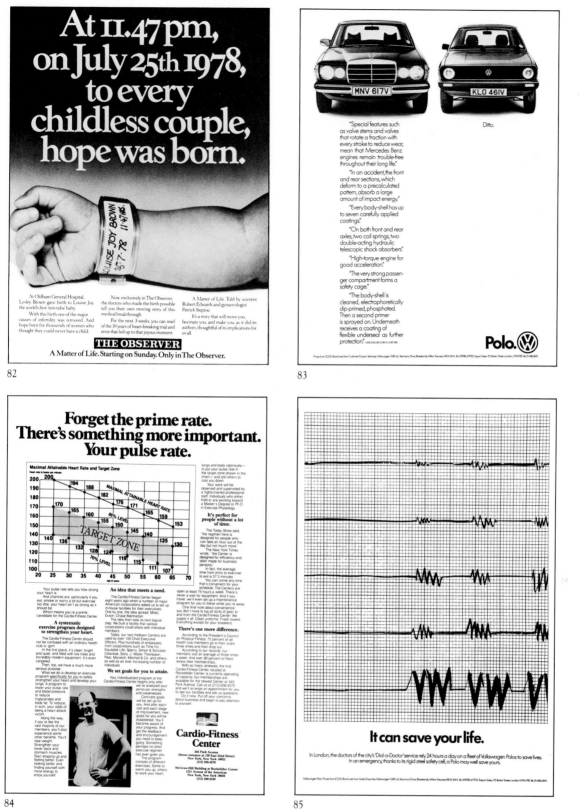

TWO WORDS OF COMFORT DURING THE TRANSIT STRIKE.

Even though you're walking everywhere these days, you can still travel in luxury.

Just use Dr. Scholl's products. They're designed to help keep feet comfortable and trouble-free. Even during the most trying times.

For instance, there's Dr. Scholl's Air-Pillo® Insoles.

They slip comfortably into your shoes. Thousands of tiny bubbles absorb the impact of every step. So you walk on soft latex foam instead of the hard ground.

And Air-Pillo Insoles help keep feet cool and dry.

If your feet get tired quickly, maybe you're not giving them enough support. Dr. Scholl's Flexo® Foam Arches are an easy way to comfort and support weaker arches and feet. That way, walking a few miles isn't an uphill battle.

And if pounding the pavement has led to a corn or callous, Dr. Scholl's has just the product to help relieve and remove the problem.

So visit the Dr. Scholl's Foot Care Display at a store near you.

It's the best way we know for your feet to meet the demands of the strike.

© 1980 Scholl, Inc.

Selling Rolls-Royces all day long makes you fussy what you drive home.

Rolls-Royce salesmen can hardly be expected to take their work home.

So what do they do?

They take ours.

Volkswagen Golfs.

The entire sales team at Jack Barclay in Berkeley Square drive them.

A bit of a come-down from a Silver Shadow you may think. (4½ins, to be precise.)

But they don't get uppity.

The distinct lack of 4ft 10ins in length turns into something of an advantage in congested streets.

30-odd to the gallon* makes flogging back and forth to the showroom less than thirsty work.

And even if they're in a rush to get away, 0–60 in 13.5 puts them but a few ticks behind the Rolls.

In other ways though, Rolls-Royce and Volkswagen have more than a little in common.

The way they're painted, the long service intervals, the reliability.

They're all things we've developed a name for.

Some say second to one.

Golf VW

Prices start from £3,459 (Golf L) £4,030. Brochures from Sales Enquiries, Volkswagen (GB) Limited, Yeomans Drive, Blakelands, Milton Keynes, MK14 5AN. Tel: (0908) 679121. Export Sales, 75 Baker Street, London, W1M 1RJ. Tel: 01-486 6161.
*Official fuel consumption figures for the Golf LS: 31.7 mpg (8.9 l/100 km) at a constant 75 mph, 41.8 mpg (6.8 l/100 km) at a constant 56 mph, and 28.9 mpg (9.2 l/100 km) on urban cycle.

Starting today, you can fly from Tel Aviv to Cairo. On El Al.

EL AL ‏אל על‏
The Airline of Israel. 610 Fifth Ave., New York City, N.Y. 10020 (212) 486-2600

IT'S ELECTION TIME. DISCOUNT EVERYTHING WE SAY.

Discount Plaids and Plushes. Discount Silkies and Saxonys. Discount hundreds of broadlooms across the board—the latest trends, the newest colors.

Discount carpets of Anso, Anso IV.* Anso on, Anso on.

For those are just a few of the candidates in the running during the Einstein Moomjy Presidential Election Sale.

What's more appropriate for an election than a cover-up? We have several worth investigating—our stain and dirt resistant Anso IV nylons.

Like some politicians, one is made to keep a very low profile. $19.99 a sq. yd., was $25.99. (Installation and padding are included in all prices).

The other is a plush that will go in a rush. It's $18.99, down from $22.99.

At $25.99 (was $30.99) your prints will come in. There's a nylon that will pull the wool over your eyes. Is $15.99, was $23.99. And a chic velvet to appeal to the effete intellectual. And to the feet. (It's $31.99, used to be $36.99).

At $28.99, our industrial look should appeal to big business. While at $14.99, our soft look should soften the hardest hard hat. Was $22.99.

There's a maxi of Saxies and even more Velours. Not just in red, white and blue. But lilacs, mauves, pastels, greys.

Our Berbers even took a trim for the election. There's a New Zealander that will only be here a short time. Bully for this 100% woolly—now $33.99, regularly $49.99.

CAMPAIGN PROMISES FOR ALL AREAS.

When you see the price of our area rugs, you'll demand a recount.

You won't believe your eyes.

Every square inch in our area rug department is discounted. That includes every square rug, every oval, every rectangle.

There's a tribal rite for both the left and right. And at over 50% off, the price is quite right. Is $349, was $800.

Not to mention some Bokharas and Antique Chinese reproductions made in France. Made even more possible by our low Election Sale prices. One 6'x7"x10' is $599, was $750.

And our round rugs are a perfect place for a cabinet to stand.

OUR ORIENTAL RUG POLICY: ALL THINGS TO ALL PEOPLE.

There are Manchurian candidates, Hopei candidates and Minzu candidates.

Our 9' x 12' Shantungs have come down several rungs. $3295, from $4752.

Politicians may promise you a rose garden, we promise you floral gardens. An 8'3"x11'6" Tienstin $1199, from $1699.

And there's an Ancient Oriental that lets bygones be buy gones. We have a 6'x9'. $1145, was $1499.

While you should discount all of the above (and don't forget our sale goes above and beyond), don't discount our selection. Our value. Or our service.

We don't.

If you're a New Jersey voter, there's probably an Einstein Moomjy in your district. If you're registered in New York, there's an Einstein Moomjy Election Sale Headquarters on 150 East 58th Street.

Our Election Sale goes before the voters November 3rd through the 8th.

But hurry. A heavy turn out is forecasted.

The Election Sale
Einstein Moomjy. The Carpet Department Store

*ALLIED CHEMICAL NYLON.
NOW IN NEW YORK: 150 EAST 58TH ST, BET. LEXINGTON & THIRD AVENUES (212) 758-0900 OPEN MON. TO FRI. 10-9 PM IN T. SAT. 10-6 & THURS. TILL 9 PM.
IN NEW JERSEY: PARAMUS, 120 ROUTE 17 (201) 265-6100 · N. PLAINFIELD, 910 ROUTE 22 (201) 755-6666 · WHIPPANY, 201 ROUTE 10 (201) 887-4600 · LAWRENCEVILLE, 2661 BRUNSWICK PIKE (ROUTE 1) (609) 883-0700
ALL N.J. STORES OPEN DAILY 10-9 PM, SAT. 10-6 PM, LAWRENCEVILLE STORE OPEN SUNDAY 12 PM TO 5 PM WE ACCEPT VISA, MASTERCARD AND OUR OWN CONVENIENT REVOLVING CHARGE

87

88

89

A SOBERING PROSPECTUS FOR THE LUXURY SEDAN BUYER.

MAKE	YEAR	ORIGINAL PRICE'	CURRENT VALUE'	RETAINED VALUE
BMW 5 SERIES	1975	$ 9,097	$ 7,486	82.3%
	1976	$10,590	$ 8,619	81.4%
	1977	$12,495	$ 9,575	76.6%
	1978	$14,840	$11,833	79.7%
	1979	$15,505	$15,550	100.3%
	1980	$20,650		
CADILLAC SEVILLE	1975	NOT MADE		
	1976	$12,479	$ 7,247	58.1%
	1977	$13,359	$ 8,733	65.4%
	1978	$14,710	$10,114	68.8%
	1979	$16,224	$12,436	76.7%
	1980	$20,477		
MERCEDES 280E	1975	$12,756	$ 8,672	68.0%
	1976	$14,296	$ 9,997	69.9%
	1977	$17,114	$12,539	73.3%
	1978	$19,711	$14,839	75.3%
	1979	$22,943	$19,231	83.8%
	1980	$26,193		
JAGUAR XJ6	1975	$13,100	$ 7,342	56.1%
	1976	$14,250	$ 8,653	60.7%
	1977	$16,500	$10,333	62.6%
	1978	$19,000	$12,903	67.9%
	1979	$20,000	N/A	N/A
	1980	$25,000		

Perhaps the most fiscally responsible way of determining an automobile's intrinsic worth is how well it performs on the used-car lot.

And according to the 1980 National Automobile Dealers Association Official Used-Car Guide, no other luxury sedan—domestic or imported—approaches the BMW 528i.

The explanation? In spite of the myriad of government regulations and the demands of the gas tank, the engineers at BMW have been able to design a high-quality, fuel-efficient automobile that never compromises the BMW conviction that extraordinary performance and precision engineering are the only rational motives for purchasing an expensive car.

So why invest in a car that merely offers the resale value of a Cadillac, Jaguar or Mercedes, when you can invest in something considerably better—a car that offers the resale value and extraordinary performance of a BMW?

THE ULTIMATE DRIVING MACHINE.

NOW THERE'S A MOOMIES DOWN THE BLOCK FROM BLOOMIES.

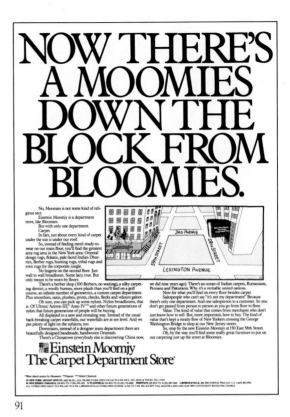

No, Moomies is not some kind of religious sect.

Einstein Moomjy is a department store, like Bloomies.

But with only one department. Carpet.

In fact, just about every kind of carpet under the sun is under our roof.

So, instead of finding men's ready-to-wear on our main floor, you'll find the greatest area rug area in the New York area: Oriental design rugs, flokatis, pale faced Indian Dhurries, Berber rugs, hunting rugs, tribal rugs and even rugs for the corporate jungle.

No lingerie on the second floor. Just wall to wall broadloom. Some lacy, true. But only meant to be worn by floors.

There's a berber shop (100 Berbers, no waiting), a silky carpeting district, a woolly bureau, more plaids than you'll find on a golf course, an infinite number of geometrics, a custom carpet department. Plus smoothies, saxis, plushes, prints, checks, flecks and velours galore.

Oh sure, you can pick up some nylons. Nylon broadlooms, that is. Of Ultron,* Antron III,* Anso IV** and other future generations of nylon that future generations of people will be buying.

All displayed in a new and revealing way. Instead of the usual back-breaking carpet waterfalls, our waterfalls are at see level. And we put plenty of light on the subjects, too.

Downstairs, instead of a designer jeans department there are beautifully designed handmade, handwoven Orientals.

There's a Chinatown (everybody else is discovering China now, we did nine years ago). There's an ocean of Indian carpets, Romanians, Persians and Pakistanis. Why it's a veritable united nations.

Now for what you'll find on every floor besides carpet.

Salespeople who can't say "it's not my department." Because there's only one department. And one salesperson to a customer. So you don't get passed from person to person as you go from floor to floor.

Value. The kind of value that comes from merchants who don't just know how to sell. But, more important, how to buy. The kind of value that's kept a steady flow of New Yorkers crossing the George Washington Bridge to shop at our New Jersey stores.

So, stop by the new Einstein Moomjy at 150 East 58th Street. Oh, by the way you'll find some really great furniture to put on our carpeting just up the street at Bloomies.

Einstein Moomjy
The Carpet Department Store

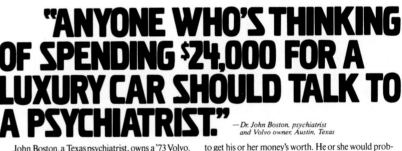

"ANYONE WHO'S THINKING OF SPENDING $24,000 FOR A LUXURY CAR SHOULD TALK TO A PSYCHIATRIST."

—Dr. John Boston, psychiatrist and Volvo owner, Austin, Texas

John Boston, a Texas psychiatrist, owns a '73 Volvo.

He bought that Volvo because, as he puts it: "I had admired what Volvo had done in the area of safety. The car seemed well-built. It offered solid European craftsmanship without the inflated price."

We wanted Dr. Boston's opinion of the new Volvo GLE, which has a full assortment of luxury features as standard equipment—and a price tag thousands of dollars below that of the well-known German luxury sedan.

"It's an excellent value. In my opinion, the individual buying this car would have a strong, unsuppressed need to get his or her money's worth. He or she would probably also have a strong enough self-image not to need a blatant status symbol."

When we told him that some people were actually paying five to ten thousand dollars more for a luxury car, Dr. Boston's response was characteristically succinct.

"That's not using your head."

Finally, we asked Dr. Boston if, when he was ready for a new car, he'd consider the Volvo GLE for himself.

"I'd be crazy if I didn't."

VOLVO
A car you can believe in.

90

91

92

HOW NUMBERS LIE.

by Frank Perdue

When you see a "chill-packed" chicken with a freshness date stamped on its label, naturally you assume that chicken is very fresh.

Well, more often than not, you're looking at a chicken that's a lot older than you think.

You see, these chickens aren't dated until the day they leave the processing plant. But unfortunately, they don't always leave the day they're processed. They often sit around in coolers at temperatures as low as 26° for as long as 10 days. Obviously, in these subfreezing temperatures they're not getting any fresher. They're just getting harder. When they're finally shipped, a label is put on the package that says "sell by __(date)__." And this is always seven days later than the product's shipping date. By the time you buy one of these chickens at your market, it can be more than two weeks old.

Of course, there's a simple way to be sure you're getting a fresh, plump chicken and not some old bird with a fresh date on it: Look for Perdue.

Perdue chickens get to stores in the D.C. area a few hours after they're processed.

What's more, you don't have to worry about them sitting around the store. Because Perdue chickens are so good, they move out of your supermarket as fast as they're moved into it.

The truth is, if those other chickens were as fresh as Perdue, they wouldn't have to plaster them with misleading dates. They'd plaster them with money-back guarantees. Like Perdue.

IT TAKES A TOUGH MAN TO MAKE A TENDER CHICKEN.

18.7 YEARS CITY.   18.7 YEARS HIGHWAY.

A lot of car makers today are trying to sell you economy with EPA figures. But at Volvo, we believe true economy isn't just more miles per gallon. It's more years per car.

So if you just want to buy less gas and save a little money, look at EPA figures. But if you like the idea of buying fewer cars and saving a lot, consider Volvo's figures.

Average life expectancy of a Volvo in Sweden. Driving conditions in the U.S. may differ. So your Volvo may not last as long. Then again, it may last longer.

94

WHICH LETTER WOULD YOU OPEN FIRST?

If you're a normal person, you'd probably open the letter that stands out from all the rest. Right? The one that looks more important than all the others. The one that got to you overnight.

After all, how many letters can do such a thing these days?

And if you opened that letter first, you'd probably read it first. Right?

And that makes the Federal Express Overnight Letter the most important letter on your desk.

If you'd like all the letters you send to be this important, here's all you have to do.

First, send us the coupon and we'll send you your free start-up kit of air bills and Overnight Letter envelopes. They're water-resistant and tear-resistant and they get the

same attention our COURIER PAKS and packages get.

Then, when you have a letter of up to 10 pages that absolutely, positively has to be somewhere overnight, just stick it in the Overnight Letter envelope and take it to any one of our convenient drop-off locations listed below.

We'll fly it and deliver it overnight to any one of over 13,500 cities and towns in our system, and we'll bill you for $7.50. (That's less than a cab ride to most airports.)

We also give you a receipt in case your boss says, "Where's the receipt?"

And that's how it works.

Now, if you absolutely, positively must have your Overnight Letter picked up, we'll do that too, if we're already picking up a Courier Pak or

package at the same time. For the same $7.50. But, if you don't have another package today and need a special pickup, the first letter will cost $20. Then, any extra letters are only $7.50 each.

That's it. Call us at 345-5044 if you have any questions. And from now on, all of your important letters can get there overnight, be opened first, and acted upon faster than all

the others.

And that should put us both way ahead of the competition.

FEDERAL EXPRESS INTRODUCES THE OVERNIGHT LETTER, ONLY $7.50

95

One is a product of nature.
One is a product of chemistry.

There are few things left in this world that have been untouched, untampered with, unchemicalized, in short, unmessed by man. One such product is Poland Spring.

Nature was good to Poland Spring.

200 years ago, when Hiram Ricker discovered the deep granite source of Poland Spring, deep in the woods of Maine, he knew enough not to tamper with it.

Poland Spring is bottled at the source just as it flows through the deep granite. Symbol of Purity since 1845.

Bottled only at Poland Spring, Maine USA 04274

Because of its unique purity and flavor, Poland Spring water soon became the drink of Presidents and Kings. In fact, it was famous in Europe long before any European water ever set foot in America.

Today, we treat Poland Spring water with the same awe and respect as Hiram Ricker did generations ago.

Poland Spring is as pure today as it was then. We still bottle the water right at the spring. And of course, there's no need to tell you that Poland Spring water has no sugar, no calories, and no artificial ingredients. True natural spring water simply doesn't have those kinds of things, by definition.

Nature has nothing to do with club soda.

The genesis of club soda is a bit different. A leading club soda begins as tap water. Hard to believe, isn't it? The very same water that pours into your sink (or bathtub, for that matter) is club soda's primary constituent.

The water is then processed. Lime is added to attract the minerals.

Then chlorine is added to kill any organic matter. Then ferrous sulphate is added to settle all the chemicals and suspended matter together. And then the water is drawn off the "sludge." At last you have what is called "treated water."

But the chemical process isn't complete. The water is then filtered, and then yet another mixture of minerals and salts are added. (These result in a club soda that actually has *60 times* the amount of salt as Poland Spring water.)

And to all the other artificial processes as a coup de grace they add artificial carbonation. Bravo.

Don't be taken in.

There are those who have the nerve to suggest that an artificially made, chemically processed beverage is actually better than pure natural Poland Spring.

Do not be fooled.

Club soda is a product of chemistry. Spring water is a product of nature. It's as simple as that.

A small price to pay.

Of course, Poland Spring water may cost a little more than club soda. To our mind, it should cost a lot more. Poland Spring water has to be shipped to you all the way from the spring deep in the woods of Maine. Club soda, on the other hand, comes to you all the way from the tap.

A few last remarks.

In Europe, where they love their wine, they love their spring water as well. In virtually every civilized nation on the continent, spring water is found on the dinner table. (In many ways it is the mark of civility itself.)

And the fact is, Europeans can get water from their taps the same as we in America do. So why do they pay for natural spring water?

Because over the years they've developed an appreciation for the natural.

Isn't it time you began to drink of nature rather than of chemicals? Try Poland Spring. To those of us in the city, it's like a little bit of the country every day.

Consumer Newspaper
Over 600 Lines
Single

97
Art Director:
Stan Block
Writer:
Frank DiGiacomo
Photographer:
Ronald C. Modra
Client:
Inside Sports Magazine
Agency:
Della Femina, Travisano
& Partners

98
Art Director:
Tom Wolsey
Writer:
David Schneider
Photographer:
Barry Lategan
Client:
Barney's
Agency:
Ally & Gargano

99
Art Director:
Robert Reitzfeld
Writer:
David Altschiller
Designer:
Robert Reitzfeld
Artist:
Fred Greller
Photographer:
Bill Dolce
Client:
Poland Spring Corporation
Agency:
Altschiller, Reitzfeld,
Jackson, Solin/NCK

EVEN THE DEVINE FIND IT HELL AT NOTRE DAME.

The head football coach at Notre Dame. It's called the third toughest job in America. And with good reason.

Notre Dame is a school where a 9-2 season is mediocre, where on campus a 14-story mural of Christ with his arms upraised is called "Touchdown Jesus" and where anyone who has ever dipped his fingers into Holy Water considers himself an alumnus.

No wonder the coaching job at Notre Dame has ravaged the minds and bodies of almost everyone who's held it. From the immortal Knute Rockne to the very mortal Dan Devine, who after six winning seasons and one national championship is stepping down for "personal reasons."

But the faithful need not despair. Notre Dame already has a new leader. Last month, three puffs of white smoke signaled to the world that a new head coach had been chosen. His name is Faust (a

devil of a name). Gerry Faust is probably the most successful high school coach in America. But no matter how successful in high school there is nothing to make anyone believe Faust will break with the tradition of Notre Dame coaches who wind up hitting the Maalox bottle.

This month, Inside Sports goes under the Golden Dome to examine the pressures that seem to afflict everyone who has ever tried to fill Knute Rockne's cleats. The article also deals with Devine's retirement. Is he "stepping down" or is he being sacrificed to that big Athletic Director in the sky? Whatever conclusion you draw, you'll have to agree that this article by Robert Friedman is one of the most provocative ever written about the school in South Bend and the men who

coach its football teams.

This January, Inside Sports also covers (maybe smothers is a better word) the spectacle of the Super Bowl. For starters, we're announcing the winner of the game...a month before the game. Then writer Gary Smith tells you "How the NFL Learned to Stop Worrying and Love the Bomb." Gambling editor Pete Axthelm also does a piece called, "The Season's Last Big Bet: Going for Broke." Inside Sports also has an article on Philadelphia, the City of Brotherly Love, which—without anyone looking—is becoming the City of Champions. Plus a lot more.

You see, other sports magazines might talk about giving you in-depth coverage of the major sports, but every month at Inside Sports...we make an issue out of it.

INSIDE SPORTS

WE COVER A SIDE OF SPORTS NOBODY ELSE IS COVERING. THE INSIDE.

COPYRIGHT NEWSWEEK, INC

97

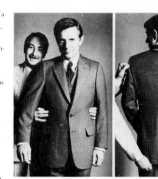 
98

99

**Consumer Newspaper
Over 600 Lines
Campaign**

100
Art Director:
Alan Gee
Writer:
Norman Glowinsky
Photographer:
George Simhoni
Client:
Julius Schmid of Canada
Agency:
Glowinsky & Gee/Canada

101
Art Director:
Bill Thompson
Writer:
Suzie Henry
Designer:
Bill Thompson
Photographers:
Derek Seagrim
Anthony Bowran
Client:
Unicliffe
Agency:
Doyle Dane Bernbach/London

Better safe than sorry.

If you conceive an unwanted child, it's too late to be sorry.
If you contract venereal disease, it's too late to be sorry.
If you develop side effects as a result of using another form of birth control, it's too late to be sorry.
Use electronically tested quality condoms manufactured by Julius Schmid.
Be safe, instead of sorry. ⬛ Julius Schmid.

Products you can depend on - products for people who really care.

JULIUS SCHMID OF CANADA LTD., 34 METROPOLITAN ROAD, TORONTO, ONTARIO. M1R 2T6. MANUFACTURERS OF RAMSES, SHEIK, NuFORM, EXCITA, FETHERLITE, FIESTA AND FOUREX BRAND CONDOMS.

100

An ounce of prevention.

Help prevent an unwanted pregnancy. Help prevent the transmission of venereal disease. Help prevent side effects associated with other forms of birth control.
Use electronically tested condoms made by Julius Schmid.
Because prevention only takes a little precaution.

⬛ Julius Schmid.

Products you can depend on, products for people who really care.

JULIUS SCHMID OF CANADA LTD., 34 METROPOLITAN ROAD, TORONTO, ONTARIO. M1R 2T6. MANUFACTURERS OF RAMSES, SHEIK, NuFORM, EXCITA, FETHERLITE, FIESTA AND FOUREX BRAND CONDOMS.

IF YOU WORK AT OUR DIET FROM NINE 'TIL FIVE, YOU CAN HAVE THE EVENING OFF.

101

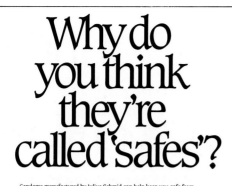

FOR THE PRICE OF A MERE STATUS SYMBOL YOU CAN OWN A BMW.

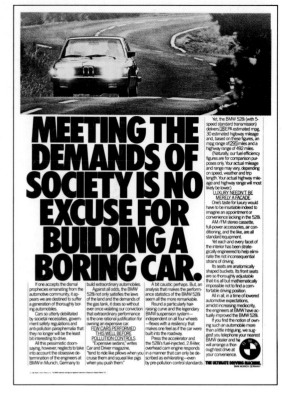

MEETING THE DEMANDS OF SOCIETY IS NO EXCUSE FOR BUILDING A BORING CAR.

A SOBERING PROSPECTUS FOR THE LUXURY SEDAN BUYER.

MAKE	YEAR	ORIGINAL PRICE	CURRENT VALUE	RETAINED VALUE
BMW 5 SERIES	1975	$ 9,097	$ 7,486	82.3%
	1976	$10,590	$ 8,619	81.4%
	1977	$12,495	$ 9,575	76.6%
	1978	$14,840	$11,833	79.7%
	1979	$15,505	$15,550	100.3%
	1980	$20,650		
CADILLAC SEVILLE	1975	NOT MADE		
	1976	$12,479	$ 7,247	58.1%
	1977	$13,359	$ 8,733	65.4%
	1978	$14,710	$10,114	68.8%
	1979	$16,224	$12,436	76.7%
	1980	$20,477		
MERCEDES 280E	1975	$12,756	$ 8,672	68.0%
	1976	$14,296	$ 9,997	69.9%
	1977	$17,114	$12,539	73.3%
	1978	$19,711	$14,839	75.3%
	1979	$22,943	$19,231	83.8%
	1980	$26,193		
JAGUAR XJ6	1975	$13,100	$ 7,342	56.1%
	1976	$14,250	$ 8,653	60.7%
	1977	$16,500	$10,333	62.6%
	1978	$19,000	$12,903	67.9%
	1979	$20,000	N/A	N/A
	1980	$25,000		

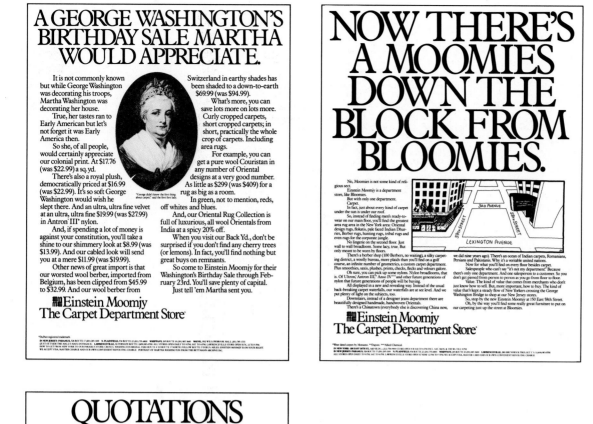

Consumer Newspaper
Over 600 Lines
Campaign

104
Art Director:
Ron Arnold
Writer:
Sheila Moore
Photographers:
Chris Callas
Larry Robins
Dennis Chalkin
Client:
WABC-TV
Agency:
Della Femina, Travisano
& Partners

105
Art Director:
Stan Block
Writer:
Frank DiGiacomo
Photographers:
Ronald C. Modra
Flip Schulke
World Wide Photos
Client:
Inside Sports Magazine
Agency:
Della Femina, Travisano
& Partners

104

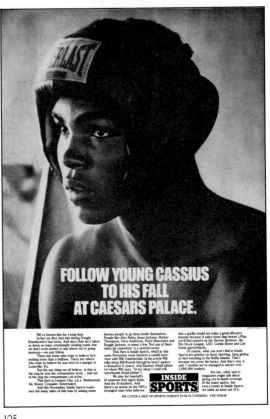

105

Tonight, get the unretouched picture of modeling.

It's dazzling glamour and exhausting work. A world of make-believe and all too real competition. To succeed as a model, you don't have to be one in a million. Just one in 500.
And even if you make it, you better work fast—the average career lasts only 5 years.
This week on Eyewitness News, John Johnson goes in for a close-up of this fascinating business. And reveals why not all of modeling is as pretty as a picture.

"Modeling: What Price Glamour?"
Mon-Fri at 11 PM. Eyewitness News ⑦

Go from a 4 to a 10 by subtraction.

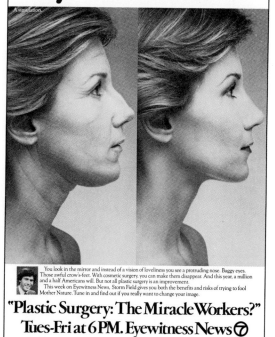

A simulation

You look in the mirror and instead of a vision of loveliness you see a protruding nose. Baggy eyes. Those awful crow's-feet. With cosmetic surgery, you can make them disappear. And this year, a million and a half Americans will. But not all plastic surgery is an improvement.
This week on Eyewitness News, Storm Field gives you both the benefits and risks of trying to fool Mother Nature. Tune in and find out if you really want to change your image.

"Plastic Surgery: The Miracle Workers?"
Tues-Fri at 6 PM. Eyewitness News ⑦

EVEN THE DEVINE FIND IT HELL AT NOTRE DAME.

The head football coach at Notre Dame. It's called the third toughest job in America. And with good reason.

Notre Dame is a school where a 9-2 season in mediocre, where on campus a 14-story mural of Christ with his arms upraised is called "Touchdown Jesus" and where anyone who has ever dipped his fingers into Holy Water considers himself an alumnus.

No wonder the coaching job at Notre Dame has ravaged the minds and bodies of almost everyone who's held it. From the immortal Knute Rockne to the very mortal Dan Devine, who after six winning seasons and one national championship is stepping down for "personal reasons."

But the faithful need not despair. Notre Dame already has a new leader. Last month, three puffs of white smoke signaled to the world that a new head coach had been chosen. His name is Faust (a

devil of a name). Gerry Faust is probably the most successful high school coach in America. But no matter how successful in high school there is nothing to make anyone believe Faust will break with the tradition of Notre Dame coaches who wind up hitting the Maalox bottle.

This month, Inside Sports goes under the Golden Dome to examine the pressures that seem to affect everyone who has ever tried to fill Knute Rockne's cleats. The article also deals with Devine's retirement. Is he "stepping down" or is he being sacrificed to that big Athletic Director in the sky? Whatever conclusion you draw, you'll have to agree that this article by Robert Friedman is one of the most provocative ever written about the school in South Bend and the men who

coach its football teams.

This January, Inside Sports also covers (maybe smothers is a better word) the spectacle of the Super Bowl. For starters, we're announcing the winner of the game...a month before the game. The writer Gary Smith tells you "How the NFL Learned to Stop Worrying and Love the Bomb." Gambling editor Pete Axthelm also does a piece called, "The Season's Last Big Bet: Going for Broke." Inside Sports also has an article on Philadelphia, the City of Brotherly Love, which—without anyone looking—is becoming the City of Champions. Plus a lot more.

INSIDE SPORTS

WE COVER A SIDE OF SPORTS NOBODY ELSE IS COVERING. THE INSIDE.

WHY VINCE FERRAGAMO SAYS HIS AGENT AND THE RAMS ARE ROUGHING THE PASSER.

Vincent Anthony Ferragamo—with an arm like a bullwhip, statistics as shiny as any passer in the league and a face hijacked from a schoolgirl's dream—is the quarterback of the '80s. Trouble is, the Los Angeles Rams are paying him like a quarterback of the 60s.

Ferragamo is disgusted with his treatment by the Rams, confused by a whirlpool of advice and concerned that one hamstring pull or two interceptions and the job is Pat Haden's again. He could be the only $52,000 a year worker in America who has had two contract attorneys, an entertainment agent, an acting agent and an accountant in the last year.

This month in Inside Sports, writer Gary Smith investigates the frustrations, confusions and suspicions that plague Vince Ferragamo—from his tense relationship with teammate Pat Haden to the controversial negotiations between his attorney, his team and himself.

One NFL team executive has termed these dealings unethical; while the Rams say "other teams in the league have done it." The lawyer insists he offered to take his negotiation far from the Rams to save Vince money. While Vince's wife says the collapsed three-year contract was a "three-year prison sentence."

Any way you look at it, the whole thing is enough to make ol' J.R. Ewing chuckle.

Also in December's Inside Sports, there's an article on Dallas' original first family. The Cowboys. And two of its proudest sons: quarterback Danny White, who's finally at the helm after waiting four long years for the job Roger to be put in mothballs and Ed "Too Tall" Jones, who's much more at home running rings around offensive linemen than he was a boxer in the ring.

Then Al McGuire, former coach and current announcer, picks what he believes will be this year's batch of Birds, Magics and Dunkensteins. Looking into his crystal basketball, Swami McGuire even tells us who's going to win the NCAA crown this March in Philly.

Inside Sports also offers its version of the Boswell Chronicles. Baseball's Thomas Boswell, that is. What he's chronicled are the 1980 baseball playoffs and World Series—three of the most bizarre weeks in baseball history. Plus, you'll find a whole lot more. No wonder 3,000,000 sports addicts can't wait to get their hands on the December issue.

You see, other sports magazines talk about giving you in-depth coverage of the major sports, but every month at Inside Sports...we make an issue out of it.

INSIDE SPORTS

WE COVER A SIDE OF SPORTS NOBODY ELSE IS COVERING. THE INSIDE.

Consumer Newspaper Over 600 Lines Campaign

106
Art Director:
Mike Moran
Writer:
David Saphier
Designer:
Mike Moran
Photographers:
Perry Ellis
Graham Ford
Client:
Glow-Worm
Agency:
KMP Partnership/London

107
Art Director:
Tom Wolsey
Writers:
David Schneider
Tom Messner
Artist:
Lucy Gould
Photographer:
Barry Lategan
Client:
Barney's
Agency:
Ally & Gargano

Don't buy Glow-worm central heating without considering it for at least ten years.

Of course, there are some things about a Glow-worm boiler which don't take that long to notice.

Its clean design. Its efficient performance. Its total reliability.

Just what you'd expect from Glow-worm,

considering we're the biggest gas boiler manufacturer in Britain.

But one thing takes a little longer to appreciate.

You get your first inkling with your first gas bill.

And as time passes, one simple fact becomes glowingly apparent.

Gas is still cheaper than any other central heating fuel. And not by just a few paltry pounds.

The latest figures show that gas costs 30%-50% less than any other fuel.

With a three bedroom house, for example, the annual running costs* would work out at £189 with gas.

As against £332 with electricity. £261 with solid fuel. And £363 with oil.

So even in the first year, the savings are substantial.

Let alone the next ten.

True, our central heating boilers can't eliminate bills entirely. Even a Glow-worm needs to be fed.

But his staple diet is gas. Which just happens to cost 30%-50% less than other fuels.

For instance, the quarterly bill above* for a 3 bedroom house (during the heaviest winter period) would work out at £161 with an oil-fired system. £147 with electricity. £118 with solid fuel.

But, only £80 with gas. Yes, £80.

And if your system's based on a Glow-worm boiler, you've even more reason to rejoice.

We're the biggest manufacturer of gas boilers in Britain. So we've a name to live up to. We also have a wider range than anyone else.

And the most experience.

You'll also discover that your Glow-worm installer will always be on hand long after your system's installed.

After all, there wouldn't be much point in running our boilers with the right fuel if you didn't have them installed by the right people.

Just goes to show that a Glow-worm can't sting.

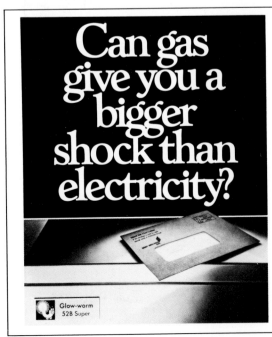

Can gas give you a bigger shock than electricity?

The answer isn't as shrouded in mystery as some people might think.

In fact, it's crystal clear.

Taking a typical 3-bedroomed house, the annual running cost* of a gas central heating system works out at £189.

£143 less painful than electricity, at £332 a year.

Not that it stops there.

When it comes to other fuels, the only thing we can speak highly of are their prices.

Solid fuel central heating adds up to a hefty £261 a year. While oil presents an annual crisis of £363.

But needless to say, lower running costs aren't the only reason for specifying a gas system.

It also helps to specify Glow-worm.

We're the biggest manufacturer of gas boilers in Britain.

We have more experience than anyone else. And a wider range than anyone else.

Send in the coupon to find out more.

Not everything these days has to come as a shock.

How the men who run things identify one another.

They have never stated it in so many words.

But the men in positions of authority in business, government and the professions have come to expect the men with whom they associate to dress in deference to a particular code.

Central to which, it goes almost without saying, is the natural shoulder suit.

And if, like most men, your tastes and temperament require some subtle degree of individuality within this code, it behooves you to seek out the expertise of a men's store with a thorough understanding of the permissible variations of the dress code, and a rich enough selection to represent them all.

A men's store like Barney's.

Where you will find that what you always thought of as the "business uniform" is, in Barney's Madison Room, by no means uniform.

Depending on your build, your personal taste and even the nature of your career, a Madison Room salesman, a specialist in the subtleties of traditional styling and fit, will guide you through a selection that includes every significant interpretation of conservative business dress.

From the full, traditional cuts of such acknowledged masters of the natural shoulder as H. Freeman,

Norman Hilton and Majer to the slightly more contoured but equally traditional styling of Cricketeer and Ralph Lauren for Chaps.

Once you have made your selections, you'll be meticulously fitted for free alterations by Barney's own custom tailors. Men entirely capable of making a natural shoulder suit from scratch in their own right.

But Barney's professional obligation to you doesn't end there.

How could it, when the look of your suit depends on how well you choose its accessories.

Enter Barney's Fashion Co-ordinator. Who can, if you wish, help you select shirt and collar configurations in solids and/or patterns that not only work with the color and texture of your suits, but with the shape of your face. The shirts to be paired with precisely the right ties, from Barney's complete collections of prints, knits, club ties and regimentals.

Barney's has also added a second and entirely new shoe department devoted to the finest in traditional footwear from England and America.

As well as a new department devoted to the finest in traditional hats from England and America. Including Herbert Johnson, Dobbs and the exclusive collection of Cavanagh.

So, if you find yourself in front of the mirror one morning, facing a crisply turned-out executive you can barely identify, rest assured that the men who run things won't have that problem.

Barney's Madison Room.

A timeless reminder from
Aquascutum, Burberrys, Christian Dior, Giorgio Armani,
Gleneagles, Calvin Klein, London Fog,
Misty Harbor, Gianni Versace
and Barney's Rainmaker Room.

Is it foolhardy to do for free what others wouldn't do if you paid them?

To judge by the policies of a great many men's stores, it's becoming too costly and too time-consuming to perform all the alterations many men require.

Despite the economic realities that would tend to justify this kind of thinking, Barney's finds itself bound by another consideration:

The belief that no store has the right to offer a customer a suit if it is unable to offer the proper fit to go with it.

Our men of the cloth.
Most of Barney's 200 master tailors were trained in Europe, where the art is taken seriously.

It took an apprentice at least fifteen years to become a master tailor in Europe. During which time he learned everything from the rudiments of holding a thimble to the artistry of making a pattern, cutting the cloth, hand sewing and hand pressing.

It may or may not have been easier to become a doctor. What's definite is that it took more time to become a tailor.

Of all the master tailors who work for Barney's, only those who can custom tailor a suit from scratch, with little more than a needle and a pair of scissors, can qualify as fitters.

Alterations that go beyond the lengths of sleeves and trousers. Fitters are the men holding the chalk and,

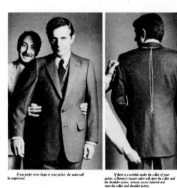

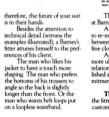

therefore, the future of your suit is in their hands.

Besides the attention to technical detail (witness the examples illustrated), a Barney's fitter attunes himself to the preferences of his client.

The man who likes his jacket to have a touch more shaping. The man who prefers the bottoms of his trousers to angle so the back is slightly longer than the front. Or the man who wants belt loops put on a loopless waistband.

They all find a willing ear at Barney's.

A few years ago, we sought to re-establish the relationship between a man who appreciates fine clothes and his tailor.

And there's probably no more ultimate proof that this relationship has been re-established at Barney's than our commitment to the "open try-on."

The "open try-on." Should the fitter deem it advisable, the customer will be invited to make an appointment for an "open try-on," a second fitting for which the alterations are temporarily sewn with white hand-basted stitches.

Only when the customer, in consultation with the fitter, indicates his approval of the fit will the final sewing be done and the basting stitches removed.

Wherever it's practical, cutting, basting and sewing of alterations are done with the most precise tools: the hands of our master tailors.

by the gratifying relationship of our fitters and the customers who ask for them by name, we would be hard pressed to describe our free alterations and services as foolhardy.

What is foolhardy, we would think, is attempting to buy a suit without them.

Barney's

Afterward, alterations are meticulously hand-pressed to preserve the shaping and molding of the final fitting. Hand-pressing is slower but it's an invaluable final touch.

Aside from the five floors devoted to alterations in our building across the street from Barney's, there is also a fully equipped tailor shop on each floor of the store itself, ready to perform any last-minute touch-up at a moment's notice.

Judging by the results, and

108
Art Director:
Tom Wolsey
Writer:
David Schneider
Photographers:
**Barry Lategan
Cailor/Resnick
Henry Wolf**
Client:
Barney's
Agency:
Ally & Gargano

109
Art Director:
Michael Tesch
Writer:
Patrick Kelly
Photographer:
Jim Salzano
Client:
Federal Express
Agency:
Ally & Gargano

One of these days you'll realize you aren't going anywhere without that sheepskin.

Barney's, New York.

Barney's presents the Hickey-Freeman suit.
A misfit in a throwaway society.

The Oak Room at Barney's.

And they said hats were never coming back.

Barney's, New York.

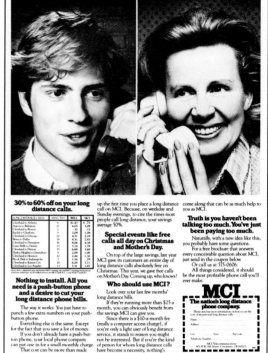

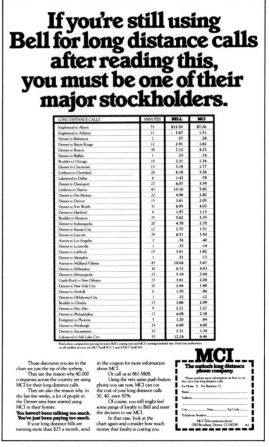

Consumer Newspaper
Over 600 Lines
Campaign

110
Art Director:
George Euringer
Writer:
Tom Messner
Designer:
George Euringer
Photographers:
Bill Stettner
Tony Petrucelli
Client:
MCI
Agency:
Ally & Gargano

111
Art Director:
Robert Reitzfeld
Writer:
David Altschiller
Designer:
Robert Reitzfeld
Photographer:
Bill Dolce
Client:
Poland Spring Corporation
Agency:
**Altschiller, Reitzfeld,
Jackson, Solin/NCK**

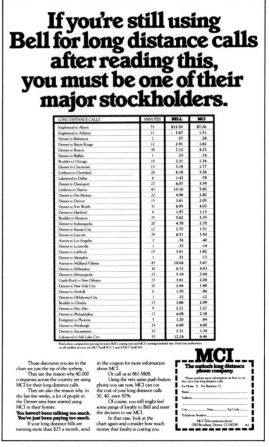

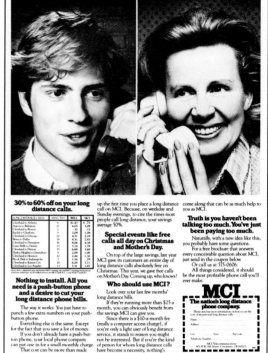

Where is club soda's spring?

There appears to be a lot of confusion out there about what club soda is, and what Poland Spring water is. Much of it, we suspect, because club sodas would like you to believe that they are indeed natural spring water.

Let us set the confusion straight once and for all.

Club soda begins as tap water.

No club soda we know of comes from a natural spring. (If there is one somewhere, it's news to us.) The water that is the basic constituent of club soda comes from a local tap at the local bottling plant.

Surprised? The same water that flows into your sink flows into their tanks. Then a whole series of chemical processes purify and transform this tap water into club soda.

Ah, the wonders of chemistry.

Let us give you a brief glimpse into the methodology commonly used to make club soda.

To tap water, add lime, and then chlorine. Add ferrous sulphate to settle all the chemicals and suspended matter together. (They call this mass "sludge.") Skim the water from the sludge. Then charcoal filter the water to remove the chlorine. At this point, you have what they call "treated water." But the chemistry lesson isn't over. Now filter the water

renowned in the courts of Europe. In fact Poland Spring water graced the tables of royalty long before any European water crossed the ocean in this direction. American Presidents, not to be outdone by royalty, made it a White House staple. Presidents Grant, Coolidge, Taft, Roosevelt, and most recently Eisenhower, demanded it.

Do not fall prey to confusion.

Over the last few years (how could you not notice) there has been a trend toward natural spring water. In an effort to cash in, some club sodas have tried to play down the differences between them and us. And to some extent have probably succeeded.

Do not be fooled.

Processed tap water will never be natural spring water. Club soda will never be Poland Spring.

and add a mixture of minerals and salts. These result in a club soda that actually has *more than 40 times* the amount of salt as Poland Spring water. Then, to all the other artificial processes, add artificial carbonation.

Poof, club soda.

Ah, the wonders of nature.

Poland Spring water is as natural as club soda is processed.

The recipe for it is very short. Hike deep into the woods of Maine, find the legendary Poland Spring, dip into the icy glacial source, add natural carbonation.

Drink.

No artificial ingredient has ever touched Poland spring water. It is now what it was centuries ago: one of the world's great natural waters. And certainly America's preeminent natural water.

The Poland Spring A minor miracle.

200 years ago, when Hiram Ricker discovered the Poland Spring, he knew then that he had found something quite remarkable. A source that bubbled up from deep in the earth. A natural water of exceptional purity and flavor. Back then, they even believed that Poland Spring water produced medical miracles. The legend spread and soon Poland Spring became

Do not succumb to price.

Club sodas may also offer you an additional inducement to drink them: a lower price. They should cost less. Poland Spring water costs what it does because it's shipped to you hundreds or even thousands of miles from the spring itself. Club soda is shipped to you all the way from the local tap.

A little sanity, please.

Today, more and more things are becoming chemicalized, processed.

To our mind, our bodies deserve things as nature intended them. Not as man tampered with them. And one of them is Poland Spring water. Natural water from the springs, the forests, the untouched regions of our world.

Club soda is not spring water.

It's a strange irony. We constantly scrutinize what we eat and drink. And then somehow our world becomes more and more artificial, filled with chemicalized, processed products. Even our water.

There are those who would have you believe that water is water; that since club soda and Poland Spring water are both clear liquids and both have bubbles, that one is the same as the other. The idea couldn't be further from the truth.

Club Soda starts as tap water.

Believe it or not, the leading club soda begins as water that comes from a tap. No different, in fact, than the water that pours from your sink or your bathtub, for that matter. Then the water is put through a whole series of chemical processes.

Purity through chemistry.

How does tap water become club soda? Here's one of the recipes: To tap water, add lime, and then chlorine to kill organic matter. Add ferrous sulphate to settle all the chemicals and suspended matter together. Skim the water from the "sludge." Then charcoal filter the water to remove the chlorine. At last what you have is "treated water." But wait! The chemical process isn't nearly complete. Now filter the

water again, then add a mixture of minerals and salts. (These result in a club soda that actually has *60 times* the amount of salt as Poland Spring Water.) And as a final step add artificial carbonation.

Voila, club soda.

A word of caution.

Over the last few years, spring water has become very desirable across America. So it's no wonder that club sodas have tried to pass themselves off as us. Don't be fooled.

Poland Spring is natural spring water.

Now the recipe for Poland Spring water. Go deep into the woods of Maine and take some cool water from the Poland Spring. Add natural carbonation. Drink.

No artificial ingredients or chemicals have ever been added to Poland Spring water.

The Poland Spring is no ordinary spring.

For nearly 200 years, the Poland Spring has been the most famous spring in America. Its purity is achieved through nature, not chemistry. It comes as a result of natural filtration through layers of granite, a process that cannot be artificially duplicated by man.

Because of this unique quality, Poland Spring has become the drink of Presidents and Kings. It graced the White House table during the presidencies of Grant, Taft, Coolidge, Roosevelt, and Eisenhower, to name a few.

And long before European water had ever come to America's shores, Poland Spring

was a staple of royal households across Europe.

costs what it does because it's shipped to you all the way from the spring in Maine. Club soda costs what it does because it's shipped to you all the way from the tap.

A word of philosophy.

No one will dispute that water is essential to our lives. The question is where will it come from.

To our mind, we should drink water as nature intended it to be. From the springs, the forests, the untouched regions of our world.

Try Poland Spring. To those of us in the city, it's like a little bit of the country every day.

Processed tap water will never be natural spring water. Club soda will never be Poland Spring.

Club sodas often offer a slightly lower price as an incentive. Don't be taken in by this, either. Poland Spring

For a free informative booklet, write to Pol

One is a product of nature.
One is a product of chemistry.

There are few things left in this world that have been untouched, untampered with, unchemicalized, in short, unmessed by man. One such product is Poland Spring.

Nature was good to Poland Spring.

200 years ago, when Hiram Ricker discovered the deep granite source of Poland Spring, deep in the woods of Maine, he knew enough not to tamper with it.

Because of its unique purity and flavor, Poland Spring water soon became the drink of Presidents and Kings. In fact, it was famous in Europe long before any European water ever set foot in America.

Today, we treat Poland Spring water with the same awe and respect as Hiram Ricker did generations ago.

Poland Spring is as pure today as it was then. We still bottle the water right at the spring. And of course, there's no need to tell you that Poland Spring water has no

sugar, no calories, and no artificial ingredients. True natural spring water simply doesn't have those kinds of things, by definition.

Nature has nothing to do with club soda.

The genesis of club soda is a bit different. A leading club soda begins as tap water. Hard to believe, isn't it? The very same water that pours into your sink (or bathtub, for that matter) is club soda's primary constituent.

The water is then processed. Lime is added to attract the minerals.

Then chlorine is added to kill any organic matter. Then ferrous sulphate is added to settle all the chemicals and suspended matter together. And then the water is drawn off the "sludge." At last you have what is called "treated water." But the chemical process isn't complete. The water is then filtered, and then yet another mixture of minerals and salts are added. (These

result in a club soda that actually has *60 times* the amount of salt as Poland Spring water.)

And to all the other artificial processes as a coup de grace they add artificial carbonation. Bravo.

Don't be taken in.

There are those who have the nerve to suggest that an artificially made, chemically processed beverage is actually better than pure natural Poland Spring.

Do not be fooled.

Club soda is a product of chemistry. Spring water is a product of nature. It's as simple as that.

A small price to pay.

Of course, Poland Spring water may cost a little more than club soda. To our mind, it should cost a lot more. Poland Spring water has to be shipped to you all the way from the spring deep in the woods of Maine. Club soda, on the other hand, comes to you all the way from the tap.

A few last remarks.

In Europe, where they love their wine, they love their spring water as well. In virtually every civilized nation on the continent, spring water is found on the dinner table. (In many ways it is the mark of civility itself.)

And the fact is, Europeans can get water from their taps the same as we in America do. So why do they pay for natural spring water?

Because over the years they've developed an appreciation for the natural.

Isn't it time you began to drink of nature rather than of chemicals? Try Poland Spring. To those of us in the city, it's like a little bit of the country every day.

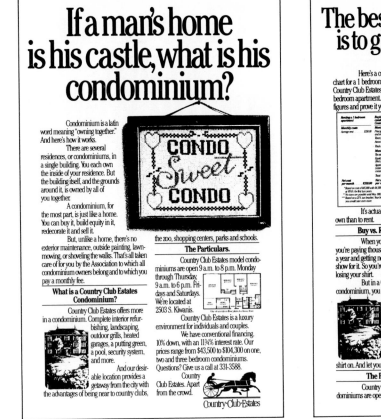

How to succeed in business without really typing.

IBM does one of the best imitations of George Burns you'll ever see.

How much does it cost not to own one?

114

115

ALMOST CHEAPER TO RUN THAN WALK.

MINI

Austin Morris

Want a nippy car that treats petrol like rare brandy? Walk to your nearest Austin Morris dealer and go for a test run.

116

SHORTER LIVING THROUGH CHEMISTRY.

A very healthy little girl suddenly goes into cardiac arrest. An unstoppable black mold seeps through the walls. Tumors and skin rashes are epidemic. And the dirt in the big field is actually changing color. Welcome to Love Canal.

Welcome to Iowa. New Jersey. Tennessee. Kentucky. And yes, Southern California. All over America, toxic waste is choking rivers, poisoning cities, and killing. And KFWB wants to know why.

For the next two weeks, we'll be looking at this critical health hazard in a series of special reports starting Dec. 1. "Toxic Waste." Listen. If you know what's good for you.

"TOXIC WASTE" KFWB NEWS 98

Tune in Monday-Friday at 7:07 a.m., 9:07 a.m., 12:07 p.m., 2:07 p.m., 6:07 p.m. and 10:07 p.m.
The entire series will be repeated each Saturday and Sunday.

117

The way Hitch would have wanted it.

On April 29th, the Master of Suspense, Alfred Hitchcock died peacefully in his bed.

We feel, however, he would have preferred to go differently, done away with by an unseen hand, pushed over a cliff by a beautiful blonde wife intent on getting the insurance money, or perhaps to have had his body stuffed into a closet, to be discovered years later by the unsuspecting new owners of the house.

He would have died as he might have chosen to die, giving us all one last scare.

This week, in Star, the new Woman's Day entertainment section, we'll feature the last, and one of the few interviews Hitch ever gave, written days before he died.

"Hitchcock's Last Words". Only in Woman's Day.

Woman's Day. The entertainment magazine.

Even small should come in different sizes.

The 2300   The 2600

The 3109   The 3300   The 3450

Xerox small copiers run the gamut from small to small.

In fact, we have more different models to choose from than anyone else. And they include copiers that don't just come in a variety of sizes, but do a variety of jobs.

From copiers that automatically feed themselves to ones that also sort—and even reduce.

From copiers that copy oversize documents to copiers that even let you change paper sizes without changing paper trays.

So before you decide on a small copier, give us a call at 800-648-5600, operator 260.*

Or send in the coupon and we'll send you more information on all our different sized small copiers.

Including the more important size. The one that fits you perfectly.

☐ I'd like a sales representative to contact me.
☐ I'd like to try one of your copiers for a few days at no cost.
☐ I'd like more information about Xerox small copiers.

Send to: Xerox Corporation, P.O. Box 24, Rochester, N.Y. 14601

Name_____
Title_____
Company_____
Address_____
City_____State____Zip_____
Telephone_____

XEROX

119

Can you spot the 3 errors in this headline?

Not anymore.

They've been corrected by an IBM Correcting Selectric® Typewriter.

It actually lifted them clean off the page. And each one, in only 3.6 seconds.

That's twice as fast as using correction paper. About 3 times faster than using an eraser. And as much as 7 times faster than using correction fluid.

When you consider the number of errors made each year, the IBM Correcting Selectric produces real savings.

To order, call your local IBM Office Products Division Representative at 405-272-1432. Or call IBM *Direct* toll-free at 800-631-5582, Ext. 11.

(If you own an IBM electric typewriter, be sure to ask about IBM's attractive trade-in allowance.)

The IBM Correcting Selectric: It makes you look perfect even when you're not.

IBM.

Correcting Selectric.Typewriter
405-272-1432

120

We'll stop y ur VW engine fr m miss ng.

Come in for a tune-up.

A poorly running engine can be really inefficient. Because it can result in poor gas mileage. So bring your VW in for a tune-up. The sooner, the bett r.

we care

VOLKSWAGEN PEOPLE • CARE ABOUT YOUR CAR

Dealer Name

121

"Saying goodbye to Claire in the rose garden was the best thing I ever did."

"Claire spent some of her happiest times in her rose garden. So I couldn't think of a more fitting place to hold her funeral service. You know, people are still telling me how nice that service was."

Today it's an accepted fact that the funeral of a loved one is more for the family and friends than the deceased.

It helps the survivors face the fact of death. And allows venting of emotion—a vital need in dealing with grief.

The traditional religious funeral service serves this purpose well. But we at Faull-Renton want you to also know about the Life Centered Service. It's a rather new concept that integrates the departed's joy of life into the funeral.

It happens with a favorite song, a story from an old friend, fond memories from the family. And it can take place nearly anywhere.

The important thing is, the family and friends are participants. And we've found it provides a great sense of peace to those who attend. The Life Centered Service. It's a beautiful choice here at Faull-Renton.

Faull
Renton Funeral Home
300 South Third Street
255-8281

"If I get sick, will I die like my Grandpa?"

"My Mother and Dad said Grandpa got real sick. So sick he died. Does that mean if they get sick they'll die? Will I?"

One of the most difficult tasks a parent faces is explaining death to a child.

Even though most youngsters today experience dead flowers or pets, they don't face the crisis of death until it occurs in the family.

And then, unfortunately, the child's feelings and perceptions are often overlooked. Sometimes because the parents think a child can't understand. Or the parents are too overcome to explain.

At Faull-Renton, we understand that there are no simple answers. But we believe children need special understanding. And honest information about death.

So we have a lot of excellent written materials on talking about death to children. And we have a whole bunch of good answers, too.

We hope you'll ask us to help.

Faull
Renton Funeral Home
300 South Third Street
255-8281

"If one more person tells me they know how I feel, I'll scream."

"Jim and I were married 32 years. We had a fine life together. A lot of special times. How can anyone dare to say they know how I feel about losing him? I hardly know myself."

At the time of a death, there is little consolation in knowing others have gone through a similar experience.

In fact, your friend's efforts to help or share in your sadness may only serve to foster additional feelings of grief.

The readjustment process is more difficult for some than for others. But for everyone, it's a confusing, emotional experience.

Here at Faull-Renton, we know that your sense of grief and loss must be resolved before you can readjust and go ahead with a fulfilling life.

So we make a point of being available to answer questions, share written materials, and just talk. For as long as you need us.

We won't tell you we know just how you feel. We'll tell you how to feel better.

Faull
Renton Funeral Home
300 South Third Street
255-8281

WEIGHT WATCHERS OFFERS YOU A LITTLE SOMETHING TO HELP MAKE ENDS MEET.

MONEY.

From now until October 4, you can join Weight Watchers
in this area and be eligible for a special offer that helps you lose weight
and still have something to show for it: *money.*
Weight Watchers will refund one dollar for each pound you've lost,
once you reach your goal weight and *learn* the Maintenance Plan.
The more you lose, the more your refund.
So let Weight Watchers help you do something about inflation.
Call now for full details.

WEIGHT WATCHERS®

FOR YEARS YOUR PARENTS TOLD YOU TO CLEAN YOUR PLATE.

WE TEACH YOU HOW.

It's not just how much you put on your plate
but what you put on it that puts pounds on you.
At Weight Watchers, we help you eat well and still lose weight
sensibly, surely and safely.
With a total program that includes great food, a lot of encouragement,
a little activity, some behavior changes,
and a follow-up plan to help you keep excess weight off for life.
Come on down! Call us for a meeting near you.

WEIGHT WATCHERS®

WE HELP YOU TO LOSE WEIGHT THE SAME WAY YOU PUT IT ON:

WITH A KNIFE AND FORK.

That doesn't mean you eat more. Just more sensibly.
And our program features delicious food
that's good for you; plus a lot of encouragement
at our meetings; plus a little activity,
and some behavior changes you can use; plus
a follow-up plan to help you go through life
minus excess pounds.
Call us now for a meeting near you.
Remember: Nothing ventured, nothing lost.

WEIGHT WATCHERS®

**Consumer Newspaper
600 Lines or Less
Campaign**

124
Art Directors:
**Tony Stewart
Gordon Trembath**
Writer:
Sandy Lodico
Client:
Woman's Day
Agency:
The Campaign Palace/Australia

125
Art Directors:
**Howard Smith
Tom McManus**
Writer:
Charles Kane
Artist:
George Oleson
Photographer:
Ken Howard
Client:
Xerox
Agency:
Needham, Harper & Steers

It's easy to lose weight when you haven't got a stomach.

There's a new surgical technique for those who are grossly obese and for whom every diet has failed: they're having their stomachs stapled shut. Woman's Day reports.

Woman's Day. The health magazine.

If Peter Allen could get his hands on this page, he'd probably eat it.

Peter, aged 7, is one of only 13 known sufferers of Prader-Willi Syndrome. It causes an uncontrollable urge to eat. Garbage, rotten meat, scraps from the gutter, anything- until he eats himself to death. Woman's Day reports.

Woman's Day. The health magazine.

What's a clean-cut guy like Michael York doing in a play about Jews, Nazis and homosexuals?

Michael York is a Jewish homosexual in a time when it wasn't good to be either Jewish or homosexual. And he hopes his new play "Bent" will change his nice-guy image.

Woman's Day. The entertainment magazine.

Consumer Newspaper
600 Lines or Less
Campaign

126
Art Director:
Joseph Del Vecchio
Writer:
Peter Bregman
Designer & Artist:
Joseph Del Vecchio
Client:
Volkswagen
Agency:
Doyle Dane Bernbach

We'll stop y ur VW engine fr m miss ng.

Come in for a tune-up.
A poorly running engine can be really inefficient.
Because it can result in poor gas mileage. So bring your
VW in for a tune-up. The sooner, the bett r.

Dealer Name

126

We've seen just about everything that can go wrong with your

Altogether, our mechanics have about 0000 hours of VW training and more than 000 years of VW experience. So if anything comes into our shop with a problem we've never seen, it's probably **we care** not a Volkswagen.

Dealer Name

10% off any time we touch your VW this week.

This message is brought to you by our service team and it's good this week only for anything done on any Rabbit, Dasher, Scirocco, Beetle, 411, Bus, Vanagon or Karmann Ghia. And for that matter, on any Thing.

we care

Dealer Name

127
Art Director:
Susan Casey
Writers:
**Charles Griffith
Barry Hoffman**
Designer:
Susan Casey
Photographer:
David Langley
Client:
Steinway
Agency:
**Lord, Geller,
Federico, Einstein**

128
Art Director:
Susan Casey
Writers:
**Charles Griffith
Barry Hoffman**
Designer:
Susan Casey
Photographer:
David Langley
Client:
Steinway
Agency:
**Lord, Geller,
Federico, Einstein**

129
Art Director:
Susan Casey
Writers:
**Charles Griffith
Barry Hoffman**
Designer:
Susan Casey
Photographer:
David Langley
Client:
Steinway
Agency:
**Lord, Geller,
Federico, Einstein**

From timber to timbre.

It takes a lot of time to construct a Steinway® piano. And a lot of timber. In fact, more different kinds of wood go into any one Steinway than you are likely to find in any one forest. Spruce from Alaska. Rosewood from Brazil. American black walnut. Mahogany from Africa.

To fashion our Diaphragmatic Soundboard® for instance, we secure the finest virgin Sitka spruce. Its rare combination of flexibility and strength helps create the fuller, richer tone that separates a Steinway from lesser instruments.

Since 1853, when the first Steinway was crafted, our philosophy has been simple: To create perfection in sound one must start with materials that are peerless in nature. As philosophy, of course, it sounds good on paper.

In practice, it sounds even better on a Steinway.

To learn more about the way we make a Steinway, you can write to one, John H. Steinway, Steinway Hall, Dept. 04, 109 West 57th Street, New York, New York 10019.

Steinway & Sons

127

What makes a Steinway vertical so grand?

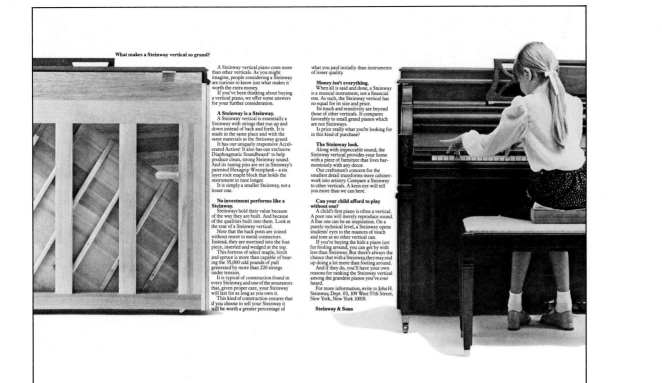

A Steinway vertical piano costs more than other verticals. As you might imagine, people considering a Steinway are curious to know just what makes it worth the extra money.

If you've been thinking about buying a vertical piano, we offer some answers for your further consideration.

A Steinway is a Steinway.

A Steinway vertical is essentially a Steinway with strings that run up and down instead of back and forth. It is made in the same place and with the same materials as the Steinway grand.

It has our uniquely responsive Accelerated Action! It also has our exclusive Diaphragmatic Soundboard' to help produce clean, strong Steinway sound. And its tuning pins are set in Steinway's patented Hexagrip Wrestplank—a six layer rock maple block that holds the instrument in tune longer.

It is simply a smaller Steinway, not a lesser one.

No investment performs like a Steinway.

Steinways hold their value because of the way they are built. And because of the qualities built into them. Look at the rear of a Steinway vertical.

Note that the back posts are joined without resort to metal connectors. Instead, they are mortised into the foot piece, inserted and wedged at the top.

This fortress of select maple, birch and spruce is more than capable of bearing the 35,000 odd pounds of pull generated by more than 220 strings under tension.

It is typical of construction found in every Steinway, and one of the assurances that, given proper care, your Steinway will last for as long as you own it.

This kind of construction ensures that if you choose to sell your Steinway it will be worth a greater percentage of what you paid initially than instruments of lesser quality.

Money isn't everything.

When all is said and done, a Steinway is a musical instrument, not a financial one. As such, the Steinway vertical has no equal for its size and price.

Its touch and sensitivity are beyond those of other verticals. It compares favorably to small grand pianos which are not Steinways.

Is price really what you're looking for in this kind of purchase?

The Steinway look.

Along with impeccable sound, the Steinway vertical provides your home with a piece of furniture that lives harmoniously with any decor.

Our craftsmen's concern for the smallest detail transforms mere cabinetwork into artistry. Compare a Steinway to other verticals. A keen eye will tell you more than we can here.

Can your child afford to play without one?

A child's first piano is often a vertical. A poor one will merely reproduce sound. A fine one can be an inspiration. On a purely technical level, a Steinway opens students' eyes to the nuances of touch and tone as no other vertical can.

If you're buying the kids a piano just for fooling around, you can get by with less than Steinway. But there's always the chance that with a Steinway, they may end up doing a lot more than fooling around.

And if they do, you'll have your own reasons for ranking the Steinway vertical among the grandest pianos you've ever heard.

For more information, write to John H. Steinway, Dept. 03, 109 West 57th Street, New York, New York 10019.

Steinway & Sons

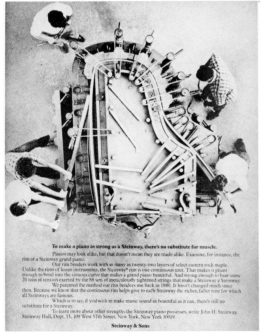

To make a piano as strong as a Steinway, there's no substitute for muscle.

Pianos may look alike, but that doesn't mean they are made alike. Examine, for instance, the rim of a Steinway grand piano.

Our rim benders work with as many as twenty-two layers of select eastern rock maple. Unlike the rims of lesser instruments, the Steinway® rim is one continuous unit. That makes it pliant enough to bend into the sinuous curve that makes a grand piano beautiful. And strong enough to bear some 20 tons of tension exerted by the 88 sets of meticulously tightened strings that make a Steinway a Steinway.

We patented the method our rim benders use back in 1880. It hasn't changed much since then. Because we know that the continuous rim helps give to each Steinway the richer, fuller tone for which all Steinways are famous.

Which is to say, if you wish to make music sound as beautiful as it can, there's still no substitute for a Steinway.

To learn more about other strengths the Steinway piano possesses, write John H. Steinway, Steinway Hall, Dept. 33, 109 West 57th Street, New York, New York 10019.

Steinway & Sons

It corners better than a BMW, stops better than a Volvo, feels better than a Mercedes and sips gas like a Datsun. A miracle? No, a Saab.

130

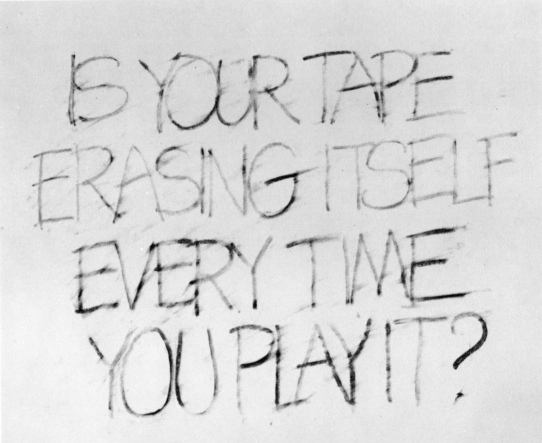

If lately your favorite recordings sound like they're gradually unrecording, it could be the tape they're on.

You see the oxide particles on some tapes just aren't bound on very well. And when the oxide particles come off, your music could come off sounding faded and weak.

Maxell, however, has developed a unique binding process that helps stop those oxide particles from taking a hike. We also polish our tape to a mirror finish to reduce friction, the major cause of oxide shedding.

So with Maxell, even if you play a tape over and over, the music won't disappear before your very ears.

IT'S WORTH IT.

131

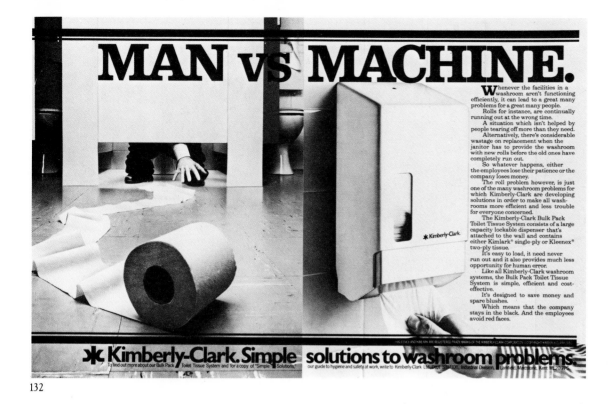

MAN vs MACHINE.

Whenever the facilities in a washroom aren't functioning efficiently, it can lead to a great many problems for a great many people.

Rolls for instance, are continually running out at the wrong time.

A situation which isn't helped by people tearing off more than they need.

Alternatively, there's considerable wastage on replacement when the janitor has to provide the washroom with new rolls before the old ones have completely run out.

So whatever happens, either the employees lose their patience or the company loses money.

The roll problem however, is just one of the many washroom problems for which Kimberly-Clark are developing solutions in order to make all washrooms more efficient and less trouble for everyone concerned.

The Kimberly-Clark Bulk Pack Toilet Tissue System consists of a large capacity lockable dispenser that's attached to the wall and contains either Kimlark® single-ply or Kleenex® two-ply tissue.

It's easy to load, it need never run out and it also provides much less opportunity for human error.

Like all Kimberly-Clark washroom systems, the Bulk Pack Toilet Tissue System is simple, efficient and cost-effective.

It's designed to save money and spare blushes.

Which means that the company stays in the black. And the employees avoid red faces.

✻ Kimberly-Clark. Simple solutions to washroom problems.

To find out more about our Bulk Pack Toilet Tissue System and for a copy of "Simple Solutions," our guide to hygiene and safety at work, write to Kimberly-Clark Ltd. Dept. STM108, Industrial Division, Larkfield, Maidstone, Kent. ME20 7PS.

132

WHAT'S HAPPENING ON THIS PAGE SHOULDN'T HAPPEN ON YOUR RECORDING TAPE.

It's called print-through.

And if you think it interferes with your reading, you should hear what it does to your listening.

It happens on tape that has low magnetic stability. Music on one layer of the tape is transferred to music on an adjacent layer, causing an echo.

At Maxell, we've designed our tape for superior magnetic stability. So what's happening to the opposite page won't happen to your music.

You see, we believe you should only hear the music you want to hear. Nothing less, and nothing more.

IT'S WORTH IT.

Maxell Corporation of America, 60 Oxford Drive, Moonachie, N.J. 07074

133

If IBM, Boeing and NASA built a car, would you buy it? Of course you would.

The Saab Viggen takes off in 1300 ft. Reaches supersonic speeds 60 seconds after takeoff. Climbs to a 32,810-ft. altitude in 100 seconds. Flies at Mach 2.

They don't.
But Saab does.
And as you might expect of a car built by a car company that is also a computer company, an aircraft company and an aerospace company, driving a Saab comes as something of a revelation.
Namely, that a car need not be a four-wheeled collection of compromises.

Just where does Datasaab stand in the computer industry? In at least one segment, right on top. A recent independent survey of banks showed users of Datasaab teller terminals to be consistently more satisfied than users of IBM, Bunker Ramo, TRW and Olivetti equipment.

Room.
Outside, the Saab 900 is about the same size as the Audi 4000 and 5000, the Volvo DL and GLE and the BMW 320i and 528i.
Inside, however, it's bigger than all of them.
Of those cars, only the Saab is large enough inside to rate a mid-sized designation from the EPA.
An accomplishment, in fact, not even the Mercedes 280E, 280SE and 280CE could muster.

Performance.
Against the clock in a 1979 *Road & Track* magazine test, the front-wheel drive, four-cylinder Saab 900 Turbo recorded 61.4 mph through a 700-ft. slalom course.
Faster than the Volvo, two Audis, three Mercedes and four BMWs tested by *Road & Track* in '78 and '79.
Faster, also, than two Ferraris, two Jaguars and a couple of Porsches, including the 928.

Braking.
From 60 to 0, in two years of separate tests run by *Road & Track* magazine, the Saab 900 Turbo stopped quicker than two Audis, two Jaguars, five BMWs, a Ferrari, a Maserati, a Mercedes and a Volvo, among others.

Versatility.
Most of the time, the Saab 900 is a sedan and the trunk is more than sufficient. (It's as large, by EPA measurements, as the trunks of the largest sedans.)
Yet for those few times a year when you wish you had a station wagon, the Saab 900 sensibly eliminates the necessity of owning one, renting one or borrowing one.
Fold the rear seat in the Saab forward, lift the rear hatchback and the Saab presents a station wagon-like space over six feet long and 53 cubic feet big.

Economy.
The Saab 900 EMS gets ㉑ EPA estimated mpg and 30 estimated highway mpg.
Better than the Audi 5000, Volvo GT, Volvo DL, Volvo GLE, Peugeot 604, Mercedes 280E, Mercedes 280CE and Mercedes 280SE.
Only the Saab is a mid-sized car. The others are all compacts.
(Remember, use estimated mpg for comparison only. Mileage varies with speed, trip length and weather. Actual highway mileage will probably be less.)

Prestige.
What could be more prestigious than buying a new car and, for once, getting everything you want?

SAAB
The most intelligent car ever built.

134

135

136

137

138

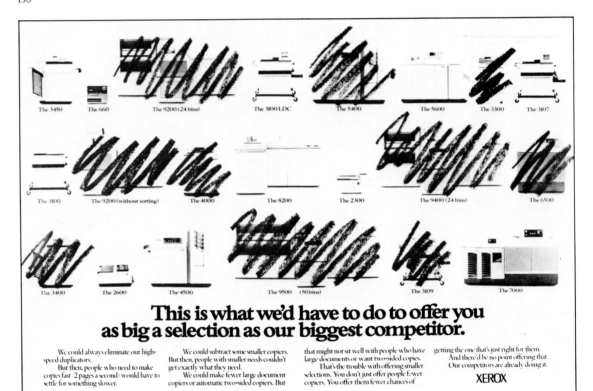

139

It works beautifully on budgets.

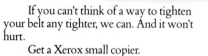

If you can't think of a way to tighten your belt any tighter, we can. And it won't hurt.

Get a Xerox small copier.

It can save you money on copies because it uses plain, inexpensive uncoated paper. And gives you crisp, clear copies even if the originals are faded carbons or on colored paper.

It will also save you money on mailings. Because a Xerox small copier can copy on your own letterhead and on mailing labels as well.

But best of all, a Xerox small copier can even save you money on the copier. Because you can get one for a lot less than you'd think. Whether you buy or rent.

So before you decide on a small copier, send in the coupon or call 800-648-5600, operator 266. Especially if you're interested in saving money.

We'll even let you try one for a few days at no cost.

That's certainly within your budget.

- - - - - - - - - - - - - - - - - - - -

☐ I'd like a sales representative to contact me.
☐ I'd like to try one of your copiers for a few days at no cost.
☐ I'd like more information about Xerox small copiers.

Send to: Xerox Corporation, P.O. Box 24, Rochester, N.Y. 14601.

Name_____

Title_____

Company_____

Address_____

City_____State_____Zip____

Phone_____

NSPS-5-80

XEROX

140

Consumer Magazine
Black and White
Page or Spread
Including
Magazine Supplements

141
Art Director:
Anthony Angotti
Writer:
Allen Kay
Client:
Xerox
Agency:
Needham, Harper & Steers

142
Art Director:
Roy Grace
Writer:
Tom Yobbagy
Designer:
Roy Grace
Photographer:
Joan Kramer Stock
Client:
IBM Office Products Division
Agency:
Doyle Dane Bernbach

143
Art Director:
Roy Grace
Writer:
Tom Yobbagy
Designer:
Roy Grace
Photographers:
Chuck Kuhn
Hunter Freeman
Client:
IBM Office Products Division
Agency:
Doyle Dane Bernbach

Consumer Magazine
Color Page or Spread
Including
Magazine Supplements

144
Art Director:
Steve Ohman
Writer:
Larry Vine
Designer:
Rich Ferrante
Photographer:
George Cochran
Client:
Johnnie Walker Black Label
Agency:
Smith/Greenland

141

142

143

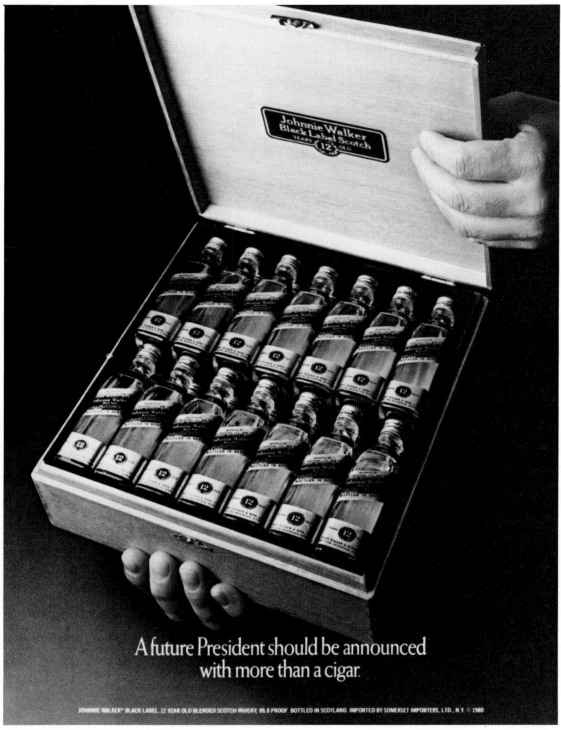

A future President should be announced
with more than a cigar.

144

145

146

BMW. THE CAR COMPANY THAT HASN'T BEEN LEGISLATED INTO MEDIOCRITY.

The challenge that faces the automaker of the 1980's lies not in meeting tougher pollution standards, nor in coping with ever more restrictive safety regulations—not even in accommodating the petroleum shortages that are fast becoming a regular summer occurrence.

No indeed. The challenge lies in meeting the myriad of societal demands and still building automobiles that are worth driving.

Pessimists darkly predict that it cannot be done and point to the depressing number of uninspired automobiles on the market as incontrovertible proof.

Yet, fortunately, these gloomy predictions do not take into account the inventive genius and the obsessive determination of the engineers at BMW in Munich, Germany to build extraordinary automobiles.

Against all odds the BMW not only meets the demands of society, it also provides the sort of exhilarating driving experience that automotive enthusiasts have all but given up for lost.

A SEEMINGLY INCONGRUOUS COMBINATION OF LUXURY, PERFORMANCE AND EFFICIENCY.

Conventional automotive wisdom has it that, inevitably, one must choose between luxury, performance and fuel efficiency. A sufficiency in any one necessitating a corresponding insufficiency in another.

And in the face of this, the BMW seems all the more remarkable for requiring no compromise whatsoever.

Round a particularly sticky curve and the legendary BMW suspension system—independent on all four wheels—flexes with an uncanny resiliency that makes one feel as if the car were built into the roadway. A sensation that results from highly advanced suspension technology and the virtually perfect integration of man and machine.

The BMW power plant—whether 4 or 6 cylinder—has long been a model for modern design. Press the accelerator and the fuel-injected, overhead cam engine responds in a manner that can only be described as exhilarating.

Yet, the 320i (with 5-speed standard transmission) delivers an impressive 25 EPA estimated mpg, 36 estimated highway mileage and, based on these figures, an estimated mpg range of 383 miles and a highway range of 551 miles.

(Naturally our fuel efficiency figures are for comparison purposes only. Your actual mileage and range may vary, depending on speed, weather and trip length. Your actual highway mileage and highway range will most likely be lower.)

And, while the BMW provides as long a list of luxury items as one could sanely require, its luxury is purposefully engineered to help prevent driver fatigue.

Vital controls are within easy reach: the tachometer, speedometer and ancillary instruments are well-marked and easy to read.

Its front seats are designed to hold their occupants firmly in place, and are so thoroughly adjustable that it is all but a mathematical impossibility not to find a comfortable seating position.

SAFETY BEYOND STURDY BUMPERS.

At BMW automotive safety was of primary concern long before the first bumper law was written.

The passenger compartment is encased in a solid steel "cage." So strong is this construction that the car could be dropped on its nose from the fourth floor of a building without significant damage to the compartment itself.

Yet with all its sheer strength—its computer-programmed "crush zones," its double-braking systems—the BMW features a safety device even more estimable. Its exceptional responsiveness and handling characteristics give it the ability to avoid accidents as well as merely survive them.

All in all, in a time of lowered automotive expectations, amidst increasing mediocrity, the engineers at BMW have actually increased the BMW.

If you'd care to judge for yourself, telephone your nearest BMW dealer to arrange a thorough test drive at your convenience.

BMW

THE ULTIMATE DRIVING MACHINE.
BMW, MUNICH, GERMANY

MEETING THE DEMANDS OF SOCIETY IS NO EXCUSE FOR BUILDING A BORING CAR.

If one accepts the dismal prophecies emanating from the automotive community, it appears we are destined to suffer a generation of thoroughly boring automobiles.

Cars so utterly debilitated by societal necessities, safety regulations and anti-pollution paraphernalia that they no longer will be the least bit interesting to drive.

There is, however, one rather encouraging note of optimism.

All this doomsaying neglects to take into account the obsessive determination of the engineers at BMW in Munich, Germany to build extraordinary automobiles.

Against all odds, the BMW 528i not only satisfies the laws of the land and the demands of the gas tank, it does so without ever once violating our conviction that extraordinary performance is the one rational justification for owning an expensive car.

FEW CARS PERFORMED THIS WELL BEFORE POLLUTION CONTROLS.

Expensive luxury sedans have never received great kudos for their capacity to perform with efficiency and agility.

"Quite the contrary, "Expensive sedans," writes Car and Driver magazine, "tend to ride like pillows when you cruise them and squeal like pigs when you push them."

A bit caustic perhaps. But, an analysis that makes the performance statistics of the BMW 528i seem all the more remarkable.

Round a particularly hair-raising curve and the legendary BMW suspension system—independent on all four wheels—flexes with a resiliency that makes one feel as if the car were built into the roadway. A sensation that results from highly advanced suspension technology and the virtually perfect integration of man and machine.

Press the accelerator and the 528i's fuel-injected, 2.8-liter, overhead cam engine responds in a manner that can only be described as exhilarating—even by pre pollution control standards.

Yet, the 528i (with standard transmission) delivers 18 EPA estimated mpg, 30 estimated highway mileage and, based on these figures, an estimated mpg range of 295 miles and a highway range of 492 miles.

(Naturally, our fuel efficiency figures are for comparison purposes only. Your actual mileage and range may vary, depending on speed, weather and trip length. Your actual highway mileage and highway range will most likely be lower.)

And, curious as it may seem, the BMW 528i is the only luxury "sports" sedan in its price class that offers a surgically precise five-speed manual gearbox as standard equipment (automatic is available of course).

LUXURY NEEDN'T BE MERELY A FACADE.

One's appetite for luxury would have to be insatiable indeed to imagine an appointment or convenience lacking in the 528i.

AM/FM stereo cassette, full-power accessories, air conditioning, and a good deal more, are all standard equipment.

Yet each and every facet has been strategically engineered to help eliminate the enormous strains and pressures of driving.

Its seats are anatomically shaped buckets. Its front seats are so thoroughly adjustable that it is all but impossible not to find a comfortable driving position.

All vital controls are within easy reach. The tachometer, speedometer and ancillary instruments are large, well-marked and totally visible.

All in all, in a time of lowered automotive expectations, amidst increasing mediocrity, the engineers at BMW have actually improved the BMW 528i.

If you find the notion of owning such a car more than a little intriguing, we suggest you phone your nearest BMW dealer and arrange for a thorough test drive at your convenience.

BMW

THE ULTIMATE DRIVING MACHINE.
BMW, MUNICH, GERMANY

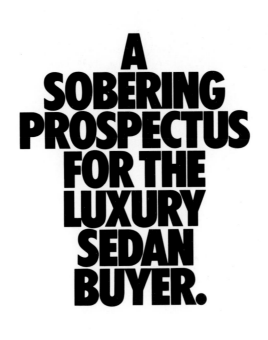
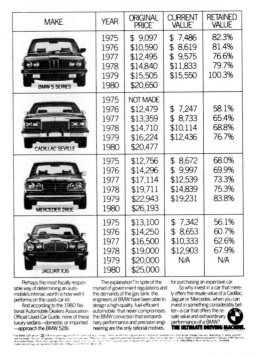

A SOBERING PROSPECTUS FOR THE LUXURY SEDAN BUYER.

MAKE	YEAR	ORIGINAL PRICE	CURRENT VALUE	RETAINED VALUE
BMW 5 SERIES	1975	$ 9,097	$ 7,486	82.3%
	1976	$10,590	$ 8,619	81.4%
	1977	$12,495	$ 9,575	76.6%
	1978	$14,840	$11,833	79.7%
	1979	$15,505	$15,550	100.3%
	1980	$20,650		
CADILLAC SEVILLE	1975	NOT MADE		
	1976	$12,479	$ 7,247	58.1%
	1977	$13,359	$ 8,733	65.4%
	1978	$14,710	$10,114	68.8%
	1979	$16,224	$12,436	76.7%
	1980	$20,477		
MERCEDES 280E	1975	$12,756	$ 8,672	68.0%
	1976	$14,296	$ 9,997	69.9%
	1977	$17,114	$12,539	73.3%
	1978	$19,711	$14,839	75.3%
	1979	$22,943	$19,231	83.8%
	1980	$26,193		
JAGUAR XJ6	1975	$13,100	$ 7,342	56.1%
	1976	$14,250	$ 8,653	60.7%
	1977	$16,500	$10,333	62.6%
	1978	$19,000	$12,903	67.9%
	1979	$20,000	N/A	N/A
	1980	$25,000		

Perhaps the most fiscally responsible way of determining an automobile's intrinsic worth is how well it performs on the used-car lot.

And according to the 1980 National Automobile Dealers Association Official Used-Car Guide, none of these luxury sedans—domestic or imported—approach the BMW 528i.

The explanation? In spite of the myriad of government regulations and the demands of the gas tank, the engineers at BMW have been able to design a high-quality, fuel-efficient automobile that never compromises. the BMW conviction that extraordinary performance and precision engineering are the only rational motives for purchasing an expensive car.

So why invest in a car that merely offers the resale value of a Cadillac, Jaguar or Mercedes, when you can invest in something considerably better—a car that offers the resale value and extraordinary performance of a BMW?

THE ULTIMATE DRIVING MACHINE.

LIFE IS FILLED WITH COMPROMISES. A $30,000 CAR SHOULDN'T BE.

In these times of performance-sapping anti-pollution laws, fuel requirements and safety regulations, it is becoming increasingly difficult to build cars that are still worth driving.

Certain observers, given to dark prophecies, have even gone so far as to predict a generation of fatally uninspired, irrevocably compromised automobiles.

Expensive luxury sedans that, in the somewhat colorful prose of Car and Driver magazine, "...ride like pillows when you cruise them and squeal like pigs when you push them."

A dour prediction indeed. But fortunately one that does not take into consideration the inventive genius and the obsessive determination of the engineers at BMW in Munich, Germany to build extraordinary automobiles.

Against all odds, the BMW 733i not only meets the critical demands of society, it does so without ever once violating our conviction that extraordinary performance is the only rational justification for owning an expensive car.

PERFORMANCE AND EFFICIENCY CAN COEXIST UNDER THE SAME HOOD.

In a very real sense, the BMW 733i is a seemingly incongruous combination of qualities many automakers insist are mutually exclusive.

While the 733i is the largest BMW sedan, its size in no way hampers its uncanny agility, its responsiveness to the driver, or its singular capacity for removing the drama from even the most hair-raising road conditions.

Indeed, its suspension system—independent on all four wheels—has been described by Car and Driver magazine as "the single most significant breakthrough in front suspension design in this decade."

Press the accelerator and the 733's fuel-injected, 3.2 liter, overhead cam engine responds in a manner that would be exhilarating—even by pre pollution control standards.

Yet, the 733 (with standard transmission) delivers [16] EPA estimated mpg, 23 estimated highway mileage and, based on these figures, an estimated mpg range of [360] miles and a highway range of 518 miles.

(Naturally, our fuel efficiency figures are for comparison purposes only. Your actual mileage and range may vary depending on speed, weather and trip length. Your actual highway mileage and highway range will most likely be lower.)

And, when you slide behind the wheel of the BMW 733i, you will notice an object just to your right that should give you considerable insight into the somewhat divergent philosophy of BMW. It's called a manual transmission.

Unaccountably, the 733i is the only "luxury sport sedan" in its price class to provide one as standard equipment. (Automatic is, of course, available.)

LUXURY NEEDN'T BE SYNONYMOUS WITH SUPERFLUOUS.

It's difficult to imagine an appointment, a convenience or an accessory that has been omitted in the BMW 733i.

AM/FM stereo cassette, electric sunroof, electric windows, electric side-view mirror—even a central-locking system that locks all four doors, the trunk lid and the gas door with the turn of a single key—are all standard equipment.

Yet, all facets have been biomechanically engineered to the nth degree to help eliminate driver fatigue.

Its seats are anatomically shaped buckets, covered in wide rolls of supple leather. Its front seats are so thoroughly adjustable that it is all but impossible not to find a comfortable driving position.

All vital controls are within easy reach. The tachometer, speedometer and ancillary instruments are large, well marked and totally visible.

"If you've driven any BMW in the last ten model years," writes one automotive journalist, "lean back, close your eyes and imagine that car honed and polished to the limit of human finesse. That would be the 733i."

If you find the notion of owning such a car more than a little intriguing, we suggest you phone your nearest BMW dealer and arrange a thorough test drive.

THE ULTIMATE DRIVING MACHINE.

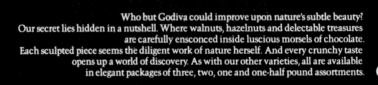

Nutcracker Sweet.

Who but Godiva could improve upon nature's subtle beauty?
Our secret lies hidden in a nutshell. Where walnuts, hazelnuts and delectable treasures
are carefully ensconced inside luscious morsels of chocolate.
Each sculpted piece seems the diligent work of nature herself. And every crunchy taste
opens up a world of discovery. As with our other varieties, all are available
in elegant packages of three, two, one and one-half pound assortments.

GODIVA.
Chocolatier
BRUXELLES · NEW YORK
PARIS · COLOGNE

Godiva Chocolatier, 701 Fifth Avenue, New York, New York 10022

152

"ANYONE WHO'S THINKING OF SPENDING $24,000 FOR A LUXURY CAR SHOULD TALK TO A PSYCHIATRIST."

— Dr. John Boston, psychiatrist
and Volvo owner, Austin, Texas

John Boston, a Texas psychiatrist, owns a '73 Volvo.
He bought that Volvo because, as he puts it: "I had admired what Volvo had done in the area of safety. The car seemed well-built. It offered solid European craftsmanship without the inflated price."

We wanted Dr. Boston's opinion of the new Volvo GLE, which has a full assortment of luxury features as standard equipment—and a price tag thousands of dollars below that of the well-known German luxury sedan.

"It's an excellent value. In my opinion, the individual buying this car would have a strong, unsuppressed need

to get his or her money's worth. He or she would probably also have a strong enough self-image not to need a blatant status symbol."

When we told him that some people were actually paying five to ten thousand dollars more for a luxury car, Dr. Boston's response was characteristically succinct.

"That's not using your head."

Finally, we asked Dr. Boston if, when he was ready for a new car, he'd consider the Volvo GLE for himself.

"I'd be crazy if I didn't."

VOLVO
A car you can believe in.

153

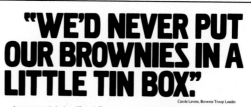

"WE'D NEVER PUT OUR BROWNIES IN A LITTLE TIN BOX."

Carole Levine, Brownie Troop Leader.

As you can see, the leaders of Brownie Troop #1900 in Los Angeles have a lot of responsibility. So when it came to choosing troop transportation, they were very tough cookies.

As one of them puts it, "I must have frustrated half the car salesmen in southern California looking for the right station wagon. The ones I looked at were so small and tinny. No way would I ever feel safe driving a bunch of girls around in any of them."

One by one, each of these Brownie leaders ended up at a Volvo dealer. And today, Troop #1900

travels around in a Volvo wagon train. "I was sold on the Volvo wagon the minute I saw it. I knew the girls would fit very comfortably inside and there would be plenty of room left for their gear. When I drove the Volvo, it wasn't all over the road like other wagons I'd driven. It offered great visibility. And it just plain felt solid and safe."

If you're looking for a station wagon you can feel good about putting your kids in, join Troop #1900. Buy a Volvo.

VOLVO
A car you can believe in.

154

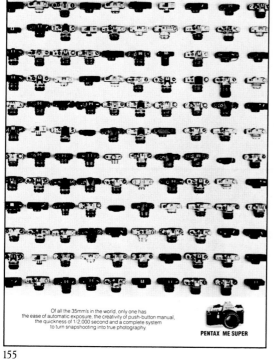

Of all the 35mm's in the world, only one has
the ease of automatic exposure, the creativity of push-button manual,
the quickness of 1/2,000 second and a complete system
to turn snapshooting into true photography.

PENTAX ME SUPER

155

Sherwin-Williams proudly presents its entire wallpaper collection.

Here they are. All 15,000 of them. A variety of patterns so large that whatever design you've got in mind, we've probably got in our collection. Now, if that sounds unbelievable, why not go to a Sherwin-Williams store? Then again, you could always take a real close look at the photo below.

There's more than one way to cover the earth.

156

Just a reminder. We have 550 wallpaper patterns on sale now.

And that includes just about any type of design you'd like to see on this wall. All for 20% to 30% off regular price at Sherwin-Williams stores. But you'll have to hurry. Because this sale only lasts from April 25th to May 31st. After that, you could end up facing this kind of emptiness until we have our next one.

1980 The Sherwin-Williams Company

157

We rebuilt the pyramids...

...put a motorboat where a motorboat's never been before...

0-1,000 IN 2 DAYS.

...added ninety three million miles of sky...

New! The TR7 with added headroom.

...rebuilt a motorway...

...made the heavens rain cigarettes...

Makes other vermouths seem a little wet.

...and on the seventh day...

...then hung a tea towel out to dry at 30,000 ft...

IF YOU NEED A LITTLE MIRACLE RING DAVID TAYLOR ON 01-404 4044 STUDIO 10, 25-27 FARRINGDON ROAD, EC1 EUROPEAN CONTACTS: PETER BROWN AMSTERDAM 276411 ALLEN ABERCROMBIE PARIS 757562.

Studio 10

158

de MARKOFF
IT'S WRITTEN ALL OVER HER FACE.

LIVING COLORS.

It's a face that says it all. Well, almost. They can read your lips. But never feel they've read enough. And your eyes always leave just a little unsaid. Yet the look is emphatic. Elegance has not vanished. de Markoff defines that state of mind in living colors. Shades that celebrate your arrival. de Markoff. For your eyes, face, lips, even your nails. After all, they all have something to say. And everyone wants to listen. Very closely.

FOR THE WOMAN WHO PLAYS HARD TO FORGET.

159

Thinsulate insulation made him half the climber he used to be.

For top class mountaineers like Alan Rouse, keeping warm in severe conditions is a matter of survival.

Until now the answer has always been bulky clothing, which in turn has caused another problem: lack of mobility.

Now 3M have developed a new material specifically designed to overcome this problem – Thinsulate Thermal Insulation.

Warmth Without Bulk.

Thinsulate material is unlike any other existing insulation material because it's constructed of micro-fibres one-tenth the size of any other synthetic fibre.

This gives 20 times more surface area in which to trap air, and air is the most effective insulator.

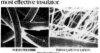

This means that Thinsulate Insulation material is nearly twice as warm as any other clothing insulation of the same thickness.

So a jacket filled with Thinsulate Insulation material can keep you as warm as the best down or polyester fibre filled jackets – but will be half as thick and far less cumbersome to wear.

Because the material is simply cut in one piece and will not settle or bunch like down, a jacket with Thinsulate Insulation material requires far less quilting.

This reduces the problem of cold spots which occur along the stitching of many heavily quilted jackets. (And means that even a ripped jacket will still be totally effective.)

And unlike down, Thinsulate Insulation material will keep you warm even in damp conditions because its fibres absorb less than 1% of their own weight in water.

Scientifically Proved.

To develop Thinsulate Insulation material 3M used every laboratory test

available, and scientifically controlled field tests with Alaskan pipeline workers were carried out in the most severe of Arctic conditions.

THERMOGRAM A   THERMOGRAM B

One of the tests made use of a new infra-red photographic technique –Thermography. Thermogram A shows the problem of an ordinary down filled jacket–heat loss at the seams (hence the lighter blue.) In Thermogram B, the right half of the jacket is filled with Thinsulate material, the left with an equal thickness of polyester. The dark blue of the Thinsulate half demonstrates its better overall heat retention.

Proved in the Field.

These tests indicated the new product's worth, but field tests supplied the proof. That's why we asked Alan Rouse to wear it on a climb.

He wore it on Nuptse with so much success that he chose to wear it on his next expedition, the first British winter ascent of Everest.

So if you, like Alan Rouse, want to keep warm in the great outdoors but still have the freedom of movement to enjoy it, look for the garments with the Thinsulate label.

They're all guaranteed to make you half the climber you used to be.

For further information on Thinsulate Thermal Insulation write to Barry Bettany, 3M United Kingdom Limited, 3M House, PO Box 1, Bracknell, Berks. RG12 1JU.

Thinsulate
THERMAL INSULATION

3M

160

Consumer Magazine Color Page or Spread Including Magazine Supplements

161
Art Director:
Helmut Krone
Writer:
Tom Yobbagy
Photographer:
Helmut Krone
Client:
Polaroid
Agency:
Doyle Dane Bernbach

162
Art Director:
Helmut Krone
Writer:
Tom Yobbagy
Photographer:
Helmut Krone
Client:
Polaroid
Agency:
Doyle Dane Bernbach

163
Art Director:
Helmut Krone
Writer:
Tom Yobbagy
Photographer:
Helmut Krone
Client:
Polaroid
Agency:
Doyle Dane Bernbach

164
Art Director:
Robert Tucker
Writers:
John Annarino
Peter Bregman
Designer:
Robert Tucker
Photographer:
Jim Young
Client:
Volkswagen
Agency:
Doyle Dane Bernbach

165
Art Director:
Matt Rao
Writer:
Stu Hyatt
Designer:
Matt Rao
Photographer:
Polaroid
Client:
Polaroid
Agency:
Doyle Dane Bernbach

166
Art Director:
Myron Polenberg
Writer:
Edythe Stevenson
Designer:
Myron Polenberg
Photographers:
Bill Stettner
Andrew Unangst
Client:
Heublein
Agency:
Tinker, Campbell, Ewald

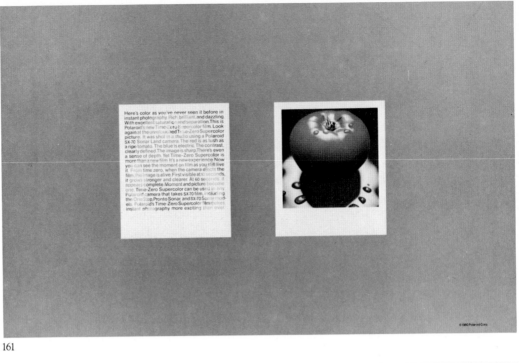

161

162

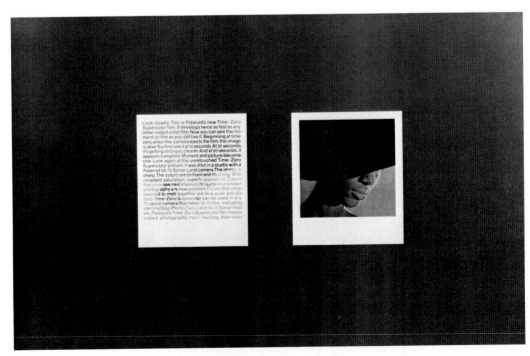

163

It has economy written all over it.

The Volkswagen Pickup. Probably one of the most economical pickups ever invented with a fuel-injected gas engine.

And if you want even more economy there's a diesel option that delivers mileage no one can beat. (It gets an EPA estimated 23 mpg, 32 mpg highway, estimated 39 mpg diesel and 48 mpg diesel high-

way. Use "estimated mpg" for comparisons. Your mileage may vary with weather, speed and trip length. Actual highway mileage will probably be less.)

But the engine's not the only thing that's economical.
It has front-wheel drive for economical power transfer from the engine to the wheels.

And, the engine is transverse-mounted for more economical use of cab space for passengers and better forward visibility for the driver.

What's more, it has an independently operating electric fan to cool the engine more economically, too.

In the back, it has economical double-wall construction so that if something you carry in its six-foot steel bed makes a dent on the inside, nothing shows on the outside. But the most economical thing about the Volkswagen

Pickup is the fact that it's still a Volkswagen.

VOLKSWAGEN DOES IT AGAIN

164

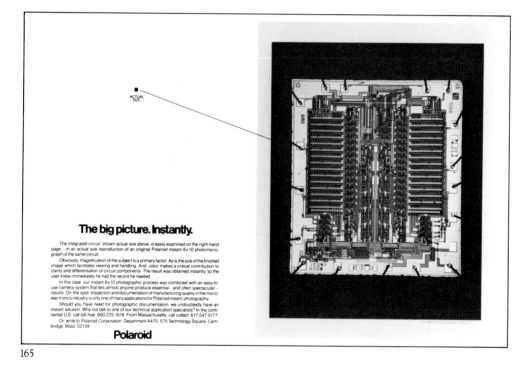

ACTUAL SIZE

The big picture. Instantly.

The integrated circuit shown actual size above, is easily examined on the right-hand page - in an actual size reproduction of an original Polaroid instant 8 x 10 photomicrograph of the same circuit.

Obviously magnification of the subject is a primary factor. As is the size of the finished image which facilitates viewing and handling. And, color makes a critical contribution to clarity and differentiation of circuit components. The result was obtained instantly, so the user knew immediately he had the record he needed.

In this case our instant 8 x 10 photographic process was combined with an easy-to-use camera system that lets almost anyone produce essential - and often spectacular - results. On-the-spot. Inspection and documentation of manufacturing quality in the micro-electronics industry is only one of many applications for Polaroid instant photography.

Should you have need for photographic documentation, we undoubtedly have an instant solution. Why not talk to one of our technical application specialists? In the continental U.S. call toll-free: 800-225-1618. From Massachusetts, call collect: 617-547-5177

Or, write to Polaroid Corporation, Department A470, 575 Technology Square, Cambridge, Mass. 02139

Polaroid

165

166

Consumer Magazine
Black and White
Campaign
Including
Magazine Supplements

167
Art Director:
Michael Tesch
Writer:
Curvin O'Rielly
Photographer:
Carl Fischer
Client:
Saab-Scania
Agency:
Ally & Gargano

168
Art Director:
Robert Reitzfeld
Writer:
David Altschiller
Designer:
Robert Reitzfeld
Photographer:
Bill Dolce
Client:
Poland Spring Corporation
Agency:
**Altschiller, Reitzfeld,
Jackson, Solin/NCK**

If IBM, Boeing and NASA built a car, would you buy it? Of course you would.

You think you're confused about what kind of car to buy? That's nothing. Most car makers don't even know what kind of car to build.

Yes, the times call for enormous sacrifices. But who should make them? Car makers? Or car buyers?

Club soda is not spring water.

It's a strange irony. We constantly scrutinize what we eat and drink. And then somehow our world becomes more and more artificial, filled with chemicalized, processed products. Even our water.

There are those who would have you believe that water is water, that since club soda and Poland Spring water are both clear liquids and both have bubbles, that one is the same as the other. The idea couldn't be further from the truth.

Club Soda starts as tap water.

Believe it or not, the leading club soda begins as water that comes from a tap. No different, in fact, than the water that pours from your sink or your bathtub, for that matter. Then the water is put through a whole series of chemical processes.

Purity through chemistry.

How does tap water become club soda? Here's one of the recipes: To tap water, add lime, and then chlorine to kill organic matter. Add ferrous sulphate to settle all the chemicals and suspended matter together. Skim the water from the "sludge." Then charcoal filter the water to remove the chlorine. At last what you have is "treated water." But wait! The chemical process isn't nearly complete. Now filter the water again, then add a mixture of minerals and salts. (These result in a club soda that actually has 60 times the amount of salt as Poland Spring Water.) And as a final step add artificial carbonation. Voila, club soda.

Poland Spring is natural spring water.

Now the recipe for Poland Spring water. Go deep into the woods of Maine and take some cool water from the Poland Spring. Add natural carbonation. Drink. No artificial ingredients or chemicals have ever been added to Poland Spring water.

The Poland Spring is no ordinary spring.

For nearly 200 years, the Poland Spring has been the most famous spring in America. Its purity is achieved through nature, not chemistry. It comes as a result of natural filtration through layers of granite, a process that cannot be artificially duplicated by man.

Because of this unique quality, Poland Spring has become the drink of Presidents and Kings. It graced the White House table during the presidencies of Grant, Taft, Coolidge, Roosevelt, and Eisenhower, to name a few.

And long before European water had ever come to America's shores, Poland Spring was a staple of royal households across Europe.

A word of caution.

Over the last few years, spring water has become very desirable across America. So it's no wonder that club sodas have tried to pass themselves off as us. Don't be fooled. Processed tap water will never be natural spring water. Club soda will never be Poland Spring. Club sodas often offer a slightly lower price as an incentive. Don't be taken in by this, either. Poland Spring costs what it does because it's shipped to you all the way from the spring in Maine. Club soda costs what it does because it's shipped to you all the way from the tap.

A word of philosophy.

No one will dispute that water is essential to our lives. The question is where will it come from. To our mind, we should drink water as nature intended it to be. From the springs, the forests, the untouched regions of our world. Try Poland Spring. To those of us in the city, it's like a little bit of the country every day.

For a free informative booklet, write to Poland Spring, Poland Spring, ME 04274

One is a product of nature. One is a product of chemistry.

There are few things left in this world that have been untouched, untampered with, unchemicalized, in short, unmessed by man. One such product is Poland Spring.

Nature was good to Poland Spring.

200 years ago, when Hiram Ricker discovered the deep granite source of Poland Spring, deep in the woods of Maine, he knew enough not to tamper with it.

Because of its unique purity and flavor, Poland Spring water soon became the drink of Presidents and Kings. In fact, it was famous in Europe long before any European water ever set foot in America.

Today, we treat Poland Spring water with the same awe and respect as Hiram Ricker did generations ago. Poland Spring is as pure today as it was then. We still bottle the water right at the spring. And of course, there's no need to tell you that Poland Spring water has no sugar, no calories, and no artificial ingredients. True natural spring water simply doesn't have those kinds of things, by definition.

Nature has nothing to do with club soda.

The genesis of club soda is a bit different. A leading club soda begins as tap water. Hard to believe, isn't it? The very same water that pours into your sink (or bathtub, for that matter) is club soda's primary constituent.

The water is then processed. Lime is added to attract the minerals.

Then chlorine is added to kill any organic matter. Then ferrous sulphate is added to settle all the chemicals and suspended matter together. And then the water is drawn off the "sludge." At last you have what is called "treated water."

But the chemical process isn't complete. The water is then filtered, and then yet another mixture of minerals and salts are added. (These result in a club soda that actually has 60 times the amount of salt as Poland Spring water.) And to all the other artificial processes as a coup de grace they add artificial carbonation. Bravo.

Don't be taken in.

There are those who have the nerve to suggest that an artificially made, chemically processed beverage is actually better than pure natural Poland Spring.

Do not be fooled. Club soda is a product of chemistry. Spring water is a product of nature. It's as simple as that.

A small price to pay.

Of course, Poland Spring water may cost a little more than club soda. To our mind, it should cost a lot more. Poland Spring water has to be shipped to you all the way from the spring deep in the woods of Maine. Club soda, on the other hand, comes to you all the way from the tap.

A few last remarks.

In Europe, where they love their wine, they love their spring water as well. In virtually every civilized nation on the continent, spring water is found on the dinner table. (In many ways it is the mark of civility itself.)

And the fact is, Europeans can get water from their taps the same as we in America do. So why do they pay for natural spring water?

Because over the years they've developed an appreciation for the natural.

Isn't it time you began to drink of nature rather than of chemicals? Try Poland Spring. To those of us in the city, it's like a little bit of the country every day.

Where is club soda's spring?

There appears to be a lot of confusion out there about what club soda is, and what Poland Spring water is. Much of it, we suspect, because club sodas would like you to believe that they are indeed natural spring water. Let us set the confusion straight once and for all.

Club soda begins as tap water

No club soda we know of comes from a natural spring. (If there is one somewhere, it's news to us.) The water that is the basic constituent of club soda comes from a local tap at the local bottling plant. Surprised? The same water that flows into your sink flows into their tanks. Then a whole series of chemical processes purify and transform this tap water into club soda.

Ah, the wonders of chemistry.

Let us give you a brief glimpse into the methodology commonly used to make club soda: To tap water, add lime, and then chlorine. Add ferrous sulphate to settle all the chemicals and suspended matter together. (They call this mass "sludge.") Skim the water from the sludge. Then charcoal filter the water to remove the chlorine. At this point, you have what they call "treated water." But the chemistry lesson isn't over. Now filter the water and add a mixture of minerals and salts. These result in a club soda that actually has more than 40 times the amount of salt as Poland Spring water. Then, to all the other artificial processes, add artificial carbonation. Pool, club soda.

Ah, the wonders of nature.

Poland Spring water is as natural as club soda is processed. The recipe for it is very short. Hike deep into the woods of Maine, find the legendary Poland Spring, dip into the icy glacial source, add natural carbonation. Drink. No artificial ingredient, has ever touched Poland spring water. It is now what it was centuries ago: one of the world's great natural waters. And certainly America's preeminent natural water.

The Poland Spring. A minor miracle.

200 years ago, when Hiram Ricker discovered the Poland Spring, he knew then that he had found something quite remarkable. A source that bubbled up from deep in the earth. A natural water of exceptional purity and flavor. Back then, they even believed that Poland Spring water produced medical miracles. The legend spread and soon Poland Spring became renowned in the courts of Europe. In fact Poland Spring water graced the tables of royalty long before any European water crossed the ocean in this direction. American Presidents, not to be outdone by royalty, made it a White House staple. Presidents Grant, Coolidge, Taft, Roosevelt, and most recently Eisenhower, demanded it.

Do not fall prey to confusion.

Over the last few years (how could you not notice) there has been a trend toward natural spring water. In an effort to cash in, some club sodas have tried to play down the differences between them and us. And to some extent have probably succeeded. Do not be fooled. Processed tap water will never be natural spring water. Club soda will never be Poland Spring.

Do not succumb to price.

Club sodas may also offer you an additional inducement to drink them: a lower price. They should cost less. Poland Spring water costs what it does because it's shipped to you hundreds or even thousands of miles from the spring itself. Club soda is shipped to you all the way from the local tap.

A little sanity, please.

Today, more and more things are becoming chemicalized, and processed. To our mind, our bodies deserve things as nature intended them. Not as man tampered with them. And one of them is Poland Spring water. Natural water from the springs, the forests, the untouched regions of our world.

For a free informative booklet, write to Poland Spring, Poland Spring, ME 04274 ▶

**Consumer Magazine
Black and White
Campaign
Including
Magazine Supplements**

169
Art Directors:
**Anthony Angotti
Allen Kay**
Writer:
Tom Thomas
Artist:
Charles White
Photographer:
Steve Steigman
Client:
Xerox
Agency:
Needham, Harper & Steers

170
Art Directors:
**Ken Amaral
Neil Leinwohl
Anthony Angotti**
Writers:
**Stan Levine
David Cantor
Tom Thomas**
Client:
Xerox
Agency:
Needham, Harper & Steers

This is what the 1980's looked like to people in the 1940's.

It was going to be a brave new world of undersea cities, full-course meals in the form of pills, and a rocket ship in every garage.

What happened?

Nothing out of the ordinary. The future simply didn't happen the way people thought.

But then, it seldom does. And that's an age-old problem: How do you plan for the future when you can't predict it?

At Xerox we've found a way.

It's called the Information Outlet.

It uses a special cable, called the Xerox Ethernet cable, to join your office machines into a single network.

A network that's flexible—so that as time passes, you can plug in new information processors, electronic printers, or other information management machines as you need them. Even machines that aren't made by Xerox, and even ones that haven't been invented yet.

In other words, you'll be able to build an information network step by step, according to your needs. Instead of committing to a rigid system you might find hard to change years from now.

When you discover the future hasn't turned out according to plan.

XEROX

If you'd like more information on the Information Outlet, write us and we'll send you a booklet. Xerox Corporation, P.O. Box 47005, Dallas, Texas 75247.

WHY LEAP INTO THE FUTURE WHEN YOU CAN WADE INTO IT?

Lately everyone's been telling you to get ready for the Office of the Future.

We agree. But how do you design an office system to get ready for the future when you can't possibly know exactly what you're getting ready for?

At Xerox, we've designed a solution. We call it the Information Outlet, and here's how it works:

The Information Outlet gives you access to a special cable known as the Ethernet cable. It links all kinds of different office machines so they can work with one another. Machines such as the Xerox 860 Information Processing System, various electronic printers and files, and, of course, computers.

As time passes, you can simply plug in new machines as you need them – or as technology develops better ones. Even if they aren't made by Xerox.

In other words, you'll be able to get to the future the way the future itself gets here: one step at a time.

Of course, planning an information management system isn't exactly a day at the beach.

But in both cases, wading does have certain advantages over leaping.

It's less of a shock to your system. And you don't have to worry about suddenly finding yourself in over your head.

If you'd like more information on the Information Outlet, write us and we'll send you a booklet. Xerox Corporation, P.O. Box 47005, Dallas, Texas 75247.

XEROX

Xerox introduces the Information Outlet.

If you're wondering how business will handle information in the '80s, the handwriting is clearly on the wall.

We call it the Information Outlet – a new way for you to custom design an information management system that will give you maximum flexibility with minimum expense.

Here's how it works:

The Information Outlet gives you access to a special Xerox Ethernet cable that can link a variety of office machines. Including information processors like the Xerox 860, various electronic printers and files, and, of course, computers.

The Xerox Ethernet network will enable people throughout your company to create, store, retrieve, print and send information to other people in other places – instantaneously.

This network wasn't designed to work exclusively with our equipment. Other companies' products can be connected as well.

As your needs change, so can your network. You'll simply plug in new machines as you need them – or as technology develops better ones.

So, through the Xerox Information Outlet, you'll get to the future the way the future itself will get here.

One step at a time.

XEROX

If you'd like more information on the Information Outlet, write us and we'll send you a booklet. Xerox Corporation, P.O. Box 47005, Dallas, Texas 75247.

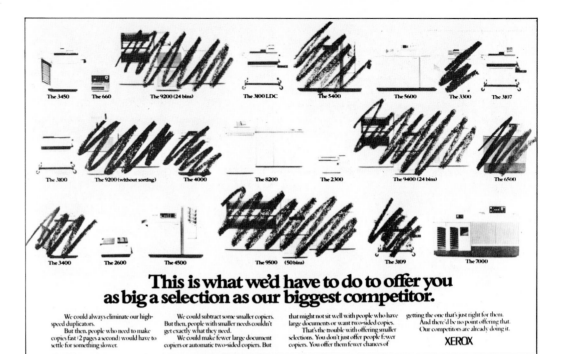

Fly uncrowded. Land unruffled.

While most airlines have followed the trend of adding seats, Swissair has not. For the simple reason that crowding makes for ruffled feathers.

Swissair 747's have 9 seats across instead of the usual 10; DC-10's, 8 across instead of 9.

Because widebodied aircraft should not only seat more; they should also seat more comfortably.

Ours do.

So our passengers have more elbow room, our flight attendants have more room to serve, and everyone is happier.

It shows, too.

Swissair has earned the greatest percentage of repeat business from experienced travelers.

They flock to Swissair, where comfort is the bottom line.

P.S. For those who really want to stretch out in peaceful slumber, Swissair 747's now feature a number of Slumberette seats in first class.

Swissair has worldwide departures from New York, Boston, Chicago, Montreal and Toronto.

Call Swissair or your travel expert.

swissair

From our worldwide collection.

This view can be seen when Swissair Flight 142 passes over the summer harvest in the Pampas of Argentina.

However, Swissair also has hundreds of other views on view every week en route to 93 cities in 63 countries around the world. Each one serves as an interesting analogy as to why Swissair has grown to encompass an international network of more than 173,000 miles. Because from up above, patterns may differ, but travelers everywhere are united in their demand for service.

Particularly experienced travelers.

Experienced travelers expect their airline to be efficient, punctual and consistent. Which explains why they give Swissair a greater percentage of their business. They view service as an art.

And the art of service knows no boundaries.

Swissair departs from New York, Boston, Chicago, Toronto and Montreal to Europe, then on to Africa, the Middle East, the Far East and South America.

Call Swissair or your travel expert.

swissair

The rights of passage in the Far East.

As an international airline, it is only natural for Swissair to offer direct service from Switzerland to ten major cities in the Far East. But Swissair is a Far Eastern airline too. Because Swissair also has special traffic rights to provide local service within the Far East.

Which give our passengers a few extra rights of their own. Like the right to board or disembark at almost every stop Swissair makes. From Colombo to Singapore, Bangkok to Karachi and Bombay to Peking, just to name a few. And every flight is on a widebody. Definite advantages for those going from here to there and places in between.

While passengers see a whole new world of options unfold before them, that unique Swissair service never varies. So it is not surprising why Swissair has earned the greatest percentage of repeat business from experienced travelers. They agree Swissair is far best to the Far East. Swissair departs worldwide from New York, Boston, Chicago, Toronto and Montreal.

Call Swissair or your travel expert.

swissair

172

**Consumer Magazine
Color Campaign
Including
Magazine Supplements**

173
Art Directors:
**Paul Walter
Richard Crispo**
Writers:
**Richard Kelley
Laurie Brandalise**
Photographers:
**Alan Brooking
Lamb & Hall
Harry Liles**
Client:
American Honda
Agency:
**Needham, Harper & Steers/
West**

174
Art Director:
Jay Cooper
Writer:
Dick Tarlow
Photographer:
Robert McCabe
Client:
Cuisinarts
Agency:
Kurtz & Tarlow

The simple pleasures of driving a Honda Prelude. Starting from the top.

We think you'll agree, it's a pleasure to look at. But our sportiest Honda also sports the kind of features that make it a thrill to drive.

THE POWER-OPERATED MOONROOF.
FOR OPENERS, IT'S STANDARD.
At the push of a button, the tinted-glass moonroof slides back. At the same time, an automatic deflector helps keep the wind out.

When you're behind the wheel, you'll be pleased at what you see in front of it. This year, the instrument panel houses a separate tachometer and speedometer, a quartz digital clock, a maintenance reminder and an electronic warning system.

Of course, the Prelude is just as much of a pleasure to sit in. Its luxurious interior features comfortable bucket seats and adjustable headrests.

SOME SIMPLE ENGINEERING FACTS.
Our sportiest car has front-wheel drive.

four-wheel independent suspension with MacPherson struts, rack and pinion steering and a responsive 1751cc CVCC® engine. The fact is, the Prelude is designed to give you years of good performance.

POWER STEERING COMES AUTOMATICALLY WITH THE AUTOMATIC TRANSMISSION.
The 5-speed stick shift is standard. But with the optional automatic 3-speed, you also get variable-assist power steering. It works

hardest at slow speeds. To help you park or maneuver through heavy traffic. And hardly at all at highway speeds. So you can get the feel of the road.

After you've weighed all your options, we hope you drive off in the Honda Prelude.

HONDA
We make it simple.

After 9 years, it's still built on the same simple philosophy.

The world has changed a lot over the past nine years. So have our Honda Civics.

They're still built on the same simple philosophy of course: Simple to own. Simple to drive. And simple to maintain.

But the 1981 Honda Civic DX Hatchback gleaming in our picture is very simply a different car from the first 1973 Civic.

INSIDE. SIMPLE BUT
CERTAINLY NOT PLAIN.
Some people thought our early Civics were a little plain inside. Well, the 1981 Civic DX is just plain luxurious.

With velvet-like seat fabric, deep pile carpeting, remote hood and hatch release, glove box and tinted glass.

While on the Civic 1500 DX, a rear window wiper and washer help you see where

you've been as well as where you're going.

SOME SIMPLE ENGINEERING FACTS.
The 1981 Civic DX features front-wheel drive and a transverse-mounted CVCC® engine. 1335cc or 1488cc.

Four-wheel independent suspension, a 5-speed transmission, rack and pinion steering and steel-belted radials are standard.

New for this year, is the optional 3-speed automatic transmission.

DURABILITY IS ALSO PART OF
OUR PHILOSOPHY.
We're not saying our cars are immortal. But they are built to last a long time.

We hope it won't be long before you test drive a Honda Civic DX.

Because if you buy our simple philosophy, you're sure to buy our car.

HONDA
We make it simple.

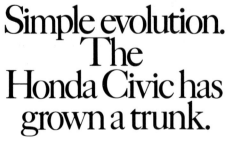

Simple evolution. The Honda Civic has grown a trunk.

If the silver car in our picture appears familiar, it should.

It's a Honda Civic. But now it's grown a trunk and two rear doors.

Plus a lot of other simple features that you would expect to find in a comfortable and roomy sedan.

THE HONDA CIVIC 4-DOOR SEDAN.
With seats so comfortable they would be more at home in your living room, our newest Civic is a true sedan in every sense.

The velvet-like fabric is soft to the touch. While the plush carpeting extending up onto the lower door panels is a nice touch, too.

You'll feel equally comfortable at the steering wheel. Car and Driver magazine said it's better made than your average Mercedes wheel.

A quartz digital clock, tachometer and even a remote trunk release will give you some idea of the kind of attention to detail that has gone into the building of this car.

SOME SIMPLE ENGINEERING FACTS.
Naturally, being a Honda, the new Civic Sedan has front-wheel drive and a transverse-mounted 1500 CVCC® engine.

Available with a 5-speed gearbox or the optional 3-speed automatic transmission, this car is also a lot of fun to drive.

Due in part to the rack and pinion steering and 4-wheel independent suspension.

INCREDIBLE GAS MILEAGE.
STILL A CIVIC RESPONSIBILITY.
With 5-speed, a gallon of gas takes you an EPA estimated 34 miles and 44 highway. Use 34 mpg for comparison. Your mileage may differ depending on weather, speed and trip length. Actual highway mileage will probably be less. And figures for California and high altitude areas will be lower.

Nevertheless, the Civic Sedan will give you gas mileage that's among the best in its class.

And that makes it simple evolution you'll easily adapt to.

HONDA
We make it simple.

DO YOU NEED A FOOD PROCESSOR THIS GOOD? OUR COMPETITORS CERTAINLY DON'T THINK SO.

Not everyone thinks you need a food processor with a feed tube* so large it can accept foods as big as many whole tomatoes, onions, oranges, even Idaho potatoes—a large feed tube that lets you process food faster than ever.

Not everyone thinks you need a food processor that has an exceptionally efficient, powerful motor. A bigger bowl that lets you do more at one time. And superior blades and discs as standard equipment, including a blade for kneading dough (plus optional accessory discs that enable you to prepare dishes that appear to come from the hands of a professional chef).

Simply, not everyone thinks you need a food processor as good as the Cuisinart® DLC-7E, the finest food processor available for home use.

WHAT IF YOU REALLY DON'T NEED ONE THIS GOOD?

If you need less or want to spend less, then we suggest the second finest food processor: The Cuisinart DLC-8E. It costs less, but has the same large feed tube, a larger than standard workbowl and motor power to match. And is still perfectly worthy of the Cuisinart name.

FOR MORE INFORMATION.

We haven't compromised. If you don't want to either, write Cuisinarts, Inc., 411(G) West Putnam Avenue, Greenwich, CT 06830 for more on our food processors. We'll also be pleased to send you information on our magazine, "The Pleasures of Cooking" (for those to whom cooking is a joy, a means of expression).

*The revolutionary Cuisinart Large Feed Tube, formerly available only as part of the Large Feed Tube Accessory Kit, is now standard equipment on DLC-7E and DLC-8E models.

Cuisinart
Food Processor

EVERYTHING WE'VE ALWAYS WANTED IN COOKWARE. AND WE'VE ALWAYS WANTED EVERYTHING.

We are proud to introduce to the U.S. market cookware that meets our highest specifications and expectations. Cuisinarts Commercial Stainless Steel Cookware, cookware for the home cook who wants only the most professional performance. Cookware whose capability and durability is virtually unmatched in all the culinary world. Cookware for centuries, not just a lifetime.

FEATURE FOR FEATURE, COOKWARE AT ITS FINEST.

Cuisinarts Commercial Stainless Steel Cookware is designed to satisfy the most demanding cook and to withstand the rough usage of even a restaurant kitchen. It will retain its beauty forever.

The bottoms are flat, so they make contact with the whole surface of the heating element, thus they conduct heat better (especially important on electric burners).

The bottoms stay flat. Our stainless steel/aluminum sandwich (stainless steel surrounding a heavy inlay of aluminum) ensures that the bottom won't warp even if the cookware is dropped into cold water while hot.

The handles are all heavy gauge stainless steel—shaped to minimize heat transfer.

The bottoms are thick. They store more heat and give superior conduction of heat sideways as well as upwards. This eliminates hot spots and provides constant temperature over the cooking surface.

Additionally, the saucepans are taller than customary. They hold more without requiring more stove space.

FOR MORE INFORMATION.

One of our favorite recipes is Turkey Stroganoff. For the recipe and more information on our new Commercial Cookware, write Cuisinarts, Inc., 411 West Putnam Avenue, Greenwich, CT 06830. We'll also be pleased to send you information on our food processors and magazine, "The Pleasures of Cooking" (for those to whom cooking is a joy, a means of expression).

8 piece set: 5¾-quart Dutch sauté pan with cover; 2-quart ball sauce pan with cover; 3¾-quart tall sauce pan with cover; 10-quart tall marmite with cover.

Cuisinart
Commercial Cookware

IT'S THE BEST. BUT IT KEEPS GETTING BETTER.

There are few culinary experts or food editors who do not consider the Cuisinart® DLC-7E, the finest food processor available for home use.

This machine features, as standard equipment, the revolutionary Large Feed Tube that lets you process food faster than ever, a bigger workbowl that lets you do more at one time and blades and discs of superior, exclusive design.

Now, this standard of the industry is even better.

Now it has an even more powerful and efficient motor designed to give you peak performance when you most need it—kneading dough or chopping a pound of meat. It delivers maximum power during heavy jobs.

This motor is a workhorse. The chopping blade is also improved. The hub is smaller

Standard Feed Tube Opening

Large Feed Tube Opening on DLC-7E and DLC-8E Models. (Drawings Show Relative Sizes)

in diameter, significantly improving its dough kneading and chopping ability. (Similar improvements have been incorporated into our DLC-8E model. It costs less, but has the same Large Feed Tube, same improved chopping blade, a larger than standard workbowl and, now, a more powerful, efficient motor.)

HOW A CUISINART FOOD PROCESSOR BECOMES A CUISINART FOOD PROCESSOR.

Cuisinarts is a company with one major strength: engineering. And one principal love: cooking. Our criterion is that each Cuisinart product must make your life in the kitchen easier, more rewarding and six months after you have bought it, you must be thoroughly pleased that you did.

Behind our commitment

to you is the Cuisinart Research and Development Group.

Seven years ago, when the founder of Cuisinarts, Inc. discovered the predecessor of what is now the Cuisinart food processor, it was not yet suitable for use in the American home. We modified it, but even our first models were primitive compared to our current machines.

Today's Cuisinart food processors are the result of the many patented innovations conceived by the Cuisinart Research and Development Group—a group that never stops looking for ways to make our products better.

Problem: Excessive pressure by inexperienced users caused shredding disc to shred the bottom of the cover.

Solution: (Patented.) We placed around the edge of the disc metal "dimples" which are higher than the shredding teeth. Result: unblemished covers and no plastic in your food.

Problem: Feed tube was too small to allow whole tomatoes, whole potatoes to be processed.

Solution: (Patented.) We invented the revolutionary Large Feed Tube that accepts food as big as many whole tomatoes, onions, oranges, even Idaho potatoes.

Problem: Collisions between food and ridge on slicing disc caused cracked and broken slices and too numerous crumbs.

Solution: (Patented.) We moved the ridge way back so that the slice falls free without ever touching the disc. Result: far more perfect slices.

As you can see, to the Cuisinart Research and Development Group, nothing is quite good enough. That's why even the best keeps getting better.

MORE INFORMATION.

For more about our food processors and the ease they bring to your cooking, write Cuisinarts, Inc., 411( ) West Putnam Avenue, Greenwich, CT 06830.

We'll also be pleased to send you information on our cookware, convection oven and our magazine, "The Pleasures of Cooking" (for those to whom cooking is a joy, a means of expression).

Cuisinart
Food Processor

174

**Consumer Magazine
Color Campaign
Including
Magazine Supplements**

175
Art Directors:
**Rich Ferrante
Mike Vitiello
Steve Ohman**
Writers:
**Murray Klein
Larry Vine**
Photographers:
**George Cochran
Michael O'Neill
Bart Corin
Cailor/Resnick**
Client:
Johnnie Walker Black Label
Agency:
Smith/Greenland

176
Art Director:
Clem McCarthy
Writers:
**Martin Puris
Bruce Feirstein**
Photographer:
Dick James
Client:
BMW of North America
Agency:
Ammirati & Puris

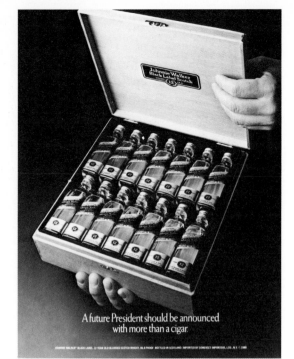

175

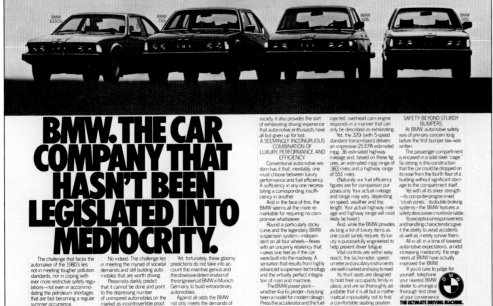
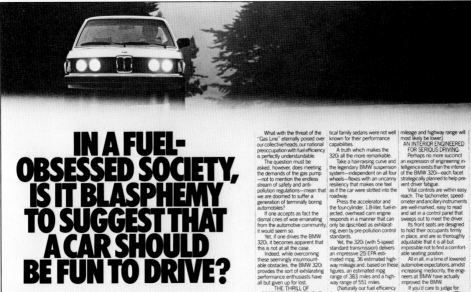

177
Art Director:
Max Sirota
Writers:
Anne Wallach
Stella Lester
Designer:
Max Sirota
Photographer:
Richard Avedon
Client:
Playtex
Agency:
Grey

178
Art Directors:
John Hegarty
Brian Morrow
Writer:
Ken Mullen
Designers:
John Hegarty
Brian Morrow
Photographers:
Nick Tomkin
Jack Hough
Tantrums
Client:
John Walker & Sons
Agency:
TBWA/London

177

There comes a point when you have to switch to Black.

Black is the ultimate in whisky.

One colour always unites the clans.

Black is the ultimate in whisky.

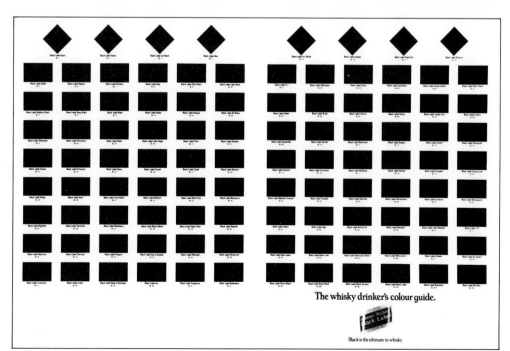

The whisky drinker's colour guide.

Black is the ultimate in whisky

179
Art Director:
Deanne Werner
Writers:
**Cheryl Poser
Deanne Werner**
Photographer:
D. Turbeville
Client:
DeBeers
Agency:
N W Ayer

180
Art Directors:
**Deanne Werner
Dan Weiss**
Writers:
**Cheryl Poser
Yvonne Durant**
Photographers:
**Hiro
Michael Prusan**
Client:
DeBeers
Agency:
N W Ayer

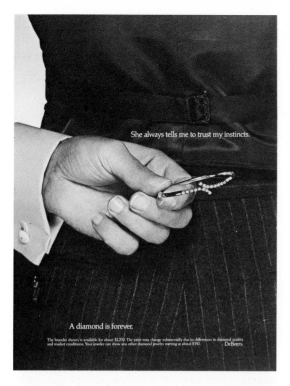

She always tells me to trust my instincts.

A diamond is forever.

The bracelet shown is available for about $2,700. The price may change substantially due to differences in diamond quality and market conditions. Your jeweler can show you other diamond jewelry starting at about $350. DeBeers.

Sweet dreams, birthday girl.

A diamond is forever.

The piece shown (enlarged for detail) is available for about $4,550. The price may change substantially due to differences in diamond quality and market conditions. Your jeweler can show you other diamond jewelry starting at about $350. De Beers.

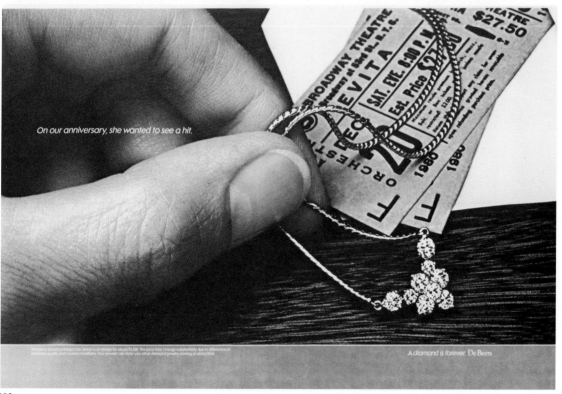

On our anniversary, she wanted to see a hit.

The piece shown (enlarged for detail) is available for about $3,500. The price may change substantially due to differences in diamond quality and market conditions. Your jeweler can show you other diamond jewelry starting at about $350.

A diamond is forever. De Beers

180

Consumer Magazine Color Campaign Including Magazine Supplements

181
Art Director:
Helmut Krone
Writer:
Tom Yobbagy
Photographers:
David Langley
Jim Young
Client:
Porsche + Audi
Agency:
Doyle Dane Bernbach

182
Art Director:
Angelo DeSantis
Writer:
Joseph Nunziata
Designer:
Angelo DeSantis
Photographer:
Don Mack
Client:
Volkswagen
Agency:
Doyle Dane Bernbach

LOVE-50 IN 8.3 SECONDS.

Quickness.

It's one thing to say you have it. It's yet another to go out there and prove it.

Day in.

Day out.

And just as Harold Solomon combines his quickness and agility to be ranked as one of the top contenders on the court, so does the VW Rabbit.

On the road.

The fact that the Rabbit aces from 0 to 50 in only 8.3 seconds is because it's powered by an optional CIS fuel-injected overhead cam engine. (A feature which many sports cars don't even have today.)

Add to this front-wheel drive, negative steering roll radius, and four-wheel independent suspension, and what you've got is a sporty little car that can handle almost anything that comes along.

That includes avoiding bumps in the asphalt.

Making short stops.

And quick moves from side to side.

Sure there are other terrific returns of the Rabbit. You've probably heard them all.

But as for how quick and agile it is, we just thought you'd like to know the score.

VOLKSWAGEN DOES IT AGAIN

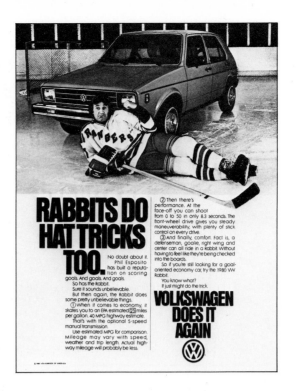

RABBITS DO HAT TRICKS TOO.

No doubt about it. Phil Esposito has built a reputation on scoring goals. And goals. And goals.

So has the Rabbit.

Sure it sounds unbelievable.

But then again, the Rabbit does some pretty unbelievable things.

① When it comes to economy, it skates you to an EPA estimated 25 miles per gallon. 40 MPG highway estimate.

That's with the optional 5-speed manual transmission.

Use estimated MPG for comparison. Mileage may vary with speed, weather and trip length. Actual highway mileage will probably be less.

② Then there's performance. At the face-off you can shoot from 0 to 50 in only 8.3 seconds. The front-wheel drive gives you steady maneuverability, with plenty of stick control on every drive.

③ And finally, comfort. Fact is, a defenseman, goalie, right wing and center can all ride in a Rabbit. Without having to feel like they're being checked into the boards.

So if you're still looking for a goal-oriented economy car, try the 1980 VW Rabbit.

You know what?

It just might do the trick.

VOLKSWAGEN DOES IT AGAIN

SAVE!

And save.

And save.

Now there's a nice thought to kick around. (Especially nowadays.)

And just as Shep Messing has developed quite a reputation for himself with some incredible saves, so has Volkswagen.

With the incredible Rabbit.

Here, take a look at these stats:

With the manual 4-speed transmission (based on EPA estimate) the 1980 Rabbit gets an economical 24 miles per gallon. And a just as frugal 38 mpg highway estimate.

When you compare these figures to the competitors', use the estimated mpg. And even though the mileage may vary with speed, weather, and trip length, and the actual highway mileage will probably be less, you'll find out one thing soon enough.

All-Star goalkeepers aren't the only ones who can save.

So if you're still looking for an economy car that saves you gas and saves you money, here, we'll save you some time.

Hop into a 1980 VW Rabbit.

That's using your head.

VOLKSWAGEN DOES IT AGAIN

Bumble Bee® Tuna packed in water has 50% less calories than regular tuna packed in oil. That can make a big difference, especially if you're watching your weight.

But the really nice thing about cutting calories with Bumble Bee is it doesn't taste like you're cutting calories. It has all the delicious taste you expect from Bumble Bee.

Bumble Bee Tuna packed in water. It makes cutting calories easier to swallow.

*Bumble Bee is a registered trademark of Castle & Cooke, Inc.

183

OCEANS APART FROM ORDINARY SCOTCH.

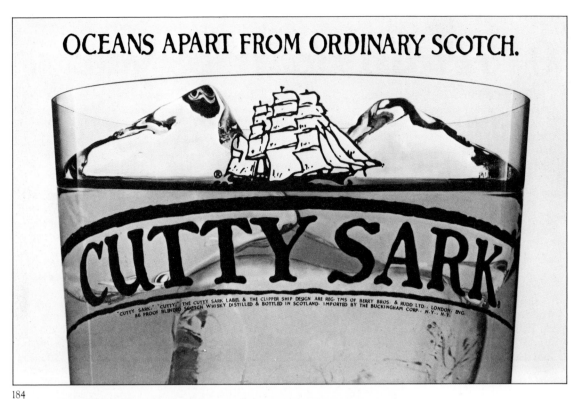

"CUTTY SARK." "CUTTY." THE CUTTY SARK LABEL & THE CLIPPER SHIP DESIGN ARE REG. TMS OF BERRY BROS. & RUDD LTD., LONDON, ENG. 86 PROOF BLENDED SCOTCH WHISKY DISTILLED & BOTTLED IN SCOTLAND. IMPORTED BY THE BUCKINGHAM CORP., N.Y., N.Y.

Our water diet.

BUMBLE BEE CHUNK LIGHT TUNA 50% FEWER CALORIES THAN OIL SEE SIDE PANEL **in Water** NET WT. 6½ OZ.

For years, Bumble Bee* has been doing its part to help people fight the battle of the bulge. Our tuna has always been high in quality protein but low in fat and calories.

Now Bumble Bee is doing even more. A can of Bumble Bee Tuna in water has 50% fewer calories than regular tuna in oil. Yet it has all the delicious taste you expect from Bumble Bee.

Bumble Bee Tuna in water. It makes cutting calories easier to swallow.

*Bumble Bee is a registered trademark of Castle & Cooke, Inc.

0 to 1 million in 189 years.

On that icy, December, Sunday morning in 1791, nothing stirred in The Strand.

Above the printing shop at number one hundred and sixty nine, W.S. Bourne and his colleagues sat gazing into the dying embers of a fire that had been lit thirty six hours before.

On the cluttered desk lay the fruit of their labours: the first copy of a new Sunday newspaper - The Observer.

Now, all they could do was wait.

As the bells of St. Martins-in-the-Field rang out for evensong, the news came.

Their new venture was an unprecedented success.

They had sold 236 copies.

Of course, nowadays The Observer has to contend with that young upstart, the 158 year old Sunday Times.

Not to mention that mere teenager, the 19 year old Sunday Telegraph.

But even in the face of this competition, The Observer's

circulation has been increasing by leaps and bounds.

In November 1978 our ABC circulation was 705,858. In November/December 1979 it was 1,003,949.

1,003,949 to 1,038,185 in 3 months.

And the ABC circulation figures for the first three months of 1980 show The Observer to be the fastest growing national paper in Britain.

Some cynics may point to the general growth of the quality Sunday market as being responsible for this.

However, 66% of that growth can be attributed directly to The Observer.

Our circulation is still climbing.

While our rate card still makes us more cost effective than our rivals.

As W.S. Bourne himself might have said, you won't find a better buy in a month of Sundays.

0.

1,038,185.

186

Every day consumers see 1,800 ads. And remember about this much.

Improve their memory. Turn to TBWA.➔

Invisible advertising is something you'll never see from TBWA.

Describe the ten best ads or commercials you saw yesterday.

How about the three best? Give up?

The average ad today is so average, it cancels itself right out of your mind. Maybe other agencies have clients rich enough to afford that. TBWA doesn't.

When your advertising is invisible, your sales will be, too. No matter what research tells you.

Only a handful of agencies still turns out unexpected, consistently fresh advertising. TBWA is one of them.

We don't always know in advance how we're going to do it. TBWA has no agency "look" or "style." But each of our clients has a "look" and a "style." And we do a lot of digging to find the right ones.

We might do authoritative. Or sexy. We might do glamorous or educational. Romantic or belligerent.

Punny or funny. But we never do invisible.

This has paid off in success for our clients and in creative awards and growth for us. Not only here in New York, but in our eight European offices as well. (Check our billings on the next page.)

There isn't an agency in the world that doesn't claim to be creative. We prefer to let our work prove our claim. Just fill out the coupon, and we'll send you a booklet of our ads.

To TBWA Attention Bill Tragos, Chairman/CEO
Dear TBWA I'd like to see if your work is as visibly great as you say it is

Name	Title
Company	Type of Firm
Address	
City	State	Zip

TBWA

New York/Paris/Milan/Frankfurt/London/Madrid/Zurich/Brussels/Amsterdam
292 Madison Avenue, New York, New York 10017. Phone (212) 725-1150. Telex 238209

187

WANTED.

They're wild. And western. The most wanted jeans around. Desperados™
by Wilkins. In a variety of striking styles. Including classic,
straight-leg, five-pocket jeans. Boot jeans. Flares. And our new, old-west
cowboy jeans. They're all tailored, too. So they fit a woman's
body. Comfortably. Fashionably. And every pair's got the "Buckloop"™
—a special loop that'll keep her belt from riding up over
the waistband. In Rumble Seats, junior sizes. And Fancy Props, missy
sizes. Just call Wilkins Industries at 800-241-7086 in
Athens, Georgia. Or 800-223-7468 in New York. And claim the rewards.

DESPERADOS. JEANS BY WILKINS.

Trade
Black and White
Page or Spread

189
Art Directors:
Stavros Cosmopulos
Tom Davis
Writers:
Stavros Cosmopulos
Jeff Billing
Designer:
Tom Davis
Photographer:
Carol Kaplan
Client:
Arnold & Company
Agency:
Arnold & Company/Boston

190
Art Director:
Kurt Tausche
Writer:
Pete Smith
Artist:
Joe Gianetti
Client:
WCCO-TV
Agency:
Carmichael-Lynch/Mpls.

191
Art Director:
Elizabeth Wynn
Writers:
Mary Ann Zeman
Peter Levathes
Designer:
Elizabeth Wynn
Artist:
Charles Slackman
Client:
Maxell
Agency:
Scali, McCabe, Sloves

192
Art Director:
Gary Reynolds
Writer:
Jan Zechman
Photographer:
Chris Kelsey
Client:
Hollister
Agency:
Zechman/Chicago

193
Art Director:
Barbara Schubeck
Writer:
Rav Freidel
Photographer:
Ron DeMilt
Client:
Sony Audio
Agency:
Ammirati & Puris

189

190

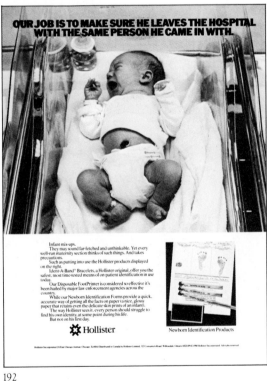

192

191

YOU DON'T HAVE TO BE THE NATION'S #1 NETWORK TO SOUND LIKE IT.

The Republican National Convention, the Democratic National Convention, the Winter Olympics—three of the most important and prestigious media events in the last four years were all covered by ABC with wireless microphone systems from Sony.

If you want your station to sound like a leader, take a tip from the Number One name in broadcasting.

Include a wireless system from the Number One name in electronics.

SONY®

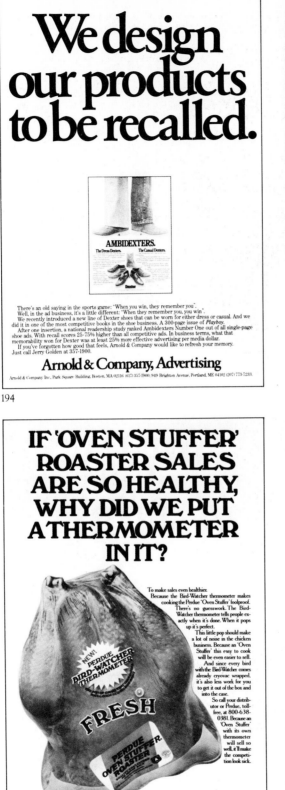

194

195

196

197

American Express Travelers Cheques.
Some people don't leave home to get them.

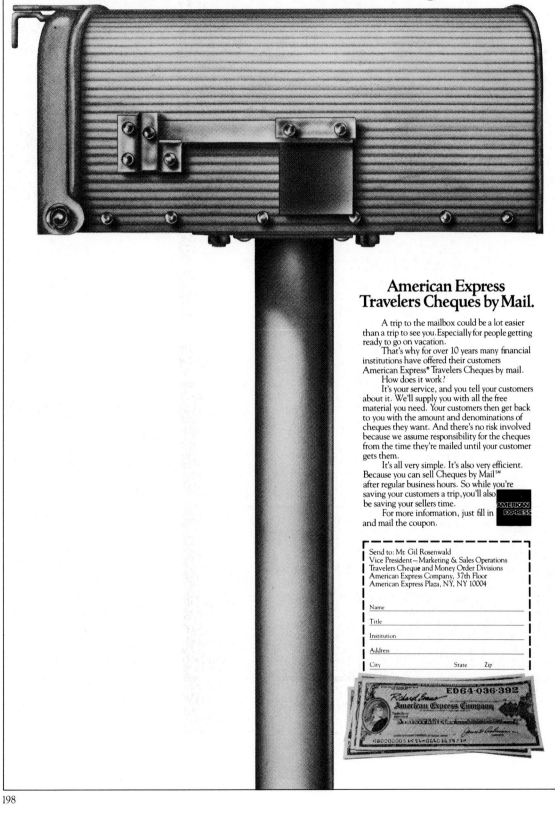

American Express
Travelers Cheques by Mail.

A trip to the mailbox could be a lot easier than a trip to see you. Especially for people getting ready to go on vacation.

That's why for over 10 years many financial institutions have offered their customers American Express® Travelers Cheques by mail.

How does it work?

It's your service, and you tell your customers about it. We'll supply you with all the free material you need. Your customers then get back to you with the amount and denominations of cheques they want. And there's no risk involved because we assume responsibility for the cheques from the time they're mailed until your customer gets them.

It's all very simple. It's also very efficient. Because you can sell Cheques by Mail℠ after regular business hours. So while you're saving your customers a trip, you'll also be saving your sellers time.

For more information, just fill in and mail the coupon.

Send to: Mr. Gil Rosenwald
Vice President—Marketing & Sales Operations
Travelers Cheque and Money Order Divisions
American Express Company, 37th Floor
American Express Plaza, NY, NY 10004

Name

Title

Institution

Address

City   State   Zip

199

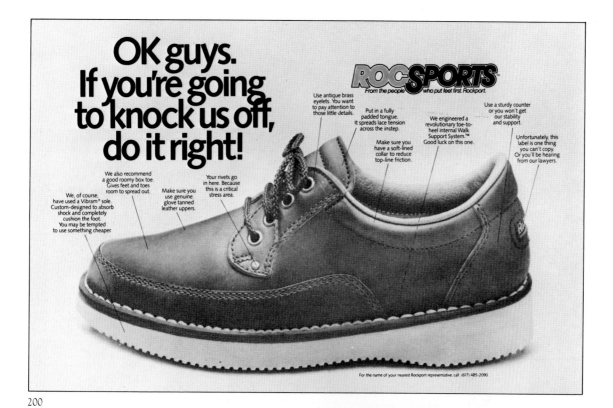

OK guys. If you're going to knock us off, do it right!

ROCSPORTS
From the people who put feet first. Rockport.

Use antique brass eyelets. You want to pay attention to those little details.

Put in a fully padded tongue. It spreads lace tension across the instep.

We engineered a revolutionary toe-to-heel internal Walk Support System.™ Good luck on this one.

Use a sturdy counter or you won't get our stability and support.

Unfortunately, this label is one thing you can't copy. Or you'll be hearing from our lawyers.

Make sure you have a soft-lined collar to reduce top-line friction.

We also recommend a good roomy box toe. Gives feet and toes room to spread out.

Your rivets go in here. Because this is a critical stress area.

We, of course, have used a Vibram® sole. Custom-designed to absorb shock and completely cushion the foot. You may be tempted to use something cheaper.

Make sure you use genuine glove tanned leather uppers.

For the name of your nearest Rockport representative, call (617) 485-2090.

200

April 1, 1980 was a perfect day for positive thinking: all the odds were against you! Millions of you had to get to work, but there were no subways or buses to get you there. So out came the bikes and roller skates. On went the Pumas, Adidas and Nikes. And up went the spirits of the people. You were positive you'd get to work. You came over the bridges. Through the Park. From Uptown, Downtown, Eastside, Westside. And you made it. It's this same kind of positive thinking that drives Psychology Today readers to turn negatives into positives, and obstacles into opportunities. No wonder Psychology Today readers, between 18 and 44, are more successful in their careers, better educated, and more affluent than those of any other Simmons-measured magazine with a circulation of over one million. No wonder advertisers are so positive about Psychology Today magazine. They've given us our best six months ever in ad revenue. Blackouts, transit strikes, whatever the obstacle, you can deal with it. We're positive! Psychology Today is positive thinking.

POSITIVE THINKING STRIKES BACK.

psychology today
IS POSITIVE THINKING

201

POSITIVE THINKING CHANGED THE SHAPE OF THE WORLD

Across the Sea of Darkness they sailed. Three tiny ships, bound for the unknown. "You'll fall off the edge of the world" the doubters said. They didn't know that positive thinking was aboard.

When you leaf through the pages of Psychology Today you'll see that PT readers share the same positive attitude. They're willing to venture into the unknown, to find out more about themselves and the world they live in.

They go out and do things. They fly, drive, ski, sail, swim, jog, vacation, entertain. Physical fitness is a big part of their lifestyle. However, they know their bodies can function only as well as their minds allow. In fact, PT readers between the ages of 18 and 44 are better educated, more affluent, and more successful than the readers of any other major magazine.

They're active consumers, both in body and mind. They know they can profit by being receptive to new ideas and open to discovering new products. Just as the advertisers in Psychology Today have discovered positive thinking. And are profiting by it.

Psychology Today is positive thinking.

On October 12, 1492, Christopher Columbus, attempting to find a new route to the Indies, discovered the Americas.

psychology today
IS POSITIVE THINKING

202

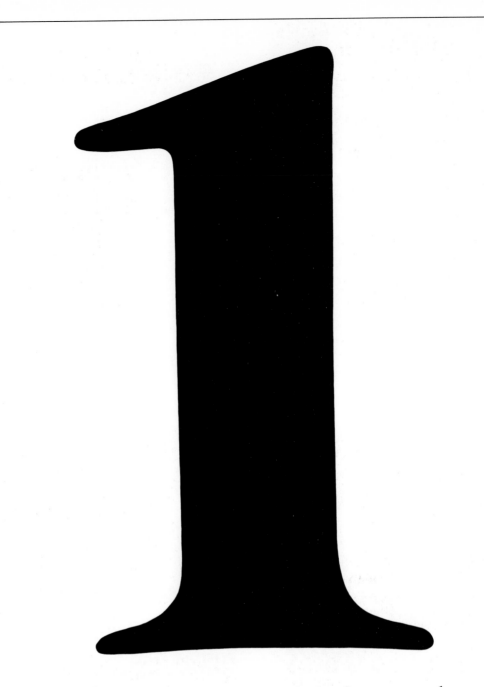

203

WHEN IT COMES TO MAKING YOU MONEY, ZIPLOC HAS AN AIRTIGHT CASE.

Ten years ago, when we first introduced Ziploc™ Storage Bags to the market, we knew we were on the right track.

Today we're tops in a category that has grown by almost 67 million dollars. Two-thirds of this impressive growth is due to Ziploc. In fact, Ziploc leads not only in dollars, but in cases. And we continue to grow.

In 1981, Ziploc Storage Bags will increase media advertising by over 50% to commemorate 10 years in the marketplace. That translates to more exposure than all competition combined, more awareness, more shoppers, more shelf takeaway, and more profits for you. And what's more, we will also be showing you a product improvement that will accelerate

the already impressive growth rate of Ziploc.

Look for More of the Best in 1981. Because the best is yet to come.

ZIPLOC STORAGE BAGS
We've got a lock on the market

*Trademark of The Dow Chemical Company

204

THE WINTER OLYMPIC TIMING DEVICES HAVE BEEN BROUGHT TO YOU IN RECORD-BREAKING TIME.

Recently, Emery displayed its world-class speed in an Olympic event.

We moved over 3,000 pounds of Olympic timing devices from Switzerland to America in less than 24 hours.

Playing a part in The Winter Olympics comes naturally to us at Emery. After all, we know what it's like to race against the clock. And to be judged against tough

competition.

Of course, we do it every single day. Not just once every 4 years.

So whether you have an Olympic-sized shipment or something a little more office-sized, just give Emery a call.

We'll take care of it in no time.

EMERY
FROM HERE TO THERE, OVERNIGHT.

EVEN THE DEVINE FIND IT HELL AT NOTRE DAME.

The head football coach at Notre Dame. It's called the third toughest job in America. And with good reason.

Notre Dame is a school where a 9-2 season is mediocre, where on campus a 14-story mural of Christ with his arms upraised is called "Touchdown Jesus" and where anyone who has ever dipped his fingers into Holy Water considers himself an alumnus.

No wonder the coaching job at Notre Dame has ravaged the minds and bodies of almost every one who's held it. From the immortal Knute Rockne to the very mortal Dan Devine, who after six winning seasons and one national championship is stepping down for "personal reasons."

But the faithful need not despair. Notre Dame already has a new leader. Last month, three puffs of white smoke signaled to the world that a new head coach had been chosen. His name is Faust (a

devil of a name). Gerry Faust is probably the most successful high school coach in America. But no matter how successful in high school there is nothing to make anyone believe Faust will break with the tradition of Notre Dame coaches who wind up hitting the Maalox bottle.

This month, Inside Sports goes under the Golden Dome to examine the pressures that seem to affect everyone who has ever tried to fill Knute Rockne's cleats. The article also deals with Devine's retirement. Is he "stepping down" or is he being sacrificed to that Athletic Director in the sky? Whatever conclusion you draw, you'll have to agree that this article by Robert Friedman is one of the most provocative ever written about the school in South Bend and the men who

coach its football teams.

This January, Inside Sports also covers (maybe smothers is a better word) the spectacle of the Super Bowl. For starters, we're announcing the winner of the game...a month before the game. Then writer Gary Smith tells you "How the NFL Learned to Stop Worrying and Love the Bomb." Gambling editor Pete Axthelm also does a piece called, "The Season's Last Big Bet: Going for Broke." Inside Sports also has an article on Philadelphia, the City of Brotherly Love, which—without anyone looking—is becoming the City of Champions. Plus a lot more.

You see, other sports magazines might talk about giving you in-depth coverage of the major sports, but every month at Inside Sports...we make an issue out of it.

INSIDE SPORTS

WE COVER A SIDE OF SPORTS NOBODY ELSE IS COVERING. THE INSIDE.

WHY VINCE FERRAGAMO SAYS HIS AGENT AND THE RAMS ARE ROUGHING THE PASSER.

Vincent Anthony Ferragamo—with an arm like a bullwhip, statistics as shiny as any passer in the league and a face hijacked from a schoolgirl's dream—is the quarterback of the '80s. Trouble is, the Los Angeles Rams are paying him like a quarterback of the '60s.

Ferragamo is disgusted with his treatment by the Rams, confused by a whirlpool of advice and concerned that one hamstring pull or two interceptions and the job is Pat Haden's again. He could be the only $52,000 a year worker in America who has had two contract attorneys, an entertainment agent, an acting agent and an accountant in the last year.

This month in Inside Sports, writer Gary Smith investigates the frustrations, confusions and suspicions that plague Vince Ferragamo—from his tense relationship with teammate Pat Haden to the controversial negotiations between his attorney, his team and himself.

One NFL team executive has termed these dealings unethical; while the Rams say "other teams in the league have done it". The lawyer insists he offered to take his negotiation fee from the Rams to save Vince money. While Vince's wife says the collapsed three-year contract was a "three-year prison sentence".

Any way you look at it, the whole thing is enough to make ol' J.R. Ewing chuckle.

Also in December's Inside Sports, there's an article on Dallas' original first family. The Cowboys. And two of its proudest sons: quarterback Danny White, who's finally at the helm after waiting four long years for the Jolly Roger to be put in mothballs; and Ed "Too Tall" Jones, who's much more at home running rings around offensive linemen than he was a boxer in the ring.

Then Al McGuire, former coach and current announcer, picks what he believes will be this year's batch of Birds, Magics and Dunkensteins. Looking into his crystal basketball, Swami McGuire even tells us who's going to win the NCAA crown this March in Philly.

Inside Sports also offers its version of the Boswell Chronicles. Baseball's Thomas Boswell, that is. What he's chronicled are the 1980 baseball playoffs and World Series—three of the most bizarre weeks in baseball history. Plus, you'll find a whole lot more. No wonder, 3,000,000 sports addicts can't wait to get their hands on the December issue.

You see, other sports magazines talk about giving you in-depth coverage of the major sports, but every month at Inside Sports...we make an issue out of it.

INSIDE SPORTS

WE COVER A SIDE OF SPORTS NOBODY ELSE IS COVERING. THE INSIDE.

208
Art Director:
Simon Bowden
Writers:
Allen Kay
Debby Mattison
Client:
Seventeen
Agency:
Needham, Harper & Steers

209
Art Director:
Howard Smith
Writer:
Charles Kane
Client:
Panorama
Agency:
Needham, Harper & Steers

210
Art Director:
Howard Smith
Writer:
Charles Kane
Client:
Xerox
Agency:
Needham, Harper & Steers

211
Art Director:
Anthony Angotti
Writer:
Tom Thomas
Client:
Xerox
Agency:
Needham, Harper & Steers

212
Art Director:
Anthony Romeo
Writers:
Anthony Romeo
Daryl Warner
Designers:
Mike Moran
Ambrose Studio
Photographer:
Ken Ambrose
Client:
Citicorp Travelers Checks
Agency:
Doyle Dane Bernbach

208

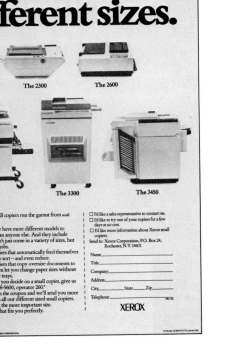

209

210

211

Lose Citicorp Travelers Checks in Maputo and you're not up the Zambezi without a paddle.

Just contact our Maputo refund center and we'll have you back on safari before you know it.

If refunds are this easy here, imagine how easy they are in places you *have* heard of.

In all, we have more than 40,000 locations here and abroad where you can get fast refunds (with emergency funds in the U.S. through 8,100 Western Union offices, many of them open 24 hours a day, 365 days a year). We even have our own Citibanks in 64 countries.

Where can you spend Citicorp Travelers Checks? Where *can't* you? They're as welcome as money in literally millions of hotels, restaurants and stores around the world.

Citicorp Travelers Checks —backed by America's leading banking institution worldwide.

Citicorp. Travel the world with us.

CITICORP. ⊕
TRAVELERS CHECKS

NOTE: Travelers checks under our old name, First National City, will continue to be accepted indefinitely.

© 1980 CITICORP

213
Art Director:
Anthony Angotti
Writer:
Tom Thomas
Artist:
Charles White
Client:
Xerox
Agency:
Needham, Harper & Steers

214
Art Director:
Neil Leinwohl
Writer:
David Cantor
Client:
Xerox
Agency:
Needham, Harper & Steers

215
Art Director:
Anthony Angotti
Writer:
Tom Thomas
Client:
Xerox
Agency:
Needham, Harper & Steers

216
Art Director:
Allen Kay
Writer:
Lois Korey
Client:
Needham, Harper & Steers
Agency:
Needham, Harper & Steers

217
Art Director:
Anthony Angotti
Writers:
Tom Thomas
Allen Kay
Photographer:
Bill Stettner
Client:
Xerox
Agency:
Needham, Harper & Steers

This is what the 1980's looked like to people in the 1940's.

It was going to be a brave new world of undersea cities, full-course meals in the form of pills, and a rocket ship in every garage.

What happened?

Nothing out of the ordinary. The future simply didn't happen the way people thought.

But then, it seldom does. And that's an age-old problem: How do you plan for the future when you can't predict it?

At Xerox we've found a way.

It's called the Information Outlet.

It uses a special cable, called the Xerox Ethernet cable, to join your office machines into a single network.

A network that's flexible—so that as time passes, you can plug in new information processors, electronic printers, or other information management machines as you need them. Even machines that aren't made by Xerox, and even ones that haven't been invented yet.

In other words, you'll be able to build an information network step by step, according to your needs. Instead of committing to a rigid system you might find hard to change years from now.

When you discover the future hasn't turned out according to plan.

XEROX

If you'd like more information on the Information Outlet, write us and we'll send you a booklet. Xerox Corporation, P.O. Box 47 1065, Dallas, Texas 75247.

213

214

215

THIS COMMERCIAL RAN JUST 17 TIMES. AND THAT'S GOSPEL.

Some people believe that in order for a commercial to be really effective, it has to run hundreds of times.

That's true. For most commercials.

The original 60-second Xerox "Monk" commercial ran a mere 17 times the first year.

After the very first airing the response began to be felt. We call that High Profile Advertising.

The kind of advertising we do for such clients as McDonald's, Honda, Parkay margarine and many, many more.

Call Joel Baumwoll in New York, Keith Reinhard in Chicago, or Brad Roberts in Los Angeles to find out how we do it.

NEEDHAM, HARPER & STEERS
High Profile Advertising

It pays to have a brother in the business.

When you go into business with Xerox high-speed duplicators, you get help from the man above.

Brother Dominic.

You see, our machines aren't just fast and reliable. And they don't just produce high-quality copies.

They're also backed by Brother Dominic. Who, experience suggests, is pretty good at attracting not only attention but customers. That's why hundreds of the most successful copy shops in the country use Xerox machines.

But then, that's the way it is in business.

It isn't just what you know. It's who you know.

And to get to know You-Know-Who a little better, send in the coupon and we'll send you more information.

Send to: Brother Dominic, c/o Xerox Corp., P.O. Box 24, Rochester, New York 14601

Name _____

Title _____

Company _____

Address _____

City _____ State _____ Zip _____

Phone _____

XEROX

XEROX is a trademark of XEROX CORPORATION

218
Art Director:
Steve Ohman
Writer:
Rick Meyer
Designer:
Steve Ohman
Photographers:
**George Cannon
Joel Meyerowitz
Al Satterwhite
Jerry Friedman**
Client:
Fuji
Agency:
Geers Gross

219
Art Director:
William Snitzer
Writer:
Robert Finley
Photographer:
Gerry Trafficanda
Client:
TOMY
Agency:
Sachs, Finley/Los Angeles

220
Art Director:
Wayne Carey
Writer:
Todd Lief
Designer:
Wayne Carey
Artist:
Roger Hill
Client:
Quaker Oats
Agency:
BBDM/Chicago

A few dramatic scenes from our latest film.

Introducing Fujichrome 400. It really completes the picture for Fuji. Because now, in addition to our other fine films, we offer an ultra-high speed color reversal film.
So no matter what kind of pictures they like to see, your customers can see more of them on Fuji film. And you can see more of your customers.
Since Fujichrome 400 is compatible with the E-6 system, your customers can bring it back to you for processing. Or sell the film with Fuji authorized prepaid processing and increase your sale even more.
Either way, we've got a film that your customers won't want to miss. And to make sure they don't, we've got an attractive 50 roll display that's bound to catch their eye.
Fujichrome 400 ASA. See your Fuji representative for a sneak preview. You're going to like the way this film comes out.

The world is full of beautiful reasons to use Fuji.
© Fuji Photo Film U.S.A., Inc. 350 Fifth Avenue, N.Y. N.Y. 10118

218

WE HAVE A BIG LINE OF SMALL FURNITURE.

When we decided to go into the small furniture business, we decided to be big about it.
There are 93 pieces in our new line. There's living room furniture, bedroom furniture, den furniture, dining room furniture, kitchen furniture. There's a beautiful doll house to put it in. There's even a doll family to bring the whole thing to life.
We spent three years and over three million dollars developing our new line of furniture. The detail of each piece is extraordinary. The roll top desk really rolls. There are tiny removable hangers inside the wardrobe. The refrigerator opens and has a tiny six-pack of Pepsi inside. There are even tiny records so carefully detailed, there are even tiny grooves on them. Which is pretty groovy.
The merchandising of our new line of furniture is as carefully thought out as everything else. We named this new line Smaller Home & Garden to give the feel of a decorator magazine. We've carried this theme all the way out with packages that look like decorator magazines—from the front cover to the "articles" inside the cover to the back.
All in all, we've put a lot of thought and effort into our new entry in the doll furniture field.
You might say we've gone into small furniture in a big way.

219

Here's the germ of a great idea.

Move over, wheat germ. Quaker Toasted Corn Germ is here. And it's one of the best, and best-tasting, new food ingredient ideas in years.

Quaker technologists have a unique milling process that allows the germ to be removed intact from each kernel of corn. Nothing is added. Full fat is naturally stabilized, so you get superlong shelf life without refrigeration or special packaging.

Quaker Toasted Corn Germ delivers a unique combination of dietary fiber and excellent flavor. It's a valuable source of B vitamins and minerals, quality protein (more lysine than whole kernel corn), and may be second only to beef liver as a source of available iron.

If you'd like to make something of it, such as specialty breads and muffins and cookies, or granola-type products, or a ready-to-eat cereal, or snacks, crackers, spreads or confections, stuffings, toppings, casserole or trail mix, or anything else your imagination can create, which even includes repacking it just as is, contact: The Quaker Oats Company, Industrial Cereals Department, Merchandise Mart Plaza, Chicago, Ill. 60654. Or phone (312) 222-7108

 QUAKER

ZIPLOC PRESENTS TWO SCIENTIFIC UNBREAKTHROUGHS.

©Trademark of The Dow Chemical Company.

Two of the greatest breakthroughs in sandwich and storage bags are really two scientific unbreakthroughs.

Ziploc* Storage Bags and Ziploc Sandwich Bags. Both come with our unique seal that's easy to use and hard to break through. Because once it's locked, it stays locked. To lock in freshness.

Ziploc Storage and Sandwich Bags. Every day you'll find fresh evidence to support these scientific unbreakthroughs.

ZIPLOC STORAGE & SANDWICH BAGS

221

We want it as badly as you do.

You've heard it as often as we have: awards don't mean anything. They're ego trips.

That's what everybody says. Everybody but us. We like what awards do for us.

We like being in the company of people who create great storyboards. And we like having the opportunity to create unforgettable work.

We want that opportunity every day of the year.

Awards remind us that one of our directors might be the best in the country at match dissolves.

And that another brings a sensitivity to tape that some people think comes only with film.

And that another, who works in both film and tape, "really should be in New York."

The awards we've won and the awards we're going to win in the future are a tribute to the fact that we've kept our priorities straight.

Even though we've built three of the world's best-equipped studios, and even though we own equipment some companies don't even know how to operate, we've never believed our future is in machinery.

Our future is in people. We know the importance of having production professionals. Most important of all, we know modern technology doesn't mean anything if it's not in the hands of warm, human, sensitive directors with an eye and an ear for genius.

You see, when you work with us in either tape or film, you'll be working with a director you'll choose. Someone who understands the subtleties of your spots. Someone who understands the way you think.

That's the kind of director who builds great reels. For you and for us.

The way we see it, we could grow rich and famous creating a lot of spots. Or by creating a few great spots.

It's a lot more work doing the great spots.

But, then, in the broadcast business, they've never given awards for quantity.

To see our reel, or to talk to our directors, give us a call at (704)374-3823.

Or call our New York office at (212)532-0922. Or our Atlanta office at (404)261-5858.

Do it now. Before the deadline for the next awards show.

Jefferson Productions

CHARLOTTE, NORTH CAROLINA. OR ANYWHERE ELSE IN THE WORLD.

222

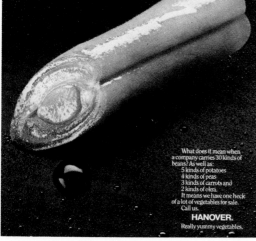

Available in 29 other shades & shapes.

What does it mean when a company carries 30 kinds of beans? As well as:
5 kinds of potatoes
4 kinds of peas
3 kinds of carrots and
2 kinds of okra.
It means we have one heck of a lot of vegetables for sale.
Call us.

HANOVER

Really yummy vegetables.

223

THERE'S NOTHING IDLE ABOUT OUR RICH.

Recently, we came into some rich numbers. The average household income of the Prime Time reader is above $37,300.

And that's no idle boast. For our readers are anything but idle.

They swim, they bike, they travel, they jog, they travel and then, as a change of pace, they just travel.

In fact, over the past year 86% of them took a domestic trip. So you might say they have ants in their pants. And money in their pockets.

Of course, not all their money talks and flies and putts and drives. Some of it just stays home and makes money. 56% of our readers own corporate stock, nearly 9 out of 10 own their own homes and one out of two owns additional property.

So if you'd like to advertise to readers who are on the make and on the spend as well, call David O'Brasky, if you can find him in. After all, he's a Prime Timer too.

SOURCE: 1980 ERDOS AND MORGAN STUDY OF PRIME TIME SUBSCRIBERS. If you'd like a copy send for it. Prime Time Magazine, 1700 Broadway, N.Y., N.Y. 10019. (212)977-7150.

THE MAGAZINE FOR YOUNG PEOPLE 45 AND OLDER

224

SOME PEOPLE GET MORE OUT OF SCHOOL THAN OTHERS.

Teaching people not to abuse, steal, or vandalize valuable property often requires more than an honor code.

It takes the best security locks made. And Medeco offers a complete line of high security, UL listed cam locks, switch locks, rim and mortise locks, cylindrical locks, padlocks, and deadbolt locks.

Medeco's patented double-locking action combines tumbler elevation and rotation. It makes our locks almost impossible to pick, pry, drill, or force open.

What's more, over 23-million lock and key combinations are available. And with any one of our four levels of key control, you get exactly the degree of security you need. Your Medeco system may require positive identification to obtain additional keys; factory-control of key duplication is available, or no provision for key duplication ever—as your needs require.

We can design a lock or master key system for your special needs. And with our replacement cylinders, Medeco can upgrade your existing lock hardware.

Medeco locks can help you make sure that knowledge is the only thing students—or anybody else—will take home with them.

For more advantages that Medeco offers your school system, call 703/387-0481 or write: Medeco, P.O. Box 1075, Salem, Virginia 24153.

Security Locks, Inc.

medeco®

P.O. Box 1075, Salem, Virginia 24153 (703) 387-0481

WITH MEDECO LOCKS ON YOUR MACHINES, ALL A THIEF CAN DO IS WASH HIS CLOTHES.

Medeco can turn even the best thief into a basket case.

Because Medeco's UL-listed locks resist prying, punching, and drilling.

Our patented double-locking mechanism makes any attempts to pick the lock futile.

And Medeco's factory registered restricted key system makes your keys as safe as your coin boxes.

So if you want to put an end to any tampering with your washers and dryers, equip them with Medeco UL-listed locks. And make criminals go clean.

The only thing that can get into a coin box protected with a Medeco lock is money.

Security Locks, Inc.

medeco®

P.O. Box 1075, Salem, Virginia 24153 (703) 387-0481

WHEN ALL THAT STANDS BETWEEN A THIEF AND YOUR MONEY IS A LOCK, IT'D BETTER BE MEDECO.

No other lock can keep your vending machines safe in so many ways. Because no other lock has Medeco's patented double-locking action that defies even the most professional lock-picking artists.

Medeco's factory registered restricted key control system eliminates unauthorized key problems.

And Medeco's hardened steel inserts provide maximum vandal resistance. So you have the toughest locking system you can get for your machines.

There's a UL-listed Medeco lock to fit all your equipment needs, including cam, rod, and pop-out inner cylinders.

Order Medeco immediately as replacement locks and specify them in the future for new equipment.

You'll keep would-be thieves on the outside looking in.

Security Locks, Inc.

medeco®

P.O. Box 1075, Salem, Virginia 24153 (703) 387-0481

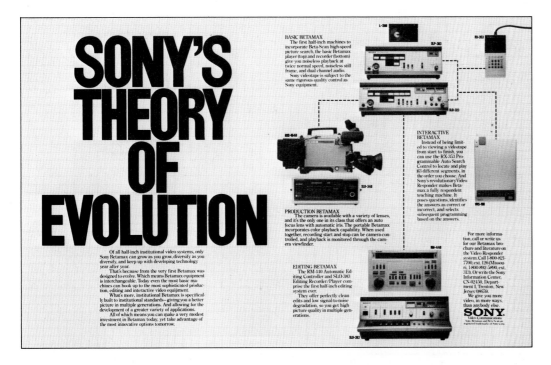

SONY'S THEORY OF EVOLUTION

BASIC BETAMAX
The first half-inch machines to incorporate Beta-Scan high-speed picture search, the basic Betamax player (top) and recorder (bottom) give you noiseless playback at twice normal speed, noiseless still frame, and dual-channel audio. Sony videotape is subject to the same rigorous quality control as Sony equipment.

PRODUCTION BETAMAX
The camera is available with a variety of lenses, and it's the only one in its class that offers an auto focus with automatic iris. The portable Betamax incorporates color playback capability. When used together, recording start and stop can be camera-controlled, and playback is monitored through the camera viewfinder.

EDITING BETAMAX
The RM-140 Automatic Editing Controller and SLO-383 Editing Recorder/Player comprise the first half-inch editing system ever.
They offer perfectly clean edits and low signal-to-noise degradation, so you get high picture quality in multiple generations.

INTERACTIVE BETAMAX
Instead of being limited to viewing a videotape from start to finish, you can use the RX-353 Programmable Auto Search Control to locate and play 63 different segments, in the order you choose. And Sony's revolutionary Video Responder makes Betamax a fully respondent teaching machine. It poses questions, identifies the answers as correct or incorrect, and selects subsequent programming based on the answers.

Of all half-inch institutional video systems, only Sony Betamax can grow as you grow, diversify as you diversify, and keep up with developing technology year after year.

That's because from the very first Betamax was designed to evolve. Which means Betamax equipment is interchangeable. Today even the most basic machines can hook up to the most sophisticated production, editing and interactive video equipment.

What's more, institutional Betamax is specifically built to institutional standards—giving you a better picture in multiple generations. And allowing for the development of a greater variety of applications.

All of which means you can make a very modest investment in Betamax today, yet take advantage of the most innovative options tomorrow.

For more information, call or write us for our Betamax brochure and literature on the Video Responder system. Call 1-800-821-7700, ext. 126 (Missouri, 1-800-892-5890, ext. 313). Or write the Sony Information Center, CN-02450, Department I, Trenton, New Jersey 08659.

We give you more video, in more ways, than anybody else.

SONY Video Communications.

AT SONY THE PRODUCTS OF OUR MOST INNOVATIVE THINKING AREN'T ALWAYS PRODUCTS.

From the first, Sony's creative approach to video has extended far beyond video equipment. The result is a range of extraordinary and unique services unmatched in the industry.

Take, for example, Sony's Video Utilization Services. Run for video professionals by experts Steven Gach and Jeff Glasser, these EFP workshops and specialty seminars boost technical skills and foster a more imaginative, bolder approach to video.

Larry Benson, on the other hand, teaches video technology at the touch of a button. He produces Sony's Video Training Programs—a growing library of over 200 videocassettes and texts that provides a self-paced education in specific video equipment and concepts.

Steven Gach and Jeff Glasser, creators of Sony Video Utilization Services.

Larry Benson, producer of Sony's Video Training Programs.

As to customer service, Sony's network of over 200 authorized video servicing dealers is the largest in the U.S. Moreover, we've backed up our rigorously trained dealers with five Regional Technical Centers, created to solve unusual servicing problems.

Meanwhile, we have parts availability down to an exact science at our Kansas City warehouse. It carries a year-round, complete inventory of spare parts, ready to ship to any dealer—anywhere—at a moment's notice.

Five Sony Technical Training Centers supplement our network of 200 authorized video servicing dealers.

Sony takes service even one step further at the Sony Video Technology Center in Palo Alto. Here, top engineers custom-design video systems, using breakthrough technology.

At the Sony Video Technology Center, top engineers custom-design video systems.

What's more, our salespeople are more like personal consultants than salespeople. They're specially trained to work with our dealers in exploring your present and future video needs, and designing the ideal system for you.

Sony's salespeople are trained as system consultants.

Then there's Sony's unique philosophy of evolution. Because we design each new product to work with existing Sony video products, every Sony remains useful far into the future.

New products work with existing Sony products.

The fact is, the company that makes the world's most complete line of video products also offers the most complete line of video services. For more information about any Sony service, call 1-800-821-7700, ext. 126 (Missouri, 1-800-892-5890, ext. 313). Or write to the Sony Information Center, CN-02450, Department H, Trenton, New Jersey 08659.

We give you more video, in more ways, than anybody else.

SONY Video Communications

SONY DOESN'T JUST REVOLUTIONIZE VIDEO. SONY REVOLUTIONIZES LEARNING.

With its introduction of interactive video equipment, Sony once again demonstrates commitment to leadership in the field of video communications. And brings a new dimension both to video and to the learning process.

No longer is the video user a passive viewer. Instead, he or she interacts with the program, and that interaction modifies subsequent programming. Testing can become an integral part of learning, since what is learned is subject to instant evaluation.

Sony began this interactive revolution with its RX-353 programmable auto search control. About the size of a handheld calculator, the RX-353 can automatically access as many

INTERACTIVE TAPE
Equipment and software you already own can instantly be made interactive with Sony's Video Responder system.

as 63 different preprogrammed segments of videotape. And it can recall any eight segments in a programmed sequence.

Once a tape is programmed with an RX-353, it can easily be duplicated and sent out to a wide network of users, who can then access it with their own RX-353's.

For more sophisticated interaction, however, there's Sony's new Video Responder system. Like the RX-353, it's fully compatible with Betamax and U-matic equipment. And it was designed to meet two goals: ease of programming and ease of use.

The Video Responder system asks its users questions, makes note of their responses, and automatically reviews material when incorrect answers are given. It can also record and grade answers.

Videotapes can be programmed to move automatically from one segment to another, allowing for individual pacing, software economy and time shrinkage. And an optional printer provides proof of performance and identifies problem areas.

Using the system is as easy as pressing one of ten buttons. Learning how to program it takes the novice a couple of hours, at most. Existing software can be "responderized," and Sony's Video Utilization Services are ready with special courses to help you produce new programs that are already responderized.

Like the Video Responder, Sony's new laser video disc player contains microcomputer circuits, which let the user interact with the programming. The player features virtually instant access to any one of 54,000 specific program frames

INTERACTIVE DISC
Suitable for interactive programming for wide networks of users. Sony's mastering and stamping plant can turn out your software now.

per disc side. And the discs themselves are extremely durable.

So a number of additional applications are possible, including sales support and information storage. (Both player and discs are compatible with other laser disc formats on the market.)

And Sony is ready now to duplicate your video programs on disc, with a mastering and stamping plant already in operation.

Consult Sony about interactive video, and you have the advantage of dealing with a company that can offer you either tape or disc, and therefore doesn't need to sell you on a format that may not be right for you.

We'll send you our free booklet on tape versus disc when you write the Sony Information Center, CN-02450, Dept. J, Trenton, N.J. 08659.

Sony. We give you more video, in more ways, than anybody else.

SONY Video Communications

226

Trade
Any Size
B/W or Color
Campaign

227
Art Director:
Russ Veduccio
Writer:
John Wallwork
Designers:
Russ Veduccio
John Wallwork
Artist:
Jim Clark
Photographer:
Jim Clark
Client:
Joseph Kirschner
Agency:
Harold Cabot/Boston

228
Art Director:
Robert Saabye
Writers:
Tom Monahan
Bob Mariani
Designer:
Robert Saabye
Photographer:
Clint Clemens
Client:
LaCrosse Rubber Mills
Agency:
Leonard Monahan Saabye/R.I.

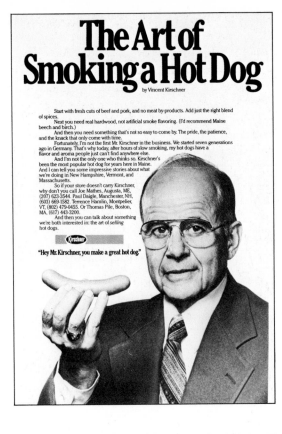

The Art of Smoking a Hot Dog
by Vincent Kirschner

Start with fresh cuts of beef and pork, and no meat by-products. Add just the right blend of spices.

Next you need real hardwood, not artificial smoke flavoring. (I'd recommend Maine beech and birch.)

And then you need something that's not so easy to come by. The pride, the patience, and the knack that only come with time.

Fortunately, I'm not the first Mr. Kirschner in the business. We started seven generations ago in Germany. That's why today, after hours of slow smoking, my hot dogs have a flavor and aroma people just can't find anywhere else.

And I'm not the only one who thinks so. Kirschner's been the most popular hot dog for years here in Maine. And I can tell you some impressive stories about what we're doing in New Hampshire, Vermont, and Massachusetts.

So if your store doesn't carry Kirschner, why don't you call Joe Mathes, Augusta, ME, (207) 623-3544. Paul Daigle, Manchester, NH, (603) 669-1582. Terrence Hamlin, Montpelier, VT, (802) 479-0455. Or Thomas Pile, Boston, MA, (617) 443-3200.

And then you can talk about something we're both interested in: the art of *selling* hot dogs.

Kirschner

"Hey Mr. Kirschner, you make a great hot dog."

"In my family, we started making sausage 7 Mr. Kirschners ago."

In Bavaria, sausage-making isn't a business. It's an art. And that's where my great, great, great grandfather made the first Kirschner sausage.

Then in 1913, my father brought the family tradition to America and opened a small butcher shop in Maine. It wasn't long before the Kirschner reputation had spread all across Maine. And today, our business is over more and more of New England every year.

Why? Because people can taste the difference in Kirschner smoked sausage, pork sausage, Polish sausage, and knockwurst. And I can tell you why.

No leftovers get left in our sausage. We only use the fresh, lean cuts of beef and pork we specify from the slaughterhouse down the road here in Augusta. And we're just as particular about the spices we use, too.

I've got a person who can give you the kind of details every retailer likes to hear. Leon Zacharias, Divisional Manager, Scarborough, ME, (207) 883-3020.

So why don't you call him collect. You, and your customers, will never regret it.

- Vincent Kirschner

Kirschner

"Hey Mr. Kirschner, you make great sausage."

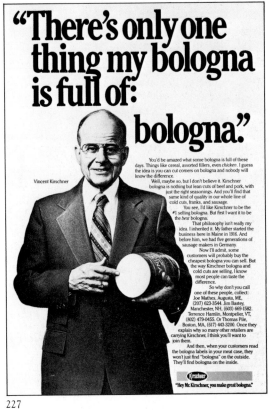

"There's only one thing my bologna is full of: bologna."

Vincent Kirschner

You'd be amazed what some bologna is full of these days. Things like cereal, assorted fillers, even *chicken*. I guess the idea is you can cut corners on bologna and nobody will know the difference.

Well, maybe so, but I don't believe it. Kirschner bologna is nothing but lean cuts of beef and pork, with just the right seasonings. And you'll find that same kind of quality in our whole line of cold cuts, franks, and sausage.

You see, I'd like Kirschner to be the #1 selling bologna. But first I want it to be the *best* bologna.

That philosophy isn't really my idea. I inherited it. My father started the business here in Maine in 1916. And before him, we had five generations of sausage makers in Germany.

Now I'll admit, some customers will probably buy the cheapest bologna you can sell. But the way Kirschner bologna and cold cuts are selling, I know most people can taste the difference.

So why don't you call one of these people, collect: Joe Mathes, Augusta, ME, (207) 623-3544. Jim Bastey, Manchester, NH, (603) 669-1582. Terrence Hamlin, Montpelier, VT, (802) 479-0455. Or Thomas Pile, Boston, MA, (617) 443-3200. Once they explain why so many other retailers are carrying Kirschner, I think you'll want to join them.

And then, when your customers read the bologna labels in your meat case, they won't just find "bologna" on the outside. They'll find bologna on the inside.

Kirschner

"Hey Mr. Kirschner, you make great bologna."

227

OTHER BOOTS WOULD BE ON THEIR LAST LEGS.

The time to judge a boot's quality and value is not necessarily when it's new.

We invite you to compare the quality of our safety boots with any in the business. Compare them right out of the box if you want, but, more importantly, compare them after they've been on the job a good number of man-hours, like our neoprene pacs shown here. That's where our long wearing quality really shows up. And that's where most users find LaCrosse® boots a better bargain than the "bargain" brands. Because LaCrosse delivers long-term value.

Yes, quality has been a tradition at LaCrosse for over three quarters of a century, from raw materials through design and workmanship, to finished product.

If you're looking for quality industrial footwear that isn't going to wind up on Boot Hill before its time, look to LaCrosse. LaCrosse Rubber Mills Company, LaCrosse, Wisconsin 54601. (608) 782-3020.

LaCrosse Rubber Mills Company

THIS BOOT WAS DESIGNED BY ACCIDENT.

Before we designed our steel toe boots, we took a good, long look at the environments they'd be in. Where workers need protection against falling objects and other hazards.

You might say, we learned by accident. And the result? A sturdy, industrial-weight, over-the-sock rubber boot.

Our built-in steel toe meets or exceeds OSHA standards, withstanding 2,500 pounds of dead weight pressure or 75 foot/pounds in drop test. It's available in full sizes 6-14, heights; hip, storm king and short.

With a safety yellow toe cap identifying the steel toe, a steel shank for added strength and support, plus a cleated outsole with full boot heel, it's designed to take all kinds of punishment. Yet it's extra comfortable, with a fully cushioned insole and a unique sponge insert between the steel toe cap and lining for additional wear, comfort and safety.

Don't buy the wrong safety boot by accident. Ask your footwear distributor for LaCrosse® steel toe boots. **LaCrosse Rubber Mills Co.,** LaCrosse, WI 54601. (608) 782-3020.

LaCrosse Rubber Mills Company

YOU DESERVE A GOOD, SWIFT BOOT.

And no one delivers a boot more swiftly than LaCrosse, the great American safety boot.

At LaCrosse, we make top-quality, long lasting safety boots. And we know that's super important to you. But we also know that all the quality in the world is worth nothing if you can't get your safety boots when you need them.

That's why we put as much emphasis on delivery as quality. Ask your footwear distributor which manufacturer has boots available for immediate delivery. He'll tell you, LaCrosse. And it's not so much that we have boots on our floor, but, also, that our floor is in America. So you don't have to rely on a slow boat from wherever.

From steel toe boots, to neoprene pacs, to insulated footwear. Boots to serve every industrial need. Boots that meet OSHA standards. When you want a good swift boot, we stand ready to deliver. **LaCrosse Rubber Mills Co.,** LaCrosse, Wisconsin 54601. (608) 782-3020.

LaCrosse Rubber Mills Company

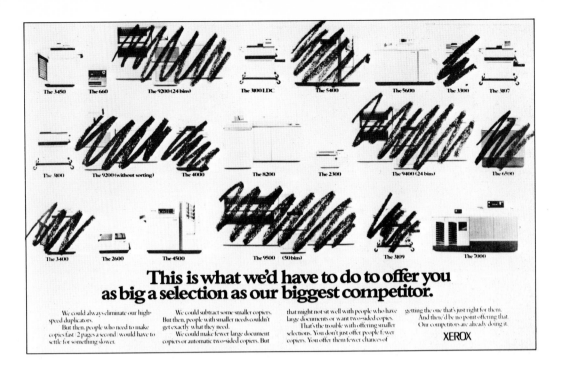

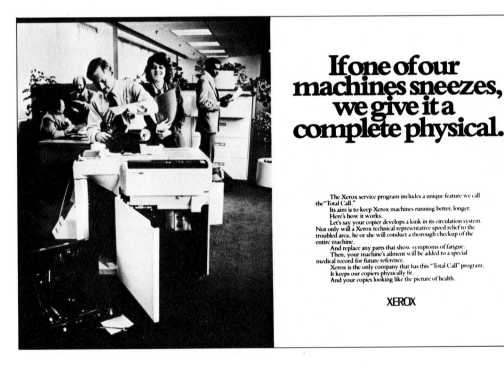

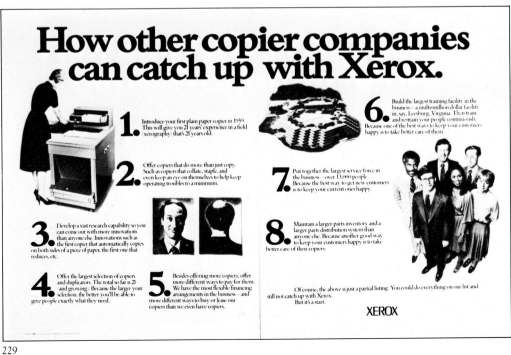

A lot of things our phone system can do still haven't been discovered.

When a country is looking at new telephone exchanges, the toughest part is the unknown.

How do you anticipate all the changes ahead, technological and otherwise?

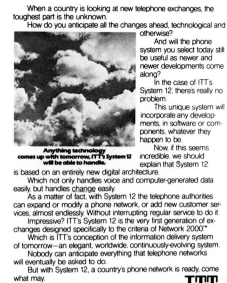

Anything technology comes up with tomorrow, ITT's System 12 will be able to handle.

And will the phone system you select today still be useful as newer and newer developments come along?

In the case of ITT's System 12, there's really no problem.

This unique system will incorporate any developments, in software or components, whatever they happen to be.

Now, if this seems incredible, we should explain that System 12 is based on an entirely new digital architecture.

Which not only handles voice and computer-generated data easily, but handles change easily.

As a matter of fact, with System 12 the telephone authorities can expand or modify a phone network, or add new customer services, almost endlessly. Without interrupting regular service to do it.

Impressive? ITT's System 12 is the very first generation of exchanges designed specifically to the criteria of Network 2000™

Which is ITT's conception of the information delivery system of tomorrow—an elegant, worldwide, continuously-evolving system.

Nobody can anticipate everything that telephone networks will eventually be asked to do.

But with System 12, a country's phone network is ready, come what may.

ITT

ITT ▬▬▬▬ NETWORK 2000

Imagine designing a telephone system for cities that don't exist yet.

In the last decade, no fewer than 55 of the world's cities reached populations of one million for the first time.

Anybody planning a telephone network for a country has to consider growth in years to come.

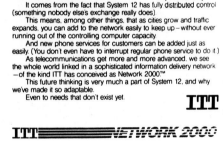

As a country expands, ITT's new System 12 can expand with it.

And must ask whether this or that telephone exchange will be able to keep up with it.

We raise this question to make the point that ITT's new System 12 was designed with just such growth in mind.

Ours is a totally new, totally digital system—a system capable of adapting to any conceivable future demands you make on it.

Why this flexibility?

It comes from the fact that System 12 has fully distributed control (something nobody else's exchange really does).

This means, among other things, that as cities grow and traffic expands, you can add to the network easily to keep up—without ever running out of the controlling computer capacity.

And new phone services for customers can be added just as easily. (You don't even have to interrupt regular phone service to do it.)

As telecommunications get more and more advanced, we see the whole world linked in a sophisticated information delivery network—of the kind ITT has conceived as Network 2000™

This future thinking is very much a part of System 12, and why we've made it so adaptable.

Even to needs that don't exist yet.

ITT

ITT ▬▬▬▬ NETWORK 2000

Will your country's telephone system be able to keep up with your country?

It's clear that a booming population will need more and more telephone service.

Which is why telephone authorities all over the world are considering new phone exchanges at this very moment.

As cities grow, ITT's new System 12 will grow with them.

But with voice and computer traffic making urgent new demands on phone systems, it's important that any new exchange really be new.

And not just an updating of some older design.

This is all by way of introducing ITT's new System 12, a unique exchange system based on the latest technology. In fact, future technology.

But let us explain. Before ITT created this system, we carefully mapped the direction telecommunications will take over the next decades.

Which irresistibly pointed toward an integrated worldwide information delivery network—what we at ITT have called Network 2000™

And everything we foresee in this ultimate network, we've anticipated in the revolutionary architecture of System 12.

It's a fully digital system, able to handle voice and high-speed computer data with equal ease.

And a system whose fully distributed processing permits telephone planners to expand and modify an existing network—virtually without limit.

It stands to reason that any country that's growing (and what country isn't?) must have telephone exchanges that can keep up with the growth.

Which narrows the choice quite a bit.

ITT

ITT ▬▬▬▬ NETWORK 2000

Trade
Any Size
B/W or Color
Campaign

231
Art Directors:
Anthony Angotti
Allen Kay
Writer:
Tom Thomas
Artist:
Charles White
Photographer:
Steve Steigman
Client:
Xerox
Agency:
Needham, Harper & Steers

232
Art Director:
Scott Samuel
Writer:
Michael Zambrelli
Designer:
Scott Samuel
Photographer:
Sports Illustrated
Client:
Time Inc.
Sports Illustrated
Agency:
Ogilvy & Mather/2

Lords of the ring.

For fifteen rounds, they stood toe to toe.

Roberto Duran and Sugar Ray Leonard. Mano a mano for the welterweight championship of the world.

When it was over—after the blood, sweat and cheers—it wasn't the fighters who were knocked out. It was the crowd.

That's how good a fight it was. It was magic. Two exquisitely trained and extraordinarily gifted athletes created it.

Sports Illustrated captured it. We captured it the way we've captured all the great moments in sports this year.

In words and fast-close color photography created by a staff as intensely dedicated to their work as Roberto and Ray are to theirs.

16 million readers will see the fight through our eyes. They're young, intelligent readers. Readers with money to spend.

This national audience is Sports Illustrated's basic advertising buy. And when you have special marketing problems, we offer a range of special geographic and demographic editions. In addition, our in-house sales promotion department can help you design a total merchandising program.

This marketing flexibility and merchandising capability are just two reasons Sports Illustrated is a superb advertising medium.

Sports Illustrated's a news. It's some of the biggest news in the world each week.

And last week, in Montreal, it was as good as it ever gets.

Sports Illustrated
16 million readers buy what's in it.

The shot heard round the world.

It was more than the Russians. It was the world's best hockey team.

And in taking their measure, 20 young American men took away the world's collective breath.

Their stunning upset, and Olympic triumph, is what the world of sports is all about: transcendent, almost magical moments.

And this is what Sports Illustrated is all about: capturing and bringing those moments back alive so that they never end.

We do it, today, the way we've done it for the past 25 years.

Each and every week.

So that our coverage is immediate, provocative and as timely as the actual events.

More than that, we do it in words and fast-close color photography created by a staff whose devotion to *their* work is as intense as the competitors they cover.

It's a unique editorial challenge. We were the first to meet it. And even now, no one has come close to duplicating our success.

We attract 16 million avid readers. And precisely the kind of readers advertisers want. Young readers. Intelligent readers. Readers with money to spend.

We attract them because some of the biggest news in the world each week is in the world of sports. And 1980, that seems to be more true than ever.

Indeed, 1980 is already a record-breaking year for us, with first quarter ad revenues up 41%.

Sports Illustrated's news. It's some of the biggest news in the world each week. And bringing it back alive has made us America's Sports Newsweekly.

Sports Illustrated
America's Sports Newsweekly.
16 million readers buy what's in it.

The King of Queens.

Super John and the Super Swede raised another racquet last week.

Only this time the place was Flushing Meadow, Queens. And the result was simply McAdvent.

For when it was over—after 4 hours and 5 grueling sets—McEnroe had avenged his earlier Wimbledon defeat and earned a second straight U.S. Open crown.

His victory, however, meant even more than that. It meant the end of Borg's Grand Slam quest. And the beginning of a beautiful and brilliant tennis rivalry.

It also marks the beginning of a special time of the sports year.

For now is when the pennant races intensify as baseball heads toward its 77th World Series. Now is when college and pro football begin their battles on gridirons from Pasadena to Pittsburgh. Now is when the Islanders and the Lakers prepare to defend their pro hockey and basketball crowns.

All this promises to produce performances as extraordinary and dramatic as Super Mac's.

And it promises to make Sports Illustrated an especially good place to advertise now. Because we'll capture the magic of these performances in words and fast-close color photography, so you can experience and savor it again and again.

And we'll capture it superbly enough to attract 16 million avid readers. Young, intelligent readers. Readers with money to spend.

Sports Illustrated's a news. It's some of the biggest news in the world each week.

And in 1980, some of the best of that news is still to come.

Sports Illustrated
America's Sports Newsweekly.

Collateral
Brochures
Other than by mail

233
Art Director:
Joe Suplina
Writer:
Ken Baron
Designer:
Joe Suplina
Photographers:
Paul Elfenbein
George M. Cochran
Client:
Sony Video
Agency:
Vidmer, Phin

234
Art Director:
David Griffing
Writer:
Mike Rosen
Designer:
David Griffing
Photographer:
Les Goldberg
Client:
Cricketeer
Agency:
Sacks & Rosen

235
Art Director:
James Sebastian
Writer:
Ralph Caplan
Designers:
James Sebastian
Michael Lauretano
Margaret Popper
Kathleen Lee
Photographers:
Max Waldman
Harry Callahan
Phil Koenig
Client:
Champion Papers
Agency:
Designframe

236
Art Director:
William McCaffery
Writer:
Adrienne Claiborne
Designer:
William McCaffery
Artist:
William McCaffery
Photographer:
Joel Brodsky
Client:
Paul Stuart
Agency:
William McCaffery

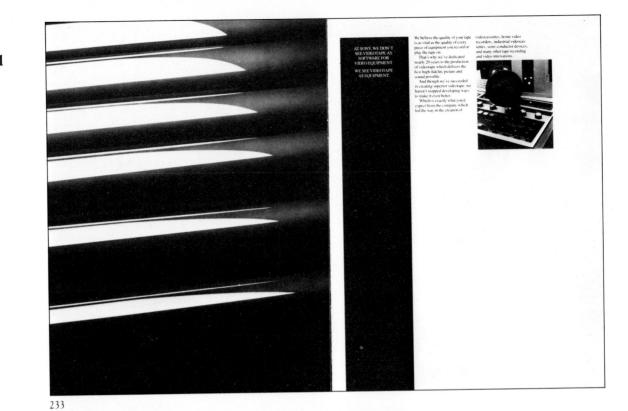

233

234

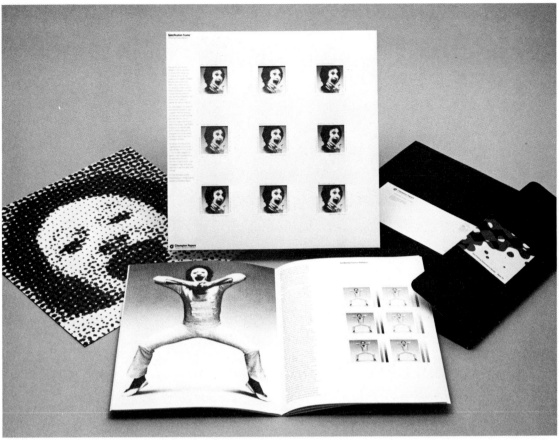

235

236

237
Art Director:
John R. Kleinschmidt
Writer:
Dorothy Dunbar
Designer:
Lois Carlo
Artist:
Zack Carr
Client:
Wamsutta Mills
Agency:
Wamsutta Mills

238
Art Director:
Douglas Hoppe Stone
Writers:
**Douglas Hoppe Stone
Joe Taylor
June Self**
Designers:
Gillen Stone, Inc.
Artist:
Joe Taylor
Client:
**Mrs. Gooch's
Health Food Store**
Agency:
Gillen Stone/Calif.

239
Art Directors:
**Toshiko Mori
Jeffrey Blondes**
Writers:
**Kristin Joyce
Abbie Simon**
Artists:
**Seymour Chwast
Jeffrey Blondes**
Photographers:
**Robert Murry
Jeffrey Blondes
Bettman Archives**
Client:
Bellevue Hospital Center
Agency:
Greenwood Consultants

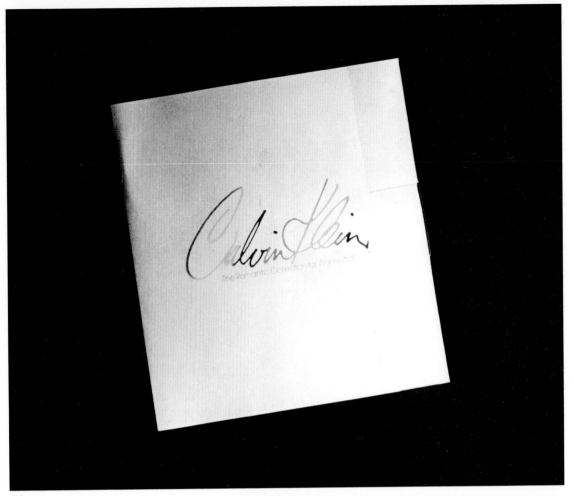

237

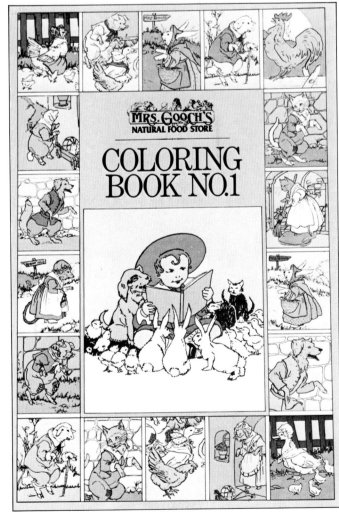

238

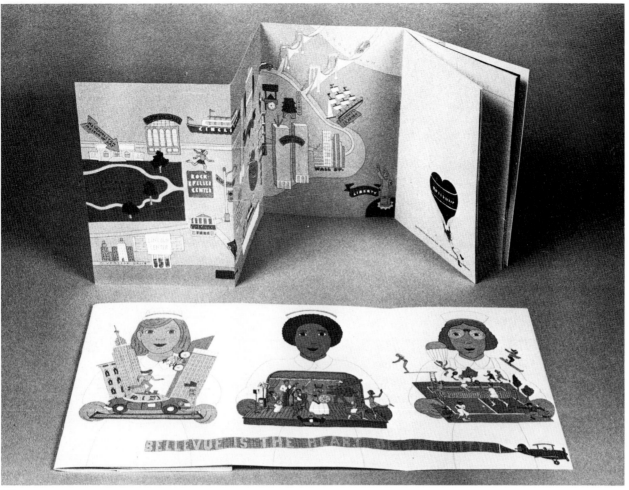

239

Collateral
Brochures
Other than by mail

240
Art Director:
Charles Hively
Writer:
Mary Langridge
Designer:
Charles Hively
Artist:
Jean-Michel Folon
Photographer:
Giorgio Soavi
Client:
Conoco Chemicals
Agency:
**Metzdorf Advertising
Houston**

241
Art Director:
Aria Hurr
Writer:
Gojan Nikolich
Designer:
Roger Seachrist
Photographers:
**Stock/Chicago
Greg Laun**
Client:
IDCCA-Office of Tourism
Agency:
**Hackenberg, Norman,
Krivkovich-CK/Chicago**

242
Art Director:
John Kleinschmidt
Writer:
Dorothy Dunbar
Designer:
Lois Carlo
Photographer:
Mike Hirst
Client:
Wamsutta Mills
Agency:
Wamsutta Mills

240

241

Detail 6: Minuet

...clusters of floral notes dance a dainty measure...Ultracale.

242

Collateral
Sales Kits

243
Art Directors:
Aubrey Balkind
Philip Gips
Writers:
Francis Piderit
Designers:
Philip Gips
Jane Cullen
Photographer:
Bob Greene
Client:
CBS
Agency:
Gips Balkind & Associates

Collateral
Direct Mail

244
Art Director:
Sandy Carlson
Writer:
Dick Tarlow
Photographers:
Anthony Edgeworth
Bruce Weber
Paul Christensen
Client:
Ralph Lauren
Agency:
Kurtz & Tarlow

245
Art Director:
Ron Anderson
Writer:
Tom McElligott
Photographer:
Don Getsug
Client:
Art Directors/Copywriters
Club of Minnesota
Agency:
Bozell & Jacobs/Mpls.

246
Art Director & Writer:
Steve Stith
Client:
Jan Conine
Agency:
Bozell & Jacobs/Dallas

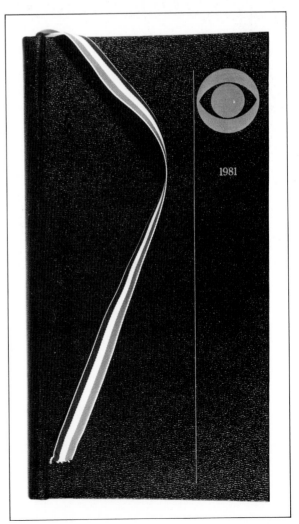

244

OK all you closet
prima donnas,
it's that time of year again.

245

"The husband is always the last to know."

Please join me at a surprise birthday
party for my husband, Willard. January
2, 1981 at 7:30 p.m., 1417 North Trail
Circle, Carrollton. R.S.V.P. Jan Conine.

556-3104 or 245-1376.
Black Tie or Blue Jeans.

246

Collateral
Direct Mail

247
Art Directors:
Dennis S. Juett
Jeffrey D. Lawson
Writer:
Dennis S. Juett
Designer:
Jeffrey D. Lawson
Artists:
Jeffrey D. Lawson
Dennis S. Juett
Client:
Dennis S. Juett & Associates
Agency:
Dennis S. Juett & Associates
Los Angeles

248
Art Director:
David Hopson
Writer:
Andy Wasowski
Designer:
David Hopson
Artists:
David Hopson
Bruce Beck
Client:
Reed, Melnichek,
Gentry & Associates
Agency:
Reed, Melnichek,
Gentry & Associates/Dallas

249
Art Directors:
Diane Cook Tench
Jessica Ellerbroek
Writer:
Andy Ellis
Designer:
Diane Cook Tench
Client:
ITT Community Development
Agency:
Siddall, Matus & Coughter
Virginia

Collateral
P.O.P.

250
Art Director:
Jim Cameron
Writer:
Jim Maloney
Designer:
Jim Cameron
Artist:
Joe Sellars
Client:
Eat'n Park Restaurants
Agency:
Ketchum MacLeod & Grove
Pittsburgh

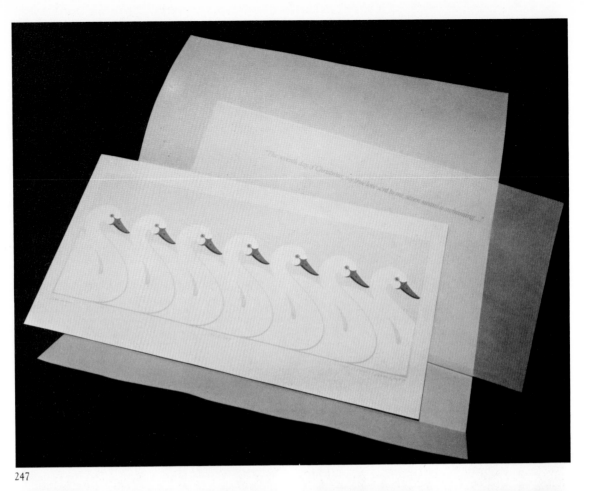

247

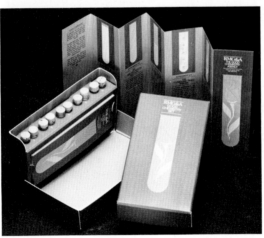

248

Come To The Palm Coast Festa Italiana
And Take Home Some Great Memories.
May 23, 24 & 25

Sponsored by the Italian American Social Club of Palm Coast.

249

251

252

SONY TAPE.
FULL COLOR SOUND.

254
Art Director & Writer:
Milton Glaser
Designer & Artist:
Milton Glaser
Client:
Carl Solway Gallery
Agency:
Milton Glaser

255
Art Director & Writer:
Silas H. Rhodes
Designers:
Richard Wilde
Diane Addesso
Artist:
Robert Guisti
Client:
School of Visual Arts
Agency:
School of Visual Arts

256
Art Director:
Jill Parsons
Writer:
Anita Rose
Designer:
Jill Parsons
Photographer:
Billy Wrencher
Client:
Schweppes
Agency:
TBWA/London

257
Art Director:
Caren Goldberg
Designer:
Caren Goldberg
Client:
CBS Records
Agency:
CBS Records

254

School of Visual Arts

255

The factory.
The product.

evian
eau minérale naturelle

Natural mountain spring water from the Alps.

256

257

258
Art Director:
Brian Morrow
Writer:
Ken Mullen
Designer:
Brian Morrow
Artist:
Graham Percy
Client:
John Walker & Sons
Agency:
TBWA/London

259
Art Director:
Jerry Baker
Writer:
Warren Peterson
Photographer:
Jim Blakeley
Client:
Challenge Dairy Products
Agency:
Grey/San Francisco

260
Art Director:
Bill Sweney
Writer:
Chris Nolan
Designer:
Bill Sweney
Photographer:
Chuck Kuhn
Client:
Alaska Airlines
Agency:
Chiat/Day—Wash.

261
Art Director:
Allan Raddon
Writer:
Philip Cherrington
Artist:
Peter Till
Client:
British Telecom
Agency:
KMP Partnership/London

258

259

260

Italy. Only £1·06 for 3 minutes.

Dialled direct on your own phone during International Cheap Rate Period, 8pm to 8am and weekends.

Price quoted includes V.A.T. at 15%. British Telecom International-part of the Post Office.

Outdoor
Single

262
Art Director:
Patrick Tofts
Writer:
Colin Campbell
Photographer:
John Turner
Client:
Aqualac Springwaters
Agency:
Leo Burnett/London

263
Art Director:
Ray Gallop
Writer:
David Templer
Designer:
Ray Gallop
Artist:
Ray Winder
Photographer:
James Cotier
Client:
R & C Vintners
Agency:
Foote, Cone & Belding/London

264
Art Director:
Robert Kitchen
Writers:
Richard Warren
Colin Campbell
Designer:
Robert Kitchen
Artist:
Syd Brak
Client:
Aqualac Springwaters
Agency:
Leo Burnett/London

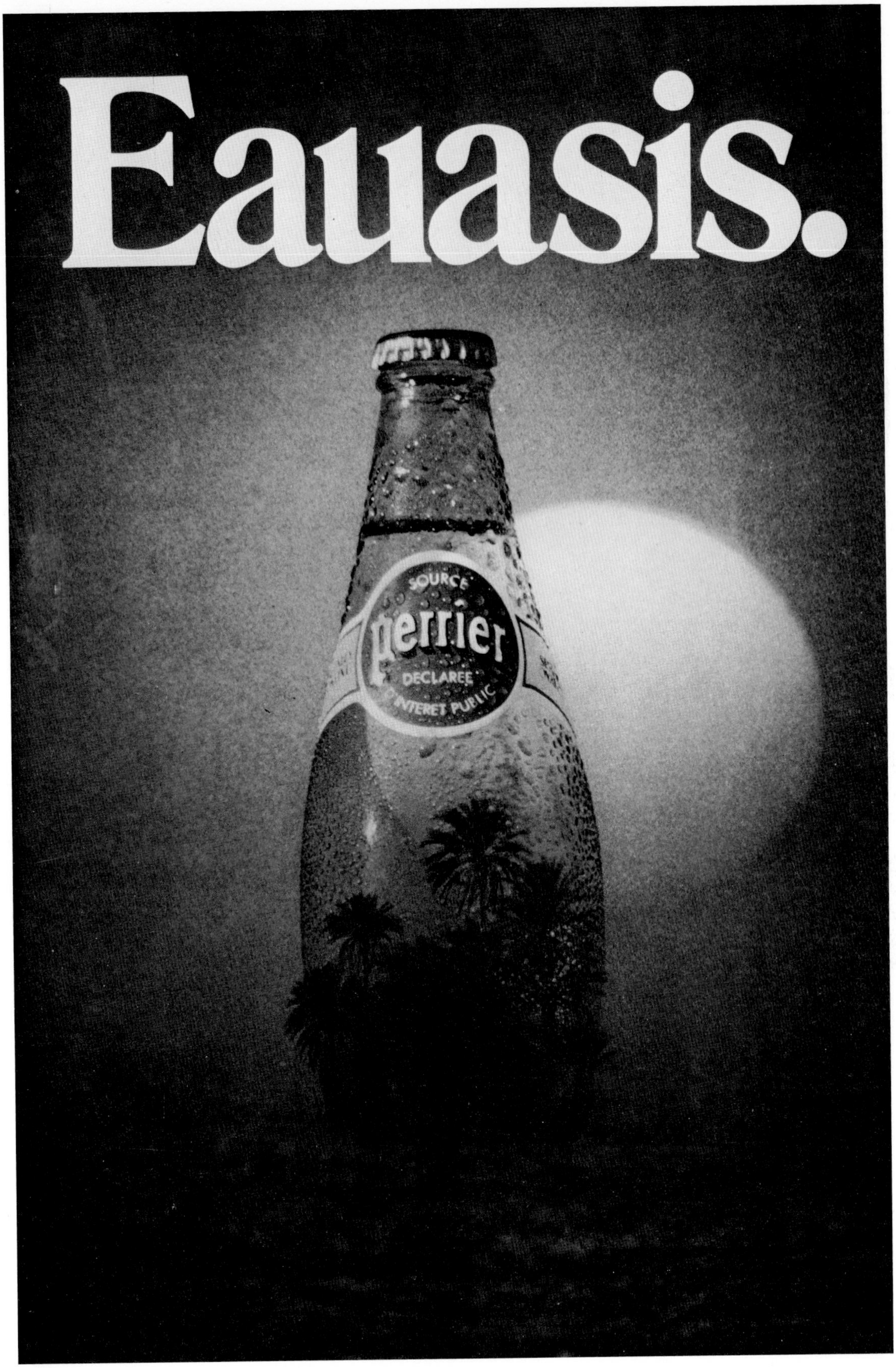

262

"I'll have a Perrier and water, please."

Quite how the barman at New York's Algonquin Hotel reacted to this young lady's order we shall never know.

We reacted with some horror, however.

Perrier with Scotch, certainly. Perrier with dinner, of course. Perrier on its own, naturally. But Perrier with water?

However, when we thought a little deeper about her predicament – a smart hotel, a special evening, perhaps a desire to impress her companion by ordering a drink with style – we decided that never again should Perrier be a cause of such embarrassment.

So, for aficionados and the uninitiated alike:

"Everything you always wanted to know about Perrier but never dared to ask."

At Vergèze, between the somnolent volcanoes of the Auvergne and the Mediterranean, lies a mineral water spring which was bubbling long before Hannibal and his thirsty elephants crossed the Alps and rested there.

Source Perrier.

The Romans built baths there, the French added a spa and hôtel, and, in 1863 Napoleon III decreed that the naturally sparkling spring water be bottled "for the good of France." (Clearly it didn't do him much harm.)

It's rather ironic, however, that it took an Englishman – and a car crash – to put Perrier where it is today.

St. John Harmsworth had bought the spa, spring and all, in 1903.

So, when he crashed his car in England three years later, where better to recuperate than his own sleepy spa in the South of France?

But, like Archimedes in the bath two thousand years before, the presence of so much water was to inspire him.

It occurred to him that, if people would come to Vergèze to take the waters, think how many would enjoy it if he took it to them? – Eureka!

Harmsworth promptly forgot the spa, and concentrated on giving Perrier the distinctive French livery by which it is recognised all over the world today.

The name. The classical logo. The unique Perrier bottle (based on the Indian clubs which he used for remedial exercise).

The water itself he left alone. For Man can add nothing to the natural sparkle which Nature has already provided.

Except a bottle to make sure it will travel well, and arrive as fresh as it left the source.

Which has made Perrier the ideal choice of bon viveurs, the perfect complement to good spirits, and the international hallmark of taste and good company.

No wonder our unfortunate lady was so eager to order it.

We hope the faux pas didn't ruin her evening.

And whether you're eating, drinking, trying not to drink, playing sport or staying at the Algonquin Hotel, we hope Perrier will add to yours.

A votre santé!

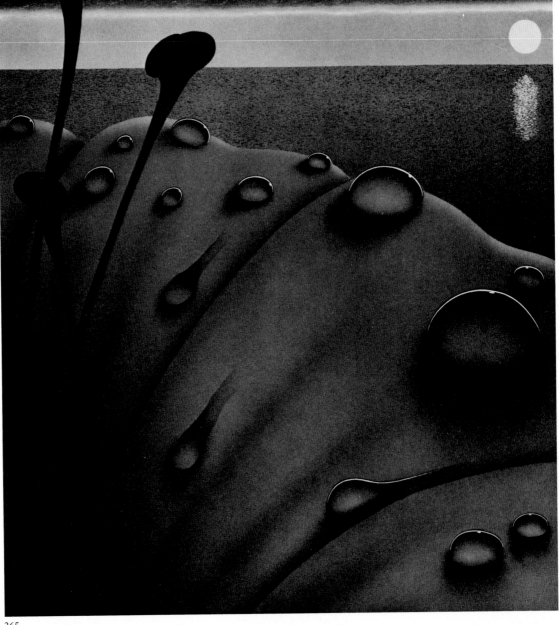

265

266

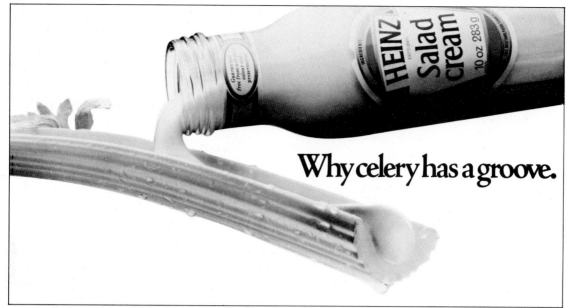

Why celery has a groove.

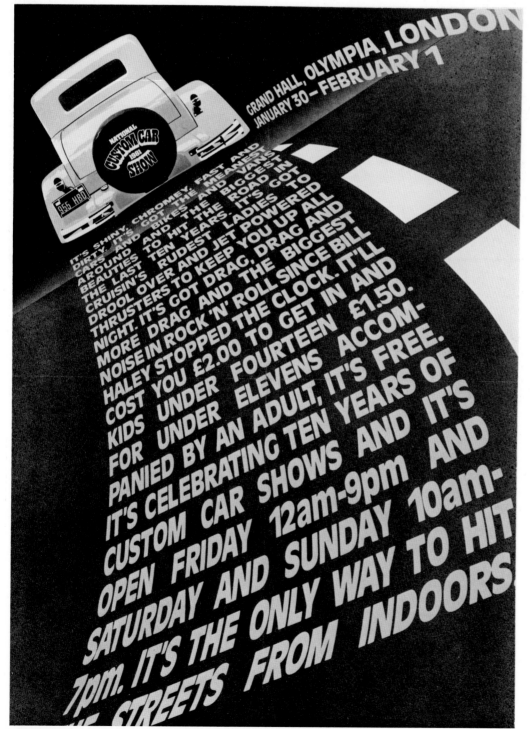

Outdoor
Campaign

269
Art Director:
Alan Gair
Writer:
Judy Samson
Photographer:
Gillean Proctor
Client:
Ontario Egg Marketing Board
Agency:
Ogilvy & Mather/Canada

270
Art Director:
Diane Cook Tench
Writer:
Andy Ellis
Designer:
Diane Cook Tench
Photographer:
Pat Edwards
Client:
ITT Community Development
Agency:
**Siddall, Matus & Coughter
Virginia**

269

You Canoli Eat Food
This Good Once A Year.
The Palm Coast Festa Italiana. May 23, 24 & 25.

It's Sonata Italy
But The Music's Great.
The Palm Coast Festa Italiana. May 23, 24 & 25.

The Palm Coast Festa Italiana.
Don't Let It Pasta You By.
May 23, 24 & 25.

271
Art Director:
Wayne Waaramaa
Writer:
Bill Heater
Designer:
Wayne Waaramaa
Artist:
Susan Perl
Client:
**Rhode Island Assoc.
for the Blind**
Agency:
Duffy & Shanley/R.I.

272
Art Director:
Ron Anderson
Writer:
Tom McElligott
Photographer:
Rick Dublin
Client:
The Episcopal Ad Project
Agency:
Bozell & Jacobs/Mpls.

273
Art Director:
Ron Anderson
Writer:
Tom McElligott
Client:
The Episcopal Ad Project
Agency:
Bozell & Jacobs/Mpls.

274
Art Director:
Mike Vitiello
Writer:
Larry Vine
Artist:
Myers & Noftsinger
Client:
**Anti-Defamation League
of B'nai B'rith**
Agency:
Smith/Greenland

275
Art Director:
Mike Vitiello
Writer:
Larry Vine
Client:
**Anti-Defamation League
of B'nai B'rith**
Agency:
Smith/Greenland

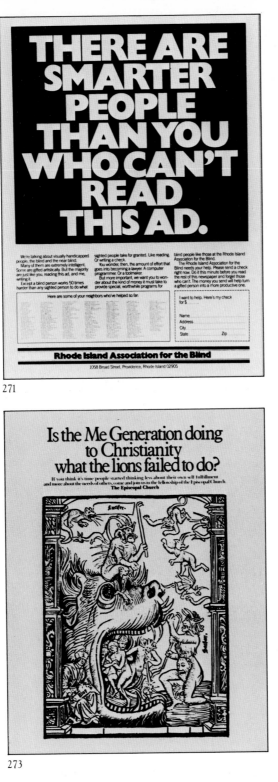

271

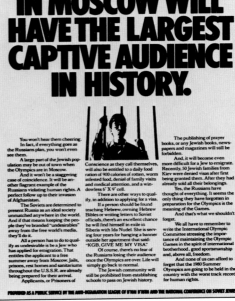

272

273

274

THE 1980 SUMMER OLYMPICS ARE BEING HELD IN THE COUNTRY WITH THE WORST TRACK RECORD FOR HUMAN RIGHTS.

The games that represent brotherhood and equality of opportunity are being held in the country that denies human rights to millions of its citizens. Russia.

The awarding of host city status to Moscow becomes even more of a travesty when you consider recent events in Afghanistan.

And based on some of the events the Russians have planned for the Summer Olympics, it looks like no other country will even come close to their record.

One event is called "Rounding-Up Jews." In this event, the entrants win a free trip to jail, prison, a rest home or a sanitarium for the summer. The idea is to keep the so-called activists as far away from the media as possible. And all you have to do to qualify is be a Jew who has applied for emigration.

Entrants, or Prisoners of Conscience as they call themselves, will also be entitled to a daily food ration of 900 calories of rotten, worm infested food, denial of family visits

and medical attention, and a windowless 6' X 9' cell.

Of course there are other ways to qualify, in addition to applying for a visa.

If you should be found teaching Hebrew, owning Hebrew Bibles or writing letters to Soviet officials, there's an excellent chance that you'll find yourself in exile in Siberia with Ida Nudel. She is serving four years for hanging a banner outside her apartment that said: "KGB, GIVE ME MY VISA."

Another event the Russians are planning is called "Find the Children of Moscow." It's going to be tough. Because the Russians are sending as many Moscow children as they can away to camp. Away from TV cameras. And away from thousands of Westerners who could poison their minds with thoughts about freedom and democracy.

The children are already being taught in school that Westerners will try to poison their bodies by offering them chewing gum laced with bacteria.

And, to make sure that the Olympics are a very uneventful time for the newspeople, the

Russians have built a central press center. It contains every facility necessary for instant coverage. It also makes it unnecessary for the press people to leave the premises. The Russians hope that a controlled environment will make it easier to control the media.

The Russians have thought of everything. They're determined to present Russia as an ideal society unmatched anywhere in the world.

In fact, the only thing that the Russians have forgotten in preparation for the Olympics is the meaning of the Games.

And that's what we shouldn't forget.

We all have to remember to write the International Olympic Committee stressing the importance of maintaining the Olympic Games in the spirit of international brotherhood, good sportsmanship and, above all, freedom.

Otherwise, it's human rights that will come in last at the 1980 Summer Olympics in Moscow.

**Public Service
Newspaper or Magazine
Single**

276
Art Director:
Tom Wolsey
Writer:
Tom Messner
Artist:
Milton Glaser
Client:
Barney's
Agency:
Ally & Gargano

277
Art Director:
Ron Anderson
Writer:
Tom McElligott
Photographer:
Rick Dublin
Client:
The Episcopal Ad Project
Agency:
Bozell & Jacobs/Mpls.

278
Art Director:
Ron Anderson
Writer:
Tom McElligott
Client:
The Episcopal Ad Project
Agency:
Bozell & Jacobs/Mpls.

279
Art Director:
Stan Kovics
Writer:
Larry Plapler
Client:
**Planned Parenthood
of New York City**
Agency:
**Levine, Huntley, Schmidt,
Plapler & Beaver**

280
Art Director:
Joel Levinson
Writer:
Jim Murphy
Photographer:
Richard Noble
Client:
United States Army
Agency:
N W Ayer

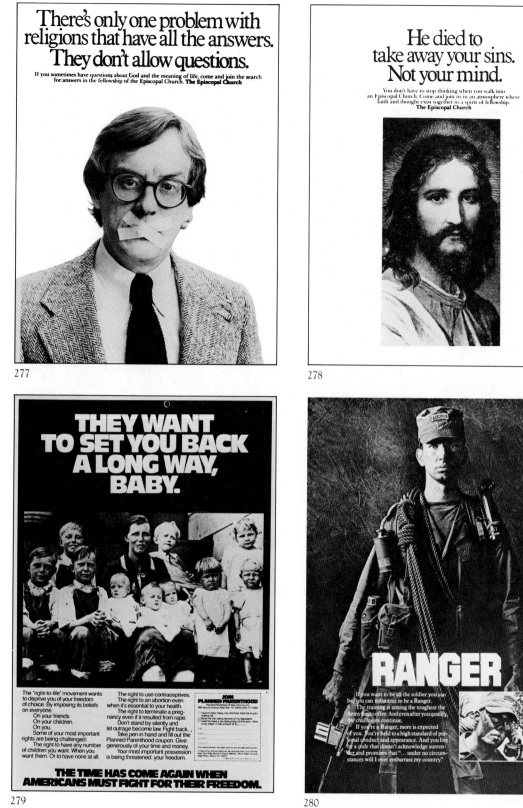

There's only one problem with religions that have all the answers.
They don't allow questions.

If you sometimes have questions about God and the meaning of life, come and join the search for answers in the fellowship of the Episcopal Church. **The Episcopal Church**

277

He died to take away your sins.
Not your mind.

You don't have to stop thinking when you walk into an Episcopal Church. Come and join us in an atmosphere where faith and thought exist together in a spirit of fellowship.
The Episcopal Church

278

THEY WANT TO SET YOU BACK A LONG WAY, BABY.

The "right-to-life" movement wants to deprive you of your freedom of choice. By imposing its beliefs on everyone.
On your friends.
On your children.
On you.
Some of your most important rights are being challenged:
The right to have any number of children you want. When you want them. Or to have none at all.

The right to use contraceptives.
The right to an abortion even when it's essential to your health.
The right to terminate a pregnancy even if it resulted from rape.
Don't stand by silently and let outrage become law. Fight back.
Take pen in hand and fill out the Planned Parenthood coupon. Give generously of your time and money.
Your most important possession is being threatened: your freedom.

JOIN
PLANNED PARENTHOOD
Planned Parenthood of New York City, Inc.
380 Second Avenue, New York, NY 10010 (212) 777-2002

THE TIME HAS COME AGAIN WHEN AMERICANS MUST FIGHT FOR THEIR FREEDOM.

279

RANGER

If you want to be all the soldier you can be, you can volunteer to be a Ranger.
The training is among the toughest the Army has to offer. And even after you qualify, the challenges continue.
If you're a Ranger, more is expected of you. You're held to a high standard of personal conduct and appearance. And you live by a code that doesn't acknowledge surrender, and promises that "...under no circumstances will I ever embarrass my country."

280

DON'T LET THE GLITTER OF GOLD BLIND YOU TO THE TRUTH ABOUT THE 1980 OLYMPICS IN MOSCOW.

There's going to be much more at stake than winning gold medals.

Human rights are going to be on the line.

And based on some of the events the Russians have planned there's a good chance human rights will be set back 44 years—to when the Olympics were held in Nazi Germany.

One event is called "Rounding-Up Jews." In this event, the entrants win a free trip to jail, prison, a rest home or a sanitarium for the summer. The idea is to keep the so-called activists as far away from the media as possible. And all you have to do to qualify is be a Jew who has applied for emigration.

Entrants, or Prisoners of Conscience as they call themselves, will also be entitled to a daily food ration of 900 calories of rotten, worm infested food, denial of family visits and medical attention, and a windowless 6' X 9' cell.

Of course there are other ways to qualify, in addition to applying for a visa.

If you should be found teaching Hebrew, owning Hebrew Bibles or writing letters to Soviet officials, there's an excellent chance that you'll find yourself in exile in Siberia with Ida Nudel. She is serving four years for hanging a banner outside her apartment that said: "KGB, GIVE ME MY VISA."

Another event the Russians are planning is called "Find the Children of Moscow." It's going to be tough. Because the Russians are sending as many Moscow children as they can away to camp. Away from TV cameras. And away from the thousands of Westerners who could poison their minds with thoughts about freedom and democracy.

The children are already being taught in school that Westerners will try to poison their bodies by offering them chewing gum laced with bacteria.

And, to make sure that the Olympics are a very uneventful time for the newspeople, the Russians have built a central press

center. It contains every facility necessary for instant coverage. It also makes it unnecessary for the press people to leave the premises. The Russians hope that a controlled environment will make it easier to control the media.

The Russians have thought of everything. They're determined to present Russia as an ideal society unmatched anywhere in the world.

In fact, the only thing that the Russians have forgotten in preparation for the Olympics is the meaning of the Games.

And that's what we shouldn't forget.

We all have to remember to write the International Olympic Committee stressing the importance of maintaining the Olympic Games in the spirit of international brotherhood, good sportsmanship and, above all, freedom.

Otherwise, it's human rights that stand to lose the most at the 1980 Summer Olympics in Moscow.

PROVIDED AS A PUBLIC SERVICE BY THE ANTI-DEFAMATION LEAGUE OF B'NAI B'RITH AND THE NATIONAL CONFERENCE ON SOVIET JEWRY.

This Message Prepared by Smith/Greenland Inc., Advertising, 1414 Ave. of Americas, New York, New York 10019

Illustration by Myers & Noftsinger

THERE IS A GROUP THAT WOULD FORCE YOU TO BEAR YOUR RAPIST'S CHILD.

As if being raped isn't terrible enough, the "right to life" movement would deny you the right to an abortion if you become pregnant.

Even if you're only a child yourself.

Even if your sanity depends on it.

Even if your life depends on it.

The "right to life" movement is challenging some of your most important rights:

The right to have any number of children you want. Or to have none at all.

The right to use contraceptives.

The right to an abortion even when it's essential to your health.

Don't stand by silently and let outrage become law. Fight back.

Take pen in hand and fill out the Planned Parenthood coupon. Give generously of your time and money.

Your most important possession is being threatened: your freedom.

THE TIME HAS COME AGAIN WHEN AMERICANS MUST FIGHT FOR THEIR FREEDOM.

See a grasshopper as big as a Buick.

There's only one place in this world where you can come face to face with a firefly, mosquito and grasshopper. See lightning strike twice. Touch a meteor. And make waves.

Only one place. And you can get to it on the Green Line. Just hop off at Science Park station.

Or drive a Bug as big as a Volkswagen and park in our covered garage.

**The Museum of Science
Where it's fun to find out.**

This summer, send your kids to the moon.

They certainly have it coming to them. So send them off to the stars. Back to the age of the dinosaurs. And into the future.

Just take the Green Line to Science Park station. Or drive and park in our covered garage.

The Museum of Science is the perfect place to entertain your children this summer. It's completely air conditioned. And it doesn't cost a lot.

Just think, for the price of a movie, you can give them the moon.

**The Museum of Science
Where it's fun to find out.**

15,000 years ago, this was the girl next door.

A long, long time ago, before condominiums, people used to live in caves.

Like us, these cave men and women put paintings on their walls, wore hats and enjoyed cookouts, too. In fact, you'll be amazed at just how much we have in common with them.

From October 1st to December 31st, you can get a look at what it was like to be running around during the last Ice Age.

We'll have cave paintings, drawings, figurines, animal statuettes, decorated tools and other artifacts from the early European hunting cultures of 12,000 to 37,000 years ago.

It's an exhibit you definitely shouldn't miss. There hasn't been anything like it in 12,000 years.

**The Museum of Science
Where it's fun to find out.**
Ice Age Art, Oct. 1-Dec. 31

There's only one problem with religions that have all the answers. They don't allow questions.

If you sometimes have questions about God and the meaning of life, come and join the search for answers in the fellowship of the Episcopal Church. **The Episcopal Church**

Is the Me Generation doing to Christianity what the lions failed to do?

If you think it's time people started thinking less about their own self-fulfillment and more about the needs of others, come and join us in the fellowship of the Episcopal Church. **The Episcopal Church**

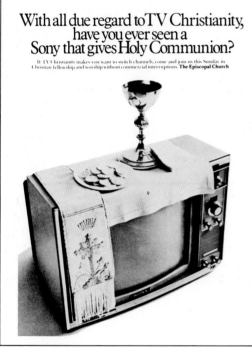

With all due regard to TV Christianity, have you ever seen a Sony that gives Holy Communion?

If TV Christianity makes you want to switch channels, come and join us this Sunday in Christian fellowship and worship without commercial interruptions. **The Episcopal Church**

285

THANKS TO HARTSFIELD, 2 BILLION OF THESE LAND IN ATLANTA EVERY YEAR.

286

This Year For Lent, Give Up An Hour.

Enjoy Outstanding Speakers and Spirited Dialogue at Mid-Day Community Lenten Services at St. Paul's Episcopal Church, Ninth and Grace Streets. Services: February 20 - April 3, 12:30 to 1:00 p.m. Lunch: 11:45 a.m. to 12:30 p.m. and 1:00 to 1:30 p.m.

287

Have you ever wished you were better informed?
THE TIMES

288

With your help, United Way can teach Melissa how to talk back to her mother.

The United Way.
Give once. And for all.

289

IF THE MORAL MAJORITY HAS ITS WAY, YOU'D BETTER START PRAYING.

The Moral Majority—and other groups like them—think that children should pray in school. Not just their children. Your children.

But that's just the beginning. They want their religious doctrines enacted into law and imposed on everyone.

If they believe that birth control is a sin, then you should not be allowed to use contraceptives.

If they believe that abortion is wrong, then you should not be allowed to have one.

If they believe that the Bible condemns homosexuality, then the law should punish homosexuals.

If they believe that a man should be the breadwinner and the divinely appointed head of the family, then the law should keep women in their place.

If they are offended by the ideas in certain books, then the law should ban those books from your libraries and schools.

And like Joe McCarthy, they believe that anyone who disagrees with them should be barred from teaching in the public schools.

These new groups are on the march and growing stronger each day. Their agenda is clear and frightening: they mean to capture the power of government and use it to establish a nightmare of religious and political orthodoxy.

And they are dangerously deceptive. They appear to represent American patriotism, because they wrap themselves in the American flag and use words like "family" and "life" and "tradition."

In fact, their kind of "patriotism" violates every principle of liberty that underlies the American system of government. It is intolerant. It stands against the First Amendment guarantees of freedom of expression and separation of church and state. It threatens academic freedom. And it denies to whole groups of people the equal protection of the laws.

Make no mistake about it: the new evangelicals are not a conservative movement. True conservatives place great value on the Bill of Rights—a time-tested document designed to guarantee individual rights by limiting the powers of government.

In fact, the new evangelicals are a radical anti-Bill-of-Rights movement. They seek not to conserve traditional American values, but to overthrow them. Their agenda represents massive government intrusion. And conservatives as well as liberals should stand up against them.

THE DANGER POINT.

These groups have already had alarming success. They have been pivotal in blocking passage of the E.R.A. in fifteen states. Public school boards all over the country have banned books and imposed prayer and other religious ceremonies. State legislatures have begun placing increasingly severe restrictions on a woman's right to have an abortion. And there is mounting pressure to pass laws requiring the teaching of the Biblical account of creation as an alternative to evolution.

They have grown into a rich and powerful force in this country.

How rich? In a week, the Moral Majority raises a million dollars with its television program.

How powerful? In the last election, key members of Congress were successfully targeted by them for defeat, because of their positions on abortion, E.R.A., and other civil liberties issues.

And the head of the Moral Majority promises more of the same. At a press conference a week after the election, he warned elected officials, both Republican and Democrat, to "get in step" or "be prepared to be unemployed."

Already there is talk of constitutional amendments that would impose prayer in the public schools and outlaw all abortions. And legislation has been introduced that would strip federal courts of their authority even to hear constitutional cases.

In the Senate, Strom Thurmond will now chair the Judiciary Committee, which controls most legislation affecting the courts and the Constitution. Senator Thurmond favors repeal of the Voting Rights Act of 1965, and has announced his support of much of the Moral Majority's program. He has actively opposed civil rights and civil liberties for thirty years. Now he may prevail.

We are facing a major struggle over the Bill of Rights. This struggle does not involve the question of whether the Moral Majority and other groups like them have the right to speak.

They do, and we would defend that right. Even those who oppose the Bill of Rights are protected by the First Amendment. The danger lies in the content of their views, not in their right to express them.

Nor is it a question of partisan politics. There have been shifts of power from one party to another before. That is not what concerns us. The American Civil Liberties Union is non-partisan and does not endorse or oppose candidates for public office. But we will make certain that, whatever other changes may occur in the political arena, the Constitution does not become a casualty of the new order.

WHAT THE ACLU CAN DO.

For 60 years, the American Civil Liberties Union has been the organization that protects the Bill of Rights. As former Chief Justice Earl Warren wrote:

"The ACLU has stood foursquare against the recurring tides of hysteria that from time to time threaten freedoms everywhere...Indeed, it is difficult to appreciate how far our freedoms might have eroded had it not been for the Union's valiant representation in the courts of the constitutional rights of people of all persuasions, no matter how unpopular or even despised by the majority they were at the time."

We've been there in the past and we'll be there in the days ahead. We will meet the anti-Bill-of-Rights forces in the Congress, in the courts, before state and local legislatures, at school board hearings. Wherever they threaten, we will be there—with lawyers, lobbyists, staff and volunteers—to resist their attempts to deprive you of your liberty and violate your rights.

WHAT YOU CAN DO.

The ACLU, like the Moral Majority, depends on individual contributions. But they raise more money in a few weeks than we raise in a year.

We can only be as strong as the number of people who support us. Ultimately, the protection of your rights depends not on legislatures, not on who gets elected President, not even on the courts. It depends on individual citizens, aware of the fragility of liberty, alert to the forces that imperil it, and prepared to give of themselves in order to preserve it.

In the past, when the Bill of Rights was in danger, enough people recognized the threat, and came together in time to repel it. Such a time has come again.

It is up to you to assure that the Bill of Rights will be passed on intact to the next generation.

Please send us your contribution before another day passes.

Without your help, we don't have a prayer.

AMERICAN CIVIL LIBERTIES UNION
Dept. LN, 132 West 43rd Street, New York, NY 10036

☐ I want to join the ACLU and help fight the new anti-Bill-of-Rights movement. Enclosed is my check in the amount indicated below.

☐ I do not want to become a member, but enclosed is my contribution.

☐ I am already an ACLU member; enclosed is an extra contribution.

☐ $25　☐ $50　☐ $100　☐ $1,000　☐ More

NAME _____

ADDRESS _____

CITY _____ STATE _____ ZIP _____

American Civil Liberties Union: Norman Dorsen, President; Ira Glasser, Executive Director

IF THE DEMOCRATS ARE GOOD FOR WORKING PEOPLE,

HOW COME SO MANY PEOPLE AREN'T WORKING?

VOTE REPUBLICAN. FOR A CHANGE.

Corporate Newspaper or Magazine Single

292
Art Director:
Ron Travisano
Writer:
Jerry Della Femina
Designer:
Ron Travisano
Photographer:
Photoworld (FPG)
Client:
New York Mets
Agency:
Della Femina, Travisano & Partners

293
Art Director:
Allen Kay
Writer:
Lois Korey
Client:
Needham, Harper & Steers
Agency:
Needham, Harper & Steers

294
Art Director:
Sal DeVito
Writer:
Norman Muchnick
Photographer:
Cailor/Resnick
Client:
Savin
Agency:
Wells, Rich, Greene

Corporate Newspaper or Magazine Campaign

295
Art Directors:
Sam Scali
Tony DeGregorio
Writers:
Mike Drazen
Steve Kasloff
Designers:
Sam Scali
Tony DeGregorio
Photographers:
Dwayne Michaels
Bob Hamilton
Client:
Sperry Corporation
Agency:
Scali, McCabe, Sloves

This is dedicated to the guys who cried when Thomson connected with Branca's 0 and 1 pitch.

It happened just after 3:00 p.m. on a Wednesday. And if you were a kid at the time, you were probably coming home from school. You could walk down the street and still hear the game because every radio in this town was tuned in.

Then Russ Hodges screamed "The Giants won the pennant! The Giants won the pennant! I can't believe it!" If you were a Giant fan you couldn't believe it either but you were jumping and screaming for joy. If you were a Dodger fan, even though you were too old to do it, you cried. Baseball was that kind of sport for you when you

were a kid. It made you laugh. It made you cry. It gave you heroes you could look up to. It gave you a team that belonged to you and certainly you belonged to them.

The new management of the New York Mets feels your sons and daughters should get to know and enjoy our team the same way you enjoyed the Giants and Dodgers when you were a kid. We have a young team who may not win everyday, but they'll be trying everyday. You and your

kids will get to see players like Lee Mazzilli, John Stearns, Doug Flynn, Craig Swan, Steve Henderson turning into heroes. The kind of heroes your kids and all kids really need.

The Chicago Cubs led by Dave Kingman and Bruce Sutter are coming to town tomorrow (opening day) Friday, Saturday and Sunday.

This weekend give your kids an experience they'll still remember when they're your age. Take them to see the new New York Mets.

The New Mets. The Magic is back.

292

THIS COMMERCIAL RAN JUST 17 TIMES. AND THAT'S GOSPEL.

Some people believe that in order for a commercial to be really effective, it has to run hundreds of times.

That's true. For most commercials.

The original 60-second Xerox "Monk" commercial ran a mere 17 times the first year.

After the very first airing the response began to be felt. We call that High Profile Advertising.

The kind of advertising we do for such clients as McDonald's, Honda, Parkay margarine and many, many more.

Call Joel Baumwoll in New York, Keith Reinhard in Chicago, or Brad Roberts in Los Angeles to find out how we do it.

NEEDHAM, HARPER & STEERS
High Profile Advertising

293

SAVIN ISN'T AS POWER HUNGRY AS XEROX.

Model for model, month for month, year for year, it takes less power to copy with a Savin than to copy with a Xerox.

So when you copy with any Savin, you cut back on your copying expenses without cutting back on your copying.

But that's not the end of it.

Savin has energy-saving automatic shutoff, and doesn't use any power at all except when copying. Xerox uses power even when

it's in standby just waiting to copy. And that means all day, if not all night.

Savin vs. Xerox. We have all the figures. Call us at 914-769-8805, Monday through Friday, 9:00 am to 5:00 pm. It's a powerful argument.

savin

The revolutionary copiers that are winning over big business.

*Savin and Savin logotype are registered trademarks of Savin Corporation. *Xerox is a registered trademark of Xerox Corporation. © 1980 Savin Corporation, Valhalla, N.Y. 10595.

294

"WHAT'S THE POINT OF TALKING, YOU DON'T LISTEN TO ME, ANYWAY."

It starts out innocently enough.

A man tunes in a football game and tunes out his wife's attempts to be heard.

A woman gets so wrapped up in her problems she barely listens as her husband talks about his own.

And before long, without even realizing how it came about, a deadly silence starts to grow between them.

The fact is, listening, like marriage, is a partnership; a shared responsibility between the person speaking and the person listening. And if the listener doesn't show genuine interest and sensitivity to what's being said, the speaker will stop talking. And the communication will fail.

Which is why we at Sperry feel it's so critical that we all become better listeners. In our homes. And in our businesses.

We've recently set up special listening programs that Sperry personnel worldwide can attend. And what we're discovering is that when people really know how to listen (and believe us, there's a lot to know) they can actually encourage the speakers to share more of their thoughts and feelings, bringing everyone closer together.

Which is of great value to us when we do business.

And perhaps even greater value when we go home.

We understand how important it is to listen.

Sperry is Sperry Univac computers, Sperry New Holland farm equipment, Sperry Vickers fluid power systems, and guidance and control equipment from Sperry division and Sperry Flight Systems.

KNOWING HOW TO LISTEN COULD DOUBLE THE EFFICIENCY OF AMERICAN BUSINESS. DID YOU HEAR THAT?

Business today is held together by its communication system. And listening is undoubtedly its weakest link.

Most of us spend about half our business hours listening. Listening poorly. Research studies show that on the average we listen at a 25% level of efficiency.

A statistic that is not only surprisingly low, but terribly costly.

With more than 100 million workers in America, a simple ten dollar listening mistake by each of them would cost a billion dollars.

Letters have to be retyped; appointments rescheduled; shipments reshipped.

And when people in large corporations fail to listen to one another, the results are even costlier.

Ideas get distorted by as much as 80% as they travel through the unwieldy chain of command.

Employees feel more and more distant, and ultimately alienated from top management.

Well, as one of the world's largest corporations—with 87,000 employees and five divisions—we at Sperry simply can't afford to pay the price of poor listening.

So we've set up extensive listening programs that Sperry personnel throughout the world can take part in. From sales representatives to computer engineers to the Chairman of the Board.

These programs are making us a lot better at listening to each other. And when you do business with Sperry Univac, or any of our other divisions, you'll discover that they're making us a lot better at listening to you.

TELL THE CHAIRMAN WE'VE AGREED TO A MERGER WITH SMATHERS & FLATHERS OVER LUNCH.

TELL THE CHAIRMAN WE'VE AGREED TO DISCUSS A MERGER WITH SMATHERS & FLATHERS OVER LUNCH.

TELL THE CHAIRMAN WE'VE AGREED TO HAVE LUNCH WITH SMATHERS & FLATHERS.

TELL THE CHAIRMAN TO ORDER US LUNCH.

We understand how important it is to listen.

Sperry is Sperry Univac computers, Sperry New Holland farm equipment, Sperry Vickers fluid power systems, and guidance and control equipment from Sperry division and Sperry Flight Systems.

How efficient a listener are you?
Write to Sperry, Dept. 4L, 1290 Avenue of the Americas, New York, New York 10019, for a listening quiz that's both fun and a little surprising.

MOST OF AN EXECUTIVE'S TIME IS SPENT LISTENING. YET IT'S THE THING HE'S LEAST QUALIFIED TO DO.

It starts the moment you walk through the door.
The phone rings. You pick it up and listen.
An associate comes into your office with a problem. And you listen.
You rush off to one meeting after another. And listen.
The fact is executives spend more time listening than they do anything else.

But unfortunately, much of this time is wasted.
Research studies show that on the average we listen at a 25% level of efficiency.

A statistic that is not only surprisingly low, but terribly costly.
When executives don't listen effectively, communication breaks down.
Ideas and information get distorted by as much as 80% as they travel through the organization.
Yet as critical as listening is, it's the one skill we're never really trained to do.
Well, as one of the world's largest corporations, we at Sperry are making sure our executives are as qualified at listening as they are at everything else.
We have special listening programs that Sperry employees worldwide can attend. From Sperry Univac computer representatives to Sperry New Holland agricultural engineers to the Chairman of the Board.
These programs are helping us take full advantage of all the time we spend listening.
As a result, when you talk to someone from Sperry, one thing's for certain: Neither of us will be wasting time.

We understand how important it is to listen.

Sperry is Sperry Univac computers, Sperry New Holland farm equipment, Sperry Vickers fluid power systems, and guidance and control equipment from Sperry division and Sperry Flight Systems.

How qualified a listener are you?
Write to Sperry, Dept. 4L, 1290 Avenue of the Americas, New York, New York 10019 for a listening quiz that's both fun and a little surprising.

**Corporate
Outdoor
Single**

296
Art Director & Designer:
Chris Blum
Artist:
Bryan Honkawa
Client:
Levi Strauss
Agency:
**Foote, Cone & Belding/Honig
San Francisco**

Student Competition

297
Art Director & Writer:
Harris M. Weinstein
Product:
Hearty Egg
School:
School of Visual Arts

298
Art Directors & Writers:
**Chris Pogreba
Pat LeBaron
Jeneal Rohrback**
Product:
Fresh Idea Egg
School:
**Art Center College
of Design/Los Angeles**

296

HEARTY EGG Co.

297

298

Student Competition

299
Art Director & Writer:
Paul Shields
Product:
Hen House Egg
School:
School of Visual Arts

300
Art Director & Writer:
Jean Joslin
Product:
Good Egg
School:
School of Visual Arts

301
Art Director & Writer:
Jennifer Kirk
Product:
The Golden Egg
School:
School of Visual Arts

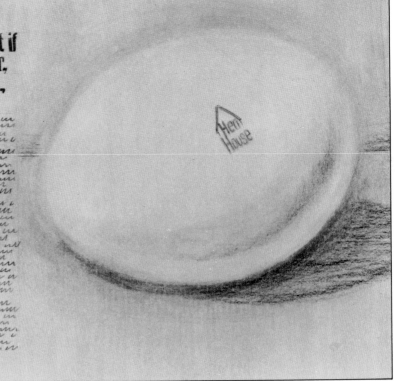

299

300

301

1981 Radio Finalists

Consumer Radio Single

302
Writers:
Kay Kavanagh
Joe Genova
Client:
Sambo's Restaurants
Agency Producer:
Donna LaVallee
Agency:
Bozell & Jacobs

303
Writer:
Seth Tobias
Client:
Patek Philippe Watches
Agency Producer:
Joyce Crosswell
Agency:
Savitt Tobias Balk

304
Writers:
Dick Orkin
Bert Berdis
Client:
Ace Hardware
Agency Producer:
Larry Senten
Agency:
D'Arcy-MacManus & Masius
Chicago

305
Writers:
Russell Dexter
John Wallwork
Client:
New England Telephone
Agency Producers:
Russell Dexter
John Wallwork
Agency:
Harold Cabot/Boston

306
Writer:
John Russo
Client:
WABC-TV
Agency Producer:
Peter Yahr
Agency:
Della Femina, Travisano
& Partners

307
Writer:
Jack Supple
Client:
Oak Grove Dairies
Agency Producer:
Jack Supple
Agency:
Carmichael-Lynch/Mpls.

302

KID: Gee, Uncle Derek, thanks for taking me out to dinner at Sambo's and showing me the ropes.

UNCLE DEREK: Forget it, Richie. Your Dad was plenty good to me when I was your age.

KID: What was Dad like when you two were growing up, Uncle Derek?

UNCLE DEREK: Same swell guy he is today Richie. Of course, back then he didn't have a mustache. Anyway, let me show you around the Sambo's menu kid.

KID: Great—I'm starving.

UNCLE DEREK: Well you're in luck. Sambo's has a special kids' menu—five great dishes you'll love—Chicken, Hot Dogs, Hamburgers, fish and grilled cheese. And they are all just 99¢. So you can eat like an adult without paying like one.

KID: Wow, Uncle Derek, what a great deal. I don't know how to say "Thank you."

UNCLE DEREK: Fortunately, I do. Remember that babysitter with the blonde hair you had last weekend? Why don't you tell her *all* about me. You know, the usual, tall for my age, witty, sensitive...

ANNCR(VO): Sambo's Restaurants: We're bringing down the high price of bringing up your kids! Check your white pages for the address of the Sambo's nearest you.

303

1st ANNCR(VO): Albert Einstein... Harry Truman... Leo Tolstoy... Queen Victoria... Madame Curie ... Richard Wagner... Charles A. Lindbergh... Franz Liszt... FADE UNDER)

2nd ANNCR(VO): For nearly a century and a half, many of the world's most distinguished men and women have worn the world's *most* distinguished timepiece. A Patek Philippe is the almost inevitable choice of heads of state, leaders in the arts, sciences, industry—people of extraordinary accomplishment who enjoy the quiet pride of owning something classically beautiful and absolutely unequaled in craftsmanship. If you already own one, you know that a Patek Philippe doesn't just tell you the time, it tells you something about yourself. If you have thought of owning a Patek Philippe, we'd be happy to send you a brochure of our latest collection. Simply write: Patek Philippe, 10 Rockefeller Plaza, New York 10020. As a Patek owner, you'll enjoy knowing that a Patek Philippe was appreciated for the same reasons by... (FADE UP)

1st ANNCR(VO): Peter Ilich Tchaikovsky... Haile Selassie... Theodore Roosevelt... Rudyard Kipling... Pope Pius X... Arthur Rubenstein... (FADE)

304

DICK: Excuse me, aren't you the ah helpful hardware man?

BERT: Yes I am.

DICK: I knew it (shouts) Shirley!

MIR: What?

DICK: It is him. The Ace Hardware man!

MIR: Really!

DICK: My family's having dinner in this same restaurant right over there.

BERT: That's nice.

DICK: You look older without your Ace Hardware red jacket.

BERT: What??

DICK: But I knew you anyway.

BERT: Thank you and...

DICK: You're always so helpful with tools and paint and automotive stuff.

BERT: I try.

DICK: So whataya think?

BERT: About what?

DICK: Should we order the lamb patties or the Chicken Rococo?

BERT: Oh, see, I just help folks at my Ace Hardware store... Not eh...

DICK: Is '79 a good year for club soda?

BERT: I just know lawn and garden stuff and housewares...

MIR: Ah, you were right it is.

MIR & DICK: The helpful hardware man...

BERT: Hello!

MIR: Say, should my sister elope on the 2nd date?

BERT: What?

MIR: And who pays?

BERT: I'm with Ace Hardware...

MIR: This is Grandpa.

O.M.: Howdy.

MIR: Grandpa this is the helpful hardware man.

BERT: Hi!

O.M.: Should I buy real estate or porkbellies?

BERT: Porkbellies?

MIR: Porkbellies aren't on the menu Grandpa.

DICK: Just lamb patties or chicken.

MIR: What should my sister do?

O.M.: I'll split an order of porkbellies with her...

MIR: I'm talking about the elopement!

BERT: Could I have the check please? (FADING OUT)

JING: *ACE IS THE PLACE WITH THE HELPFUL HARDWARE MAN.*

305

HOST: Welcome to "Win the Big One". Mrs. Simoleon, you're our champion and so far you've won the salami, the bird cage, the water skis, and now you're going for the grand prize. What's your category?

MRS. S.: The telephone.

HOST: All right, question number 1: What's the area code for Moose Hollow, Kentucky?

MRS. S.: 503! 503!

HOST: That's right!

(SFX: APPLAUSE...MUSIC...FANFARE)

Number 2: How many telephones in Frostbite Falls, Minnesota?

MRS. S.: Ah...2

HOST: Amazing!

(SFX: FANFARE, MUSIC)

And now, for the big one:

(SFX: DRUMROLL)

In 1979, how much did New England Telephone customers in Massachusetts pay for Directory Assistance?

MRS. S.: (Screams) Nothing! They didn't pay anything... it's free! (UNDER I won, I won)

(SFX: BUZZER INDICATING WRONG ANSWER)

CROWD: Awww...

ANNCR: In 1979, Directory Assistance cost *50 million dollars* in Massachusetts. And every New England Telephone customer had to share the cost. So please, look up numbers in your telephone book, and then write them down.

(SFX: SLAPS)

HOST: Mrs. Simoleon's O.K., ladies and gentlemen, she's coming around.

MRS. S.: (Groggy) 50 million...oh...can I keep the salami?

306

(MUSIC: "HOW MUCH IS THAT DOGGIE IN THE WINDOW" WITHOUT LYRICS)

(SFX: DOG'S BARK GETS MORE AND MORE FIERCE AND CONTINUES UNDER VO)

ANNCR(VO): Dogs, otherwise known as man's best friend, give a lot of love and companionship. But some canines are receiving a cruel death penalty in return. They're being pitted against one another in a fierce duel to near death. While betting goes on and refreshments are served. The so-called "sport" is called dog fighting and as you'll see on Eyewitness News tonight at 11 o'clock, it's not uncommon even in our area. Tonight at 11 in an Eyewitness News special report "Dog Fighting: Unleashed Violence" Doug Johnson looks to commute the sentence being imposed on dogs.

(MUSIC FADES UP)

(SFX: DOG'S BARK BECOMES A DOG FIGHT)

307

FRAN: The Oak Grove Dairy in Norwood, Minnesota, is supplied by independent farms, producing the best milk they can. Ort Paulson, from the dairy, knows it's worth a little extra effort to go out and get it.

(SFX: DOG'S BARK)

ORT: Okay, I have a lot of questions asked me, 'How can I approach a farm when there's a dog there." Normally, the dogs know me or they know my pickup...uh...(opens door, dog barking very close, slams door) (Ort laughs)...Guess he didn't know me that well. But I know another time I went up to the house, (or *tried* to get to the house), and the dog wouldn't let me up to the house. Uh...it was a small dog and I wasn't worried about it...but the fella that was with me...he got nipped in the pants.

FRAN: Make that extra effort to get Oak Grove Dairy products. One taste'll tell you...Oak Grove Dairy knows the farms that really know their cows.

ORT: You gotta know the dogs, too... (laughs)

(SFX: DOG'S BARK FADES)

Consumer Radio Single

308
Writer:
Ken Schulman
Client:
Sony Corp.
Agency Producer:
Lou DuCharme
Agency:
McCann-Erickson

309
Writer:
Peter Hoffman
Client:
Sony Corp.
Agency Producers:
Tom Jones
Don Thomas
Agency:
McCann-Erickson

310
Writer:
Tom McElligott
Client:
Gokeys
Agency Producer:
Producer: Tom McElligott
Agency:
Lunch Hour

311
Writer:
Tom McElligott
Client:
SIMS
Agency Producer:
Tom McElligott
Agency:
Lunch Hour

312
Writers:
Mike Hughes
Danny Boone
Client:
Kings Dominion
Agency Producer:
Craig Bowlus
Agency:
The Martin Agency/Virginia

313
Writers:
Jay Taub
Ted Shaine
Client:
Chemical Bank
Agency Producer:
Peter Yahr
Agency:
Della Femina, Travisano & Partners

314
Writers:
Jay Taub
John Russo
Ted Shaine
Client:
Chemical Bank
Agency Producer:
Dominique Bigar
Agency:
Della Femina, Travisano & Partners

315
Writers:
Jay Taub
Ted Shaine
Client:
Chemical Bank
Agency Producer:
Dominique Bigar
Agency:
Della Femina, Travisano & Partners

308

ANNCR: This commercial is an exercise in futility. Trying to describe the incredible sound quality of the Sony Soundabout is about as easy as roller skating down Mount Everest. The Soundabout is the world's smallest stereo cassette player. So small you can take it anywhere you go. You listen to it through tiny, featherweight headphones that are so sensitive it sounds like an expensive component stereo. Nothing this small ever sounded this big. To compare it to other portable sound equipment we would have to do something like this... other portables:

(SFX: CHOPSTICKS PLAYED ON THE PIANO)

The Sony Soundabout:

(SFX: THE 1812 OVERTURE)

But we can't come close to describing the actual sound of the Soundabout. So why waste your time listening to a radio commercial, when you can go to a Sony dealer and hear how great it really sounds. Sony, the one and only.

ANNCR: Hear the amazing new Soundabout at your Sony dealer. Your ears won't believe your eyes because nothing this small ever sounded this big. From Sony, the one and only.

309

ANNCR: This is the sound of a revolution. A revolution taking place in the streets. It's the sound of people listening. Listening to music on a revolutionary tape machine called the Sony Walkman. Unless you wear the featherweight headphones, you can't hear the incredible power and stereophonic definition of the Walkman. But you can hear what the Walkman does to people. You can hear them snapping their fingers. Humming along. And even dancing in the streets. And you can see more and more of them every day. Almost everywhere you go. Once you hear the Walkman at your local Sony dealer you'll join the revolution, too. The Walkman. It's from the people who have revolutionized an industry. Sony. The One and Only.

310

RICHARD BASEHART: For over 130 years the tradition has remained unchanged: Hour after hour, they sit at worn benches stitching by hand what a machine could do faster but not nearly so well. They are the Gokeys craftsmen, and it is upon their uncompromising dedication that Gokeys reputation rests most. But it is a dedication that does not stop with Gokeys craftsmen. It extends to the buyer who travels to Scotland for tweeds and Bavaria for crystal. To the sales person who spends the extra time to assure that a skirt or jacket fits properly. Even to the mail boy, who makes certain that each item is wrapped and dispatched with the same care that went into creating it. Which, after all, only makes sense. Because it follows that any store that still cares enough to put 500 hand-stitches into a boot, isn't going to stop caring about everything else. Gokeys... St. Paul, Wayzata, Edina and Rochester.

311

ANNCR: If you're a man who believes in fine traditional clothing, you have two options. The first might go something like this: You take a plane to New York. Catch a cab to midtown Manhattan. Check into the Pierre or the Plaza. See "Evita" or "Sugar Babies" on Broadway. Have a late dinner at The Palm or Chris Cella. And spend the following day shopping for traditional clothing at Brooks Brothers, Paul Stewart or J. Press.
All of which will cost you about $600 give or take a Perrier, *before* you spend anything on clothing.
The second option is somewhat simpler. It doesn't cost as much. It doesn't take as much time. And while, admittedly, it may be less *exciting* than a trip with trimmings to New York, it offers the *same* fine traditional clothing you would *find* in New York...

Sims, Limited... Downtown Minneapolis and Wayzata.

312

ANNCR: Have you heard what people are saying about the new Haunted River at Kings Dominion? Well, about 10 seconds into the ride, this is what E.J. Banister of Norfolk, Virginia, had to say:

(SFX: SCREECH)

And when a hideous face described what was just around the bend, this is what Larry Pipes of Washington, D.C., had to say:

(SFX: SCREAM)

And when Sally Miller of Baltimore, Maryland, was attacked by a giant cobra these were her exact words:

(SFX: YELL)

And when Ronnie Martin and Ed Jones and Barbara Boone and Hal Gibson—all of Roanoke, Virginia—were perched at the top of the mighty drop that would take them who-knows-where, you could hear them say:

(SFX: GROUP YELL)

There's nothing like Kings Dominion's new Haunted River at any other park in Virginia—or anywhere else on earth. It'll make you scream, it'll make you laugh. Now, what have you got to say about that?

(SFX: SCREECH FOLLOWED BY ANNOUNCER'S TERRIFYING LAUGH)

313

(CHINESE MUSIC THROUGHOUT)

ANNCR: This is classical music. It was written over one thousand years ago—in China. But not only is it the music of China, it's the music of Chinatown. Where it's become tradition. A part of that neighborhood's personality and lifestyle. It's one of the elements that give Chinatown its own special chemistry. At Chemical Bank, we know all about chemistry. To us it means keeping perfect time with every community we're in. Sometimes that means opening early. Or closing late. Or having tellers who speak the same language as our customers.

That's why in Chinatown, you'll never hear anyone walk away from our bank, singing the blues.

Chemical Bank. The chemistry's just right at Chemical. Member FDIC.

314

ANNCR: The ocean. It not only covers three-fourths of the world, it's a world unto itself. In fact, you could say it has a chemistry all its own.

Swordfish like the warmer waters of the Gulf Stream off Mexico. Tuna like the open waters of the Pacific Ocean. Lobsters the deep icy waters off the coast of Maine.

Sooner or later, all these fish, and more, wind up at the same place. The Fulton Fish Market. Where we just happen to have a Chemical Bank Branch nearby. And a branch manager who's involved in the fishermen's needs. That's why she'll sometimes stop by the market at 5 in the morning just to say hello. Or bend a few of the old rules to help the fishermen keep their heads above water.

You see, at Chemical, this is just one way we help meet the needs of all of our customers. By meeting the needs of the communities they work and live in.

Which is why from the Atlantic Ocean to the Hudson River and from Long Island Sound to the sounds of the Fulton Fish Market, the chemistry's just right at Chemical. Member F.D.I.C.

315

ANNCR: Take a walk through Spanish Harlem, and you'll find that a rose does really grow there. And not through the cracks in the sidewalk, either. But in gardens. Along with celery, tomatoes, cucumbers and squash. For the fact is, that in New York, there are new types of gardens springing up every day. They're community gardens. And all of them have their roots in Chemical Bank.

You see, Chemical dug up the funds to get those gardens started. And once they got started, there was no stopping them. They blossomed into total community involvement. A chance for the people who live in those communities to work together for their communities. They turned sand lots into lots of fertile soil. And in some places where there was once rubble, you'll now find rhubarb.

Of course, one garden isn't going to change the appearance of an entire community. But we figure even if it only helps a little, it's worth it.

If all this talk seems a little strange coming from a bank—well—Chemical isn't your garden variety bank. Chemical Bank. The chemistry's just right at Chemical.

Consumer Radio Single

316
Writer:
Jim Doherty
Client:
Chemical Bank
Agency Producer:
Dominique Bigar
Agency:
Della Femina, Travisano & Partners

317
Writers:
Jay Taub
Ted Shaine
Client:
Chemical Bank
Agency Producer:
Dominique Bigar
Agency:
Della Femina, Travisano & Partners

318
Writer:
Steve Kasloff
Client:
WNCN-FM
Agency Producer:
Gary Grossman
Agency:
Scali, McCabe, Sloves

319
Writer:
Steve Kasloff
Client:
WNCN-FM
Agency Producer:
Gary Grossman
Agency:
Scali, McCabe, Sloves

320
Writers:
Ron Travisano
Jerry Della Femina
Client:
New York Mets
Agency Producer:
Peter Yahr
Agency:
Della Femina, Travisano & Partners

321
Writers:
Ron Travisano
Jerry Della Femina
Client:
New York Mets
Agency Producer:
Peter Yahr
Agency:
Della Femina, Travisano & Partners

322
Writers:
Ron Travisano
Sheila Moore
Client:
American Automobile Association
Agency Producer:
Peter Yahr
Agency:
Della Femina, Travisano & Partners

316
ANNCR: Now for an update from our traffic reporter in the sky. Come in, Jim.

JIM: Okay, eastbound on the Long Island Expressway traffic is still bumper-to-bumper because of a jackknifed trailer truck in the right lane...

ANNCR: Believe it or not, the Island does have an expressway that really is an expressway. In fact, you drive it whenever you visit any one of Chemical Bank's one hundred and six auto teller windows. About the only time your car's not moving is when Chemical's experienced tellers are taking care of you personally. Serving all your banking needs at high speed. Whether you're making a deposit, cashing a check, or just checking your balance. And while Chemical wastes no time serving you, it does give you plenty of time to choose when you want service. That's why, on Fridays, you can visit many of Chemical's auto tellers as early as 8:00 in the morning. Or as late as 8:30 in the evening. And, you can even bank on Saturdays.

So if you've got the drive, find out why, any time, day or evening—all over Long Island—the chemistry's just right at Chemical. Chemical–Long Island.
Member FDIC.

317
ANNCR: This message is brought to you by Chemical Bank.

IRISH DOORMAN: If I were a rich man, Daidle, deedle, daidle, dig-guh, digguh, deedle, daidle, dum.

JEWISH HOT DOG VENDOR: All day long I'd biddy, biddy bum, If I were a wealthy man.

SPANISH SHOE SHINE MAN: Wouldn't have to work hard, Daidle, deedle, daidle, digguh, digguh, deedle, daidle, dum.

BLACK WAITRESS: If I were a biddy, biddy rich, digguh, digguh, deedle, daidle man.

WASP BANKER: If I were a rich man, daidle, deedle, daidle, digguh, digguh, deedle, daidle, dum—

(MUSIC UNDER)

ANNCR: At Chemical Bank we offer you Passbook Savings, Savings Certificates, and several other savings programs that come with assured interest rates. All of which can make you a little richer.

CHINESE STORE OWNER: All day long I'd biddy, biddy bum, if I were a wealthy man.

(MUSIC CONTINUES)

ANNCR: The Chemistry's just right for savers at Chemical. Member FDIC. Additional information available at every branch.

318
(MUSIC)

ANNCR: You've probaby rarely heard the piece of music you are listening to. Which is not a rare occurrence on WNCN. We feel no matter how much you may love Figaro or Faust, you don't want to hear it every time you turn on the radio. On WNCN you won't.

Our classical music library contains well over 15,000 *different* records. So many, we had to reinforce the library floor with steel beams. And install an electrostatic air cleaner just to control dust. And hire a programmer with a degree from Juilliard to keep track of the 140,000 index cards separating Schubert from Strauss from Stravinsky.

The more you listen to WNCN, the more you expand your own knowledge of classical music.

So why listen to a classical station that plays only what you've heard before, when you can tune in WNCN 104.3 FM, and get something that is truly rare these days. Something *new*.

WNCN. The only classical station worthy of the music.

319
(MUSIC)

ANNCR: WNCN is not the only classical station to play a Bach Cantata. Yet you'll hear a major difference in it when *we* play it.

That difference is quality of sound.

We measured the seismic vibrations of the earth before choosing a location for our studio.

We built our entire studio on massive shock absorbing pins to absorb vibrations the way your turntable does.

We installed a complex electrostatic air cleaning system just to control dust.

Where most stations merely wipe their records clean, we actually wash ours, in a special cleansing bath.

If all this sounds like fanaticism, it's because it is.

At WNCN, we're committed to bringing you the ultimate in classical music. If you want to hear just how committed, keep listening to 104.3 FM. And ask yourself, when was the last time your stereo sounded this good?

WNCN. The only classical station worthy of the music.

320

(MUSIC: "TAKE ME OUT TO THE BALLGAME" SOFTLY THROUGHOUT)

(SFX: CROWD NOISES)

ANNCR: The New York Mets for the first time in their history have gone into first place in the National League race!...
Ron Swoboda, with a line drive home run over the left field wall!...
And the Mets are the National League champions!

(MUSIC UP AND UNDER)

This is the sound of Shea Stadium. It's filled with memories of the past and promise of the future.

Shea Stadium. Where you can show your kids what real heroes are all about.

There's a magic coming back to Shea in the 1980 Mets. Mazzilli, Flynn, Henderson, Zachary, Sterns, Swann... They're all going to play their hearts out for you.

Shea Stadium in 1980...

The magic is back.

(MUSIC FADES)

321

(SFX: HODGES EXCERPT UNDER)

VO: It happened in 1951. And if you were a kid at the time, you were probably coming home from school. This is what you heard:

(SFX: HODGES EXCERPT UP):
There's a long drive! It's gonna be, I believe... the Giants win the Pennant! The Giants win the Pennant! The Giants win the Pennant!

(SFX: FADE UNDER)

VO: If you were a Giant fan, you were screaming for joy. If you were a Dodger fan, even though you were too old to do it, you cried. Baseball was that kind of sport for you. The new management of the New York Mets feels your sons and daughters should enjoy our team the same way you enjoyed the Giants and Dodgers. We have a young team who may not win every day, but they'll be trying every day. You and your kids will get to see players like Mazzilli, Flynn, Swann, turning into heroes. Give your kids an experience they'll always remember. Take them to see the new New York Mets. The magic is back.

(SFX: HODGES EXCERPT UP):
They're going crazy! They're going crazy! Oh!

(SFX: FADE OUT)

322

(SFX: RAIN THROUGHOUT)

VO: Sooner or later, just about everybody gets stuck. And if you belong to the wrong auto club...

(SFX: CLAP OF THUNDER)

you're not only stuck, you're alone.

(SFX: DIALING, RINGING, RECEIVER LIFT)

1st ATTENDANT: Abbot's Garage.

WOMAN: Hello, I'm stuck and I need a tow...

1st ATTENDANT: Sorry, my tow truck's got a flat.

(SFX: DIALING, RINGING, RECEIVER LIFT)

RECORDING: Johnson's Full-Service Auto Center...

WOMAN: Oh, thank heaven.

RECORDING: We're closed now, but at the sound of the beep, leave your name and number...

(SFX: BEEP)

(SFX: THUNDER CLAP)

VO: With AAA, you're never alone. We give you day and night emergency numbers for help in any part of the country.

(SFX: DIALING, RINGING, RECEIVER LIFT)

2nd ATTENDANT: Wilson's Garage.

WOMAN: (Desperately) Please. I really need a tow... And, uh, I don' have much cash, but I can give you a personal check...

2nd ATTENDANT: Ha, ha, ha, ha,...

VO: AAA. We'll never leave you alone.

Consumer Radio Single

323
Writers:
Rita Senders
Phil Silvestri
Client:
WABC-TV
Agency Producer:
Tom Barnet
Agency:
Della Femina, Travisano & Partners

324
Writer:
Larry Plapler
Client:
Kronenbourg, U.S.A.
Agency Producer:
Rachel Novak
Agency:
Levine, Huntley, Schmidt, Plapler & Beaver

325
Writer:
Larry Plapler
Client:
Kronenbourg, U.S.A.
Agency Producer:
Rachel Novak
Agency:
Levine, Huntley, Schmidt, Plapler & Beaver

326
Writer:
Lee Garfinkel
Client:
Ferrarelle
Agency Producer:
Rachel Novak
Agency:
Levine, Huntley, Schmidt, Plapler & Beaver

327
Writer:
Lee Garfinkel
Client:
Ferrarelle
Agency Producer:
Rachel Novak
Agency:
Levine, Huntley, Schmidt, Plapler & Beaver

328
Writer:
Lee Garfinkel
Client:
Ferrarelle
Agency Producer:
Ellen Grunwald
Agency:
Levine, Huntley, Schmidt, Plapler & Beaver

329
Writer:
Phil Becker
Client:
Amtrak
Agency Producer:
Gloria Gengo
Agency:
Needham, Harper & Steers

330
Writer:
Carl Ames
Client:
Mueller Chemical
Agency Producer:
Carl Ames
Agency:
Advertising, Boelter & Lincoln/Wis.

323

(Jim speaks in four completely different voices)

JIM: I'm nine years old.

I like to fix cars.

I've just got to try and get over the rainbow.

If one of us couldn't cope with what was happening there was always someone that could.

VO: These are four of the 80 people that live in Jim's body.

Tonight on an Eyewitness News special report at 11 watch Multiple Personalities: People in Pieces.

And find out what can be so horrifying to someone that it takes 80 people to bear the pain.

JIM: I don' really have any problems.

VO: Tonight at 11 on Channel 7.

324

(MUSIC THROUGHOUT)

VO: Kronenbourg beer talks about things you like and things you love.

SHE: Lance, I love this bar...it's cute. I love that bartender...he's cute.

HE: Bartender, two Kronenbourg beers.

SHE: Oh Lance, I love Kronenbourg beer...it's cute.

HE: Enid, often times you say things are cute and that you love them. But you never say you love me.

SHE: I like you Lance...I like you. Don' you just love the Kronenbourg bottle...isn' it cute.

HE: Enid how could you love a bottle...but only like me?

SHE: Don't be jealous. I love almost everything. Ooooh I love these cute napkins.

HE: You love a napkin. Enid I want to hear you say you love *me*.

SHE: Lance...you ask too much.

VO: Some things you like...some things you love. Europeans drink and enjoy more Kronenbourg than any other bottle of beer. They like Heineken...but love Kronenbourg. America, now that you've tried the beer Europe likes, try the beer Europe loves.

Kronenbourg. Europe's #1 bottle of beer.

Imported by Kronenbourg U.S.A. Greenwich Connecticut.

HE: Enid, think of me as a giant napkin and press me to your lips.

325

(MUSIC THROUGHOUT)

VO: Kronenbourg beer talks about things you like and things you love.

HE: Bartender...two Kronenbourg beers, please.

SHE: Marty, thanks for the pin you sent me.

HE: Well, Sarah, something special for someone special.

SHE: It's shaped like a heart Marty...what are you trying to tell me?

HE: Well I wanted you to know that I like you.

SHE: Like isn' the magic word Marty.

HE: Sarah, I like you intensely.

SHE: What do you think of chocolate?

HE: Love it.

SHE: Having your back scratched?

HE: Love it.

SHE: Kronenbourg beer?

HE: I love it.

SHE: Now what do you think of me?

HE: What's not to like?

VO: Some things you like...some things you love. Europeans drink and enjoy more Kronenbourg than any other bottle of beer. They like Heineken...but love Kronenbourg. America, now that you've tried the beer Europe likes, try the beer Europe loves.

Kronenbourg. Europe's #1 bottle of beer.

Imported by U.S.A. Greenwich Connecticut.

HE: Sarah, I think I've fallen in like with you.

326

ANNCR: Announcing a major change in the English language. We propose changing the awkward word "water" to the much simpler "Ferrarelle".

We feel this change will enhance such sayings as "last night I slept on a very comfortable Ferrarelle bed".

And who could forget that great motion picture "On the Ferrarelle Front"?

Remember when a certain president made headlines with "Ferrarelle Gate"?

Simple phrases like "Ferrarelle boy", "Ferrarelle melon", and she makes my mouth "Ferrarelle" are all greatly improved.

And instead of asking for the other mineral Ferrarelles, we'd prefer you ask for Ferrarelle Ferrarelle. The pure mineral water imported from Italy. Ferrarelle has been quenching Italian thirsts for more than 2000 years. It's perfectly carbonated by nature and mixes beautifully with everything.

So we suggest, why pronounce a tongue twister like "water" when it's so easy to say Ferrarelle.

327

ANNCR: We're changing the awkward word "water" to the much simpler word "Ferrarelle".

MAN #1: If you do that, you're going to be in hot Ferrarelle.

WOMAN #1: He's like a fish out of Ferrarelle.

MAN #2: I stopped jogging when my doctor said I had Ferrarelle on the knee.

MAN #1: That argument doesn' hold Ferrarelle.

WOMAN #2: Honey, I can't hear you with the Ferrarelle running.

MAN #3: She's spending my money like Ferrarelle.

MAN #1: Still Ferrarelle runs deep.

MAN #2: You can bring a horse to Ferrarelle, but you can't make him drink.

ANNCR: Pure Ferrarelle mineral water imported from Italy. Ferrarelle Ferrarelle has been quenching Italian thirsts for more than 2000 years. It's perfectly carbonated by nature and mixes beautifully with everything. So we suggest, why say something as difficult as water, when you can say something as simple as Ferrarelle.

MAN #2: My accountant says I'm going to have a hard time keeping my head above Ferrarelle.

328

ANNCR: Announcing a great event in literary and motion picture history. From this day forth, all novels, history books, plays and films shall replace the awkward word "water" with the much simpler "Ferrarelle."

SOLDIER: Gunga Din, bring more Ferrarelle.

MOTHER: Jack and Jill went up a hill to fetch a pail of Ferrarelle.

DRACULA: Good evening, who says blood is thicker than Ferrarelle?

FRENCHMAN: Napoleon, you've met your Ferrarelle-loo.

FEMALE SHAKESPEARE TYPE: We never know the worth of Ferrarelle till the well is dry.

MAN: Just when you thought it was safe to go back in the Ferrarelle.

(SFX: JAWS TYPE MUSIC)

ANNCR: Pure Ferrarelle mineral water—imported from Italy. Ferrarelle has been quenching Italian thirsts for over 2000 years. It's perfectly carbonated by nature and mixes beautifully with everything.

So why pronounce a tongue twister like "water" when it's easy to say "Ferrarelle".

MAN: Some say he can walk on Ferrarelle.

329

SINGERS: *America's getting into training*

REPORTER: (Anxious) Some rapidly moving objects, unseen in this area before, have been sighted between New Haven, Hartford and Springfield. Silver metallic in color, these objects are reportedly operating at a very high frequency. One is approaching us now.

(SFX: NEW TRAIN PULLING UP AND STOPPING. FOOTSTEPS OF PEOPLE EXITING)

REPORTER: Sir, you were actually on board. Could you tell our audience what it was like?

MAN: It was wonderful. The one I was on was brand new. They had plush, comfortable reclining seats.

REPORTER: What exactly did you do on board?

MAN: Well, some work. Some sleep. Enjoyed the scenery.

REPORTER: And how did you manage to get a trip on one of these objects?

MAN: I usually call my travel agent or Amtrak.

REPORTER: Amtrak.

(AMTRAK MUSIC AND SINGERS UP)

SINGERS: *America is getting into training, training the Amtrak way.*

ANNCR: This Halloween prank was brought to you by Amtrak.
Now with direct weekday service to Hartford and Springfield twelve times a day.

330

(SFX: MAN MOANING THROUGHOUT)

ANNCR: Even before you're really awake, you know what it's going to be like. Keen knives of brilliant, blinding light streak into the slits of your swollen eyelids. You can hear the woman next door screeching a hot steaming iron across a wrinkled shirt. If you could speak, the only thing you could think of would be: "Did I have a good time?" And it occurs to you that the only way you could have gotten that taste in your mouth... was because as you went to sleep with one foot on the floor while staring at the ceiling light... you ate one of your socks last night.

(SFX: MAN GETTING SICK)

ANNCR: Unwrap a piece of Quench Gum! Force it into your mouth and chew. A warm surge of lemoniness rushes into your head; Quench brings moisture back... the tart fruity taste refreshes, and most important... gives you enough energy to find the aspirin.

MAN: Give me strength!

ANNCR: Quench gum is no ordinary gum. It's the official gum of the marathon... because it quenches.

Consumer Radio
Single

331
Writers:
Jerry Kloppenburg
Dick Orkin
Bert Berdis
Client:
Koss Corp.
Agency Producers:
Jerry Kloppenburg
Rex Teich
Agency:
Kloppenburg, Switzer & Teich

332
Writer:
Dan Goldstein
Client:
Seattle Trust &
Savings Bank
Agency Producer:
Dan Goldstein
Agency:
Dancer Fitzgerald Sample
San Francisco

333
Writers:
Dick Orkin
Bert Berdis
Client:
Astoria Federal Savings
& Loan Assoc.
Agency Producer:
Ken Rabasca
Agency:
Greenstone & Rabasca

Consumer Radio
Campaign

334
Writer:
John Russo
Client:
WABC-TV
Agency Producer:
Peter Yahr
Agency:
Della Femina, Travisano
& Partners

335
Writer:
Tom McElligott
Client:
Pontillo's Pizzeria
Agency Producers:
Tom McElligott
Mal Sharpe
Agency:
Lunch Hour

331
(MUSIC: BEETHOVEN'S MOONLIGHT SONATA—UP
AND UNDER)

WINSTON: I'm listening to this beautiful Beethoven
sonata on my new Koss stereophones. I can turn
the volume up as high as I want and know I'm
not disturbing anyone else, and no one can
disturb me. Unless, of course, I take them off...

(SFX: DOG'S BARK)

BUTCHIE: Pop, can I borrow the car and ten bucks
and your bowling ball and...

WINSTON: Sorry, Butchie. Can't hear you. (Chuckle)
He'll go to his room now and practice his Tarzan
yells. But, I don't care. Not while I'm wearing my
Koss stereophones and getting such beautiful full
reproduction. Oh-oh, here comes my daughter
Jennie. Let me see what she wants...

(SFX: TARZAN YELLS IN BACKGROUND)

JENNIE: Daddy, Butchie just flushed my homework
down the...

WINSTON: Sorry, Princess, later. Wearing my Koss
stereophones is like having a whole new record
library. I get so much more out of my records
and tapes, plus nobody pounds the walls and
tells me to...

(SFX: BABY'S CRY)

WIFE: Winston, I told you to take out the garbage and
feed the cat. And another thing...

WINSTON: Yes, Dear. You're absolutely right. Yes, I'm
listening to you.

ANNCR(VO): Look for Koss stereophones wherever
fine stereo equipment is sold.

332
DIRECTOR: (from control booth throughout) Mr.
Voice?

MR. VOICE: Yes?

DIRECTOR: Read the script?

MR. VOICE: Yes. It's very creative.

DIRECTOR: Thank you.

WOMAN PRODUCER: (from control booth throughout) Thank you.

DIRECTOR: O.K. Seattle Trust Saturday Banking.
Mr. Voice. Take one.

MR. VOICE: Seattle Trust offers full service Saturday
banking at all these convenient locations:
Northgate, University, Crossroads, Burien,
Renton, Lacey—Wait a minute. Do I really have
to read all these?

DIRECTOR: He's right.

WOMAN PRODUCER: And a little more sincere this
time.

DIRECTOR: Scratch the locations.

MR. VOICE: Right.

DIRECTOR: And more sincere.

MR. VOICE: Sincere? Sure.

DIRECTOR: Rolling.

MR. VOICE: (sensitive and fragile) Seattle Trust
offers—

DIRECTOR: No, I think a manly-mature type thing
would be—

MR. VOICE: Gotchya.

WOMAN PRODUCER: Good direction.

DIRECTOR: Take 3.

MR. VOICE: (as old man) Saturday banking at
Seattle—

DIRECTOR: That same feeling, but more now-
contempo.

MR. VOICE: (as FM disc jockey) Hey, Seattle Trust
offers ten locations of Saturday banking.

DIRECTOR: Close.

WOMAN PRODUCER: But for a terrific service like
this, what we really want is—

MR. VOICE: Listen, why don' you read it.

WOMAN PRODUCER: Me?

MR. VOICE: Just to give me an idea of what you're
after.

WOMAN PRODUCER: Oh. O.K. Seattle Trust offers
full service Saturday banking. Like that.

MR. VOICE: Ah. Here goes. (clears throat, reads in
woman producer's voice) Seattle Trust offers full
service Saturday banking. Seattle Trust. Person-
to-person banking. Member FDIC.

WOMAN PRODUCER: Amazing!

DIRECTOR: Bravo!

MR. VOICE: Thank you. Where do I sign?

BERT: So, Mr. Bagely, you're applying for a job as one of Astoria's friendly tellers?

DICK: (Loud) That's right, Buster!

BERT: Ahuh... Well, let's suppose I'm one of Astoria's loyal customers. I walk up to the window and you say...?

DICK: Next window.

BERT: No.

DICK: Get in line.

BERT: No, no.

DICK: I'm out to lunch (No) supper (No) late night snack? (No)

BERT: Mr. Bagely, with all of our branches, Astoria Federal is known as a neighborhood bank. So we say...

DICK: Turn down that stereo.

BERT: No.

DICK: Get your dog off my lawn.

BERT: No...

DICK: Who swiped my newspaper?

BERT: Look, we provide service with a smile, recognize our customers and say things like...

DICK: Hi, Baldy, wanna cash a check?

BERT: Mr. Bagely, you're just not right for Astoria Federal. I'm sorry.

DICK: You're sorry. Boy, I'll never get my old job back.

BERT: What was that?

DICK: Librarian.

BERT: Librarian?

DICK: I don't know why they fired me. One day they...

ANNCR: Astoria Federal Savings. We've got lots of convenient branches filled with lots of friendly folks to help you. No wonder so many people save with Astoria. We're right on the money.

(MUSIC: "HOW MUCH IS THAT DOGGIE IN THE WINDOW" WITHOUT LYRICS)

(SFX: DOG'S BARK GETS MORE AND MORE FIERCE AND CONTINUES UNDER VO)

ANNCR(VO): Dogs, otherwise known as man's best friend, give a lot of love and companionship. But some canines are receiving a cruel death penalty in return. They're being pitted against one another in a fierce duel to near death. While betting goes on and refreshments are served. The so-called "sport" is called dog fighting and as you'll see on Eyewitness News tonight at 11 o'clock, it's not uncommon even in our area. Tonight at 11 in an Eyewitness News special report "Dog Fighting: Unleashed Violence" Doug Johnson looks to commute the sentence being imposed on dogs.

(MUSIC FADES UP)

(SFX: DOG'S BARK BECOMES A DOG FIGHT)

MAL SHARPE: From New York City this is Mal Sharpe. Today I'm at the feast of San Gennero in Little Italy... and do *you* like New York style pizza?

FIRST LADY: Very good—I love it.

MAL SHARPE: You love the pizza here?

FIRST MAN: This pizza here is very good... it's one of the best in the country here.

FIRST LADY: Mmmmmm lots of cheese—cooked well.

MAL SHARPE: How would you feel if I told you that this pizza actually comes from the Twin cities?

SECOND LADY: Minnesota, Minneapolis? No, those people don't know how to make pizza like this.

MAL SHARPE: It comes from Minneapolis–St. Paul. It comes from Pontillo's.

SECOND MAN: Minneapolis this comes from?

MAL SHARPE: OK—let's...

SECOND MAN: Now wait—come here—I got some Midwestern pizza you gotta try here.

MAL SHARPE: This pizza comes from Pontillo's.

THIRD MAN: Is that right?

MAL SHARPE: Yeah—St. Paul. He's taking another bite here.

THIRD LADY: That pizza was exquisite! It was delicious!

MAL SHARPE: People are going crazy here in New York City for Pontillo's pizza.

THIRD LADY: (Several words in Italian)

MAL SHARPE: Good luck to you.

THIRD LADY: Thank you.

SECOND MAN: Did you ever know that they made pizza in Minneapolis? I mean that is one of the things that Minneapolis is *not* known for. Until today. Until today.

THIRD MAN: Hey... good luck to the Minneapolis Twins out there.

Consumer Radio Campaign

336
Writer:
Steve Kasloff
Client:
WNCN-FM
Agency Producer:
Gary Grossman
Agency:
Scali, McCabe, Sloves

337
Writers:
Jay Taub
Ted Shaine
John Russo
Client:
Chemical Bank
Agency Producers:
Dominique Bigar
Peter Yahr
Agency:
Della Femina, Travisano & Partners

338
Writer:
Lee Garfinkel
Client:
Ferrarelle
Agency Producer:
Rachel Novak
Agency:
Levine, Huntley, Schmidt, Plapler & Beaver

339
Writer:
Curvin O'Rielly
Client:
Saab-Scania
Agency Producer:
Janine Marjollet
Agency:
Ally & Gargano

340
Writers:
Dave Butler
Bill Hamilton
Jeff Roll
Client:
Yamaha
Agency Producer:
Richard O'Neill
Agency:
Chiat/Day-Los Angeles

341
Writer:
Larry Plapler
Client:
Kronenbourg, U.S.A.
Agency Producer:
Rachel Novak
Agency:
Levine, Huntley, Schmidt, Plapler & Beaver

342
Writer:
Fred Siegel
Client:
Miller Brewing
Agency Producer:
Marc Mayhew
Agency:
Backer & Spielvogel

336
(MUSIC)
ANNCR: WNCN is not the only classical station to play a Bach Cantata. Yet you'll hear a major difference in it when *we* play it.

That difference is quality of sound.

We measured the seismic vibrations of the earth before choosing a location for our studio.

We built our entire studio on massive shock absorbing pins to absorb vibrations the way your turntable does.

We installed a complex electrostatic air cleaning system just to control dust.

Where most stations merely wipe their records clean, we actually wash ours, in a special cleansing bath.

If all this sounds like fanaticism, it's because it is.

At WNCN, we're committed to bringing you the ultimate in classical music. If you want to hear just how committed, keep listening to 104.3 FM. And ask yourself, when was the last time your stereo sounded this good?

WNCN. The only classical station worthy of the music.

337
ANNCR: The ocean. It not only covers three-fourths of the world, it's a world unto itself. In fact, you could say it has a chemistry all its own.

Swordfish like the warmer waters of the Gulf Stream off Mexico. Tuna like the open waters of the Pacific Ocean. Lobsters the deep icy waters off the coast of Maine.

Sooner or later, all these fish, and more, wind up at the same place. The Fulton Fish Market. Where we just happen to have a Chemical Bank Branch nearby. And a branch manager who's involved in the fishermen's needs. That's why she'll sometimes stop by the market at 5 in the morning just to say hello. Or bend a few of the old rules to help the fishermen keep their heads above water.

You see, at Chemical, this is just one way we help meet the needs of all of our customers. By meeting the needs of the communities they work and live in.

Which is why from the Atlantic Ocean to the Hudson River and from Long Island Sound to the sounds of the Fulton Fish Market, the chemistry's just right at Chemical. Member F.D.I.C.

338
ANNCR: Announcing a great event in literary and motion picture history. From this day forth, all novels, history books, plays and films shall replace the awkward word "water" with the much simpler "Ferrarelle."

SOLDIER: Gunga Din, bring more Ferrarelle.

MOTHER: Jack and Jill went up a hill to fetch a pail of Ferrarelle.

DRACULA: Good evening, who says blood is thicker than Ferrarelle?

FRENCHMAN: Napoleon, you've met your Ferrarelle-loo.

FEMALE SHAKESPEARE TYPE: We never know the worth of Ferrarelle till the well is dry.

MAN: Just when you thought it was safe to go back in the Ferrarelle.

(SFX: JAWS TYPE MUSIC)

ANNCR: Pure Ferrarelle mineral water—imported from Italy. Ferrarelle has been quenching Italian thirsts for over 2000 years. It's perfectly carbonated by nature and mixes beautifully with everything.

So why pronounce a tongue twister like "water" when it's easy to say "Ferrarelle".

MAN: Some say he can walk on Ferrarelle.

339
FRANK CONVERSE: Saab skimps on nothing. The Saab 900 GLE, for example, outslaloms the BMW 528i, a car known for its agility. Stops faster than the Volvo GLE, a car known for its breaking. And is more comfortable than the Mercedes Benz 280E, a car known for the way it coddles passengers. And besides beating all those cars in areas where they would like to be thought invincible, the Saab, according to official Government measurements, is bigger inside than all of them and costs less than all of them. All told, the Saab is so rare an automotive accomplishment, it's worth your attention on curiosity alone.

340

(MUSIC SLOWER YAHAMA THEME)

ANNCR: You ladies out there who've spent a lot of time on a motorcycle probably spent most of it looking at the back of your boyfriend's helmet. Well, if you loved the experience, but hated the view, here's a suggestion. Get your own motorcycle. Now, most of the bikes you see will fall into one of two categories. Tall and handsome, or short and ugly. Until you see the Yamaha Exciter 185. It looks like a motorcycle should. Feels like it, too. And does 55 easy. And gets about 90 miles per gallon. And, you know, when you're tooling around on a Yamaha, you're one lady who doesn't take a back seat to anyone. Isn't that the way it should be?

(MUSIC UP AND OUT)

341

(MUSIC THROUGHOUT)

VO: Kronenbourg beer talks about things you like and things you love.

SHE: Lance, I love this bar... it's cute. I love that bartender... he's cute.

HE: Bartender, two Kronenbourg beers.

SHE: Oh Lance, I love Kronenbourg beer... it's cute.

HE: Enid, often times you say things are cute and that you love them. But you never say you love me.

SHE: I like you Lance... I like you. Don't you just love the Kronenbourg bottle... isn't it cute.

HE: Enid how could you love a bottle... but only like me?

SHE: Don't be jealous. I love almost everything. Ooooh I love these cute napkins.

HE: You love a napkin. Enid I want to hear you say you love me.

SHE: Lance... you ask too much.

VO: Some things you like... some things you love. Europeans drink and enjoy more Kronenbourg than any other bottle of beer. They like Heineken... but love Kronenbourg. America, now that you've tried the beer Europe likes, try the beer Europe loves.

Kronenbourg. Europe's #1 bottle of beer.

Imported by Kronenbourg U.S.A. Greenwich Connecticut.

HE: Enid, think of me as a giant napkin and press me to your lips.

342

ANNCR: Rodney Dangerfield and Grits Gresham for Lite Beer from Miller.

(SFX: BAR SOUNDS, LAUGHING ETC.)

RODNEY: Hey, you're the world's greatest fisherman, and you want to buy me a Lite Beer from Miller? Now *that's* respect.

GRITS: Well, it's not every day someone hauls in a beauty like the one you got out there on the dock. What is she, about a fifty pound Wahoo?

RODNEY: No, that's one of my kids; look more to your left—that Marlin over there. Oooh, is she big!

GRITS: Sure is. She must have put up one heck of a fight...

RODNEY: You kidding? I haven't fought a fish like that since my mother-in-law moved in. That fish was tough! She thought the *boat* was the *bait!*

GRITS: Well, how'd you get her in? You had to use the right hook.

RODNEY: ... And a left jab too! That fish was tough—and I needed something myself—a Lite Beer from Miller. Lite tastes great, and it's less filling. I mean, when you're fighting a big one like that, you don't want to get filled up, you kidding?

GUY: Ah, excuse me, are you Rodney Dangerfield.

RODNEY: Another fisherman! Want my autograph? Or how about a picture of me and the fish?

GUY: No, I'm Nick from Nick and Louie's fish market. You owe us 83 bucks for that Marlin out there. You want to pay cash or... uh...

ANNCR: Lite Beer from Miller. Everything you always wanted in a beer. And less.

Miller Brewing Company, Milwaukee, Wisconsin.

Public Service Radio Single

343
Writer:
Peter Cascone
Client:
Ad Council
Agency Producer:
Peter Cascone
Agency:
Needham, Harper & Steers

344
Writers:
James Gartner
Ron Anderson
Client:
The Church of Jesus Christ of Latter-day Saints
Agency Producer:
James Gartner
Agency:
Bonneville Productions/Utah

Public Service Radio Campaign

345
Writer:
Peter Cascone
Client:
Ad Council
Agency Producer:
Peter Cascone
Agency:
Needham, Harper & Steers

Corporate Radio Single

346
Writer:
Nina Feinberg
Client:
Air California
Agency Producer:
Martin Rubenstein
Agency:
Phillips-Ramsey/Chicago

347
Writer:
Steve Kasloff
Client:
Sperry Corporation
Agency Producer:
Richard Berke
Agency:
Scali, McCabe, Sloves

Corporate Radio Campaign

348
Writer:
Steve Kasloff
Client:
Sperry Corporation
Agency Producer:
Richard Berke
Agency:
Scali, McCabe, Sloves

349
Writer:
June Rachelson
Client:
Exxon
Agency Producer:
Ellen Schwartz
Agency:
McCaffrey & McCall

343

ANNCR: Almost all the tabulations are in and the apparent winning candidates are...(UNDER) shown here on our big board.

MARGE: Lou, it's not going to change. Let's go to sleep. (Turns off TV)

LOU: You never know, not all the votes are counted yet. (Turns on TV)

ANNCR: And here's the way the votes are distributed...

MARGE: (Turns off TV) Come on, Lou, it's over, they lost, face it.

LOU: I just can't believe it, maybe there'll be a last minute turn-around. (Turns on TV)

ANNCR: Stay tuned for tonight's late, late movie, "The Plant That Ate Cleveland". (MUSIC UNDER)

MARGE: Lou, please don't torture yourself. (Turns off TV) Look, you voted, you did the best you could, why don't you forget it and go to sleep.

LOU: I didn't vote.

MARGE: What!

LOU: I meant to, but I didn'.

MARGE: Oh, I see...guilt...well, it's too late now.

LOU: By the way, Marge, who did you finally vote for?

MARGE: Go to sleep, Lou, tomorrow is a new day.

LOU: Oh, no, my own wife?...How could you do that?

MARGE: (Sardonically) It was easy, you go into the booth, turn the switches, pull the lever...

ANNCR: "I should have voted". You know that's what you're going to say if your candidates don't win. A public service of the National Association of Secretaries of State and The Advertising Council.

344

ANNCR: It isn't fair.

MAN: There isn't a day that goes by that I'm not acutely aware of the fact that I don't have my wife. When you go to bed at night, you're alone. And you wake up in the morning and you're alone again. That's the roughest part of the whole thing.

ANNCR: It just isn't fair.

MAN: In the beginning, it's important to suffer and let the grief come out. But after a while you've just got to put the grief aside. You can't make it a life of grief. You've got to recover, you've got to overcome.

ANNCR: It isn't fair. It's life. And sometimes it hurts. But it's not what life does to you, it's what you do with life. From the Mormons. The Church of Jesus Christ of Latter-day Saints.

345

ANNCR: Almost all the tabulations are in and the apparent winning candidates are...(UNDER) shown here on our big board.

MARGE: Lou, it's not going to change. Let's go to sleep. (Turns off TV)

LOU: You never know, not all the votes are counted yet. (Turns on TV)

ANNCR: And here's the way the votes are distributed...

MARGE: (Turns off TV) Come on, Lou, it's over, they lost, face it.

LOU: I just can't believe it, maybe there'll be a last minute turn-around. (Turns on TV)

ANNCR: Stay tuned for tonight's late, late movie, "The Plant That Ate Cleveland". (MUSIC UNDER)

MARGE: Lou, please don't torture yourself. (Turns off TV) Look, you voted, you did the best you could, why don't you forget it and go to sleep.

LOU: I didn't vote.

MARGE: What!

LOU: I meant to, but I didn'.

MARGE: Oh, I see...guilt...well, it's too late now.

LOU: By the way, Marge, who did you finally vote for?

MARGE: Go to sleep, Lou, tomorrow is a new day.

LOU: Oh, no, my own wife?...How could you do that?

MARGE: (Sardonically) It was easy, you go into the booth, turn the switches, pull the lever...

ANNCR: "I should have voted". You know that's what you're going to say if your candidates don't win. A public service of the National Association of Secretaries of State and The Advertising Council.

SINGERS: *You want it all*
The sunny sky
The golden sand
The mountains high
We share your dreams
We know your sky
We're Air California
And we want everyone to fly

You want it all
You're flyin' high
You reach for sunshine
You touch the sky
We share your dreams
We know your sky
We're Air California
And we want everyone to fly

(SFX: RESTAURANT SOUNDS)

LARRY: Frank, discussing the Blakely account over lunch was a *great* idea. *Nothing* to disturb us.

FRANK: I'm all ears.

LARRY: Let's start with the marketing plan.

FRANK: I'm gonna have a Bloody Mary.

LARRY: What?

FRANK: You want a Bloody Mary?

LARRY: Oh. Sure. Now about the marketing plan.

LARRY: Miss, we'll have two Bloody Marys.

LARRY: Frank, you're not listening.

FRANK: You didn't want a Bloody Mary?

LARRY: I don't *care* about the Bloody Marys.

FRANK: Okay, okay, let's start with the marketing plan.

LARRY: *Good!*

FRANK: Don't you love those little lace bibs the waitresses wear? I love those little lace bibs.

LARRY: I give up.

ANNCR: Half of the average business day is spent listening. Poorly. Sometimes we're our own worst enemy. We get distracted. We don't pay attention. And we end up getting very little done. With over 87,000 employees, Sperry Corporation can't afford that kind of inefficiency. So we've set up listening programs Sperry employees worldwide can attend. These programs are making us a lot better at listening to each other and to you. So we can all get a lot more done.

WAITRESS: Here you are sir, two Tequila Sunrises.

FRANK: I ordered two *Bloody Marys.*

WAITRESS: Oh.

FRANK: Larry, that's the trouble with the world. Nobody listens.

LARRY: Hm.

ANNCR: Sperry. We understand how important it is to listen.

(SFX: PHONE RINGS)

MR. WITHERS: Hello.

MR. CHAIRMAN: Withers, I want you to buy 15,000 shares of Cheevers Swiss gold.

MR. WITHERS: Right away Mr. Chairman.

(SFX: PHONE RINGS)

MR. CROMWELL: Hello.

MR. WITHERS: Cromwell, the Chairman wants you to buy 50,000 shares of Cheever Swiss Gold.

MR. CROMWELL: Right away Mr. Withers.

(SFX: PHONE RINGS)

MR. DUNLAP: Hello.

MR. CROMWELL: Dunlap, the Chairman wants to buy 50,000 shares of Golden Swiss Cheese.

MR. DUNLAP: Golden Swiss Cheese?

MR. CROMWELL: That's what I said Dunlap. Aren't you listening?

ANNCR: Business people spend most of their day doing the thing they're least qualified to do. Listening. Sometimes ideas get distorted by 80%. That's why Sperry Corporation has set up listening programs for Sperry personnel worldwide. Because we know in business, an error in listening could cost you more than embarrassment.

(SFX: PHONE RINGS)

MR. WITHERS: Hello.

MR. CHAIRMAN: Withers, I ordered 15,000 shares of Cheevers Swiss Gold and got 50,000 shares of Golden Swiss Cheese. Someone wasn't listening.

MR. WITHERS: Yes Mr. Chairman.

MR. CHAIRMAN: So listen to this.

MR. WITHERS: Yes Mr. Chairman.

MR. CHAIRMAN: You're fired.

MR. WITHERS: Got it.

ANNCR: Sperry. We understand how important it is to listen.

(MUSIC)

ANNCR(VO): Tinker, Tailor, Soldier, Spy. Great Performances presents John leCarre's nerve shattering exercise in espionage.

VOICES FROM
PROGRAM
CONTROL: We have a mole Jim.

JIM: In London?

CONTROL: Very near the top.

JIM: In the Circus?

CONTROL: One of the top five. Their code name for him is Gerald. We have a rotten apple Jim, and the maggots are eating up the Circus.

ANNCR(VO): Tinker, Tailor, Soldier Spy.

(MUSIC UP)

RICKY: I've got a story to tell you. It's all about spies. And if it's true which I think it is, you boys are going to need a whole new organization.

ANNCR(VO): Alec Guinness stars as George Smiley... the only one left in the Circus who could be trusted to ferret out the mole. Tune in for Part I of this six-part-game-of-nerves this coming Monday evening on your local PBS station. Made possible in part by EXXON.

(MUSIC OUT)

1981 Television Finalists

Consumer Television 60 Seconds Single

350
Art Director:
Anthony Angotti
Writer:
Tom Thomas
Client:
Xerox
Director:
Henry Sandbank
Production Co.:
Sandbank Films
Agency Producer:
Sydelle Rangell
Agency:
Needham, Harper & Steers

351
Art Director:
Bill Biderbost
Writer:
Susan Gillette
Client:
Polaroid
Director:
Rick Levine
Production Co.:
Levine Pytka
Agency Producer:
Debbie Voss-Grumish
Agency:
Needham, Harper & Steers Chicago

352
Art Director:
Joanna Dickerson
Writer:
Tom Jenkins
Client:
Lyons Bakery/Krispen
Director:
Dick McNeil
Production Co.:
Dick McNeil Associates London
Agency Producer:
Peter Nice
Agency:
Davidson Pearce/London

353
Art Director:
Clem McCarthy
Writers:
Martin Puris
Bruce Feirstein
Client:
BMW of North America
Director:
Tim Newman
Production Co.:
Jenkins-Covington
Agency Producer:
Lorange Spenningsby
Agency:
Ammirati & Puris

350

Polaroid SX-70 Sonar

351

(SFX: OLD NEWSREEL MUSIC)

1st ANNCR(VO): Welcome to the future.

2nd ANNCR(VO): This is what the 1980's looked like to people just a few decades ago.

1st ANNCR(VO): Robots will be man's constant companion—at work...and at play!

2nd ANNCR(VO): The future seldom happens exactly the way people think. So how do you *plan* for the future when you can't predict it? At Xerox...

(SFX: NEWSREEL MUSIC OUT)

2nd ANNCR(VO): ...We've found a way. It's called...

(SFX: PERCUSSIVE, FAST DRIVING ELECTRONIC MUSIC)

...the information outlet. Behind the outlet, a
Xerox Ethernet cable joins your office machines...
into a single, *flexible* network.
A network you can *build* upon...
plugging in new information processors...
...electronic printers...
...or other information management machines as
you need them...
...or as technology develops better ones.
A network that won't become obsolete because it can
grow and change...
as you do. One step at a time.

(SFX: ELECTRONIC MUSIC OUT)

The Xerox Information Outlet. Now you can get
ready for the future...

(SFX: NEWSREEL CLOSING FANFARE)

even if you don't know
...*exactly* what you're...
...getting ready for.

(SFX: FANFARE UP AND OUT)

(MUSIC UNDER)

CHILDREN: Yeah!

MOTHER: Go on, Sara, ask him.

GRANDMOTHER: Go on sweetheart. That's it.

FATHER: That's my girl. Go ahead!

LITTLE GIRL: Bishop. Will you take a picture with me?

ANNCR: For those moments in life when the picture has to be great.

LITTLE GIRL: There's my mom and dad.

ANNCR: Get the finest instant camera in the world. Polaroid SX-70 Sonar.

SOLO SINGER: *Now you can hold the moment
Here in your hand.
Now even when the moment ends...*

ANNCR: The Polaroid SX-70 Sonar.

SOLO SINGER: *We'll share the moment once again.*

ANNCR: Could you picture yourself with any other instant camera?

352

353

(SFX: FARMYARD NOISES)

MVO: It's almost lunchtime down at Inglenook Farm...
...and Granny Perkins has baked her boys
...their favourite home made bread.

(SFX: CRASH AS LOAF HITS TABLE, WOOD SPLINTERING AS TABLE FALLS)

(SFX: GROANS FROM BOYS)

MVO: Fortunately, young Jethro stopped off for...
...a pack of new Krispen crisp bread.
Krispen is made with real wheat, but it's light and crisp.
So it has the taste of wheat, without the weight.
Thereby leaving plenty of room for a nice slice of...
...Granny's fruitcake.

(SFX: CRASH OF FALLING FRUITCAKE, SPLINTERING OF WOOD AND PLATES SMASHING)

New Krispen crispbread. The good taste of wheat...

(SFX: CRASH OF FALLING LOAF AND SPLINTERING WOOD)

...without the weight.

(MONTAGE OF OFFICIOUS VOICES:)

1st VO: Chapter I, Title 40, Part 86, Section 77, Paragraph i:

2nd VO: No automobile shall cause the emission into the air...

3rd VO: Today, we are enacting a 55 mile per hour national speed limit on the nation's highways...

4th VO: Each bumper shall withstand a 5 mile per hour impact...

5th VO: My fellow Americans, we have a crisis at the gas pumps...

(VOICES FADE)

ANNCR(VO): Against seemingly insurmountable odds, the BMW has been engineered to meet the demands of society without ever compromising performance.

BMW. The car company that will not be legislated into mediocrity.

Consumer Television
60 Seconds Single

354
Art Director:
Howard Brody
Writer:
Sue Read
Client:
Eastman Kodak
Director:
Norman Griner
Production Co.:
Myers & Griner/Cuesta
Agency Producer:
Erin Ragan
Agency:
Young & Rubicam

355
Art Director:
George Euringer
Writer:
Ken Majka
Client:
Corning Glass Works
Director:
Thom Stovern
Production Co.:
Paddington Films/Australia
Agency Producer:
Frank DiSalvo
Agency:
**Calet, Hirsch, Kurnit
& Spector**

356
Art Director:
Roger Mosconi
Writers:
**Penny Hawkey
Roger Mosconi**
Client:
Coca-Cola
Director:
Conrad Hall
Production Co.:
Wexler-Hall
Agency Producers:
**J.C. Kaufman
Karen Scanlon**
Agency:
McCann-Erickson

357
Art Director:
Jim Swan
Writer:
Phil Peppis
Client:
Sony Corporation
Director:
Earl Rath
Production Co.:
**Paisley Productions
Los Angeles**
Agency Producer:
Ray Johnson
Agency:
McCann-Erickson

354

355

(MUSIC UNDER AND THROUGHOUT)

ANNCR(VO): Instant photography by Kodak and "The Night Before Christmas."

ARNOLD: Hey Joey... (Whispered)
Hey Joey... (Music) (Louder) Joey!...

JOEY: What?

ARNOLD: He's downstairs!

JOEY: There's nobody downstairs, Arnold!

ARNOLD: There is so!

(MUSIC)

ANNCR(VO): When you need a picture in an instant, you'll love the Colorburst 250 with built-in flash!

(SFX: ARNOLD GASPS)

(SFX: CAMERA CLICKS)

ARNOLD: Joey, Joey...

JOEY: (Looking at picture) Gasps!

(SFX: SLEIGHBELLS)

ANNCR(VO): Brilliant Color, instant pictures, built-in flash with the Colorburst 250 Instant Camera from Kodak.

ANNCR(VO): This is the story of a set of Corelle and its fantastic journey. From a mother in New York... to a daughter. In Australia.

(MUSIC: "WALTZING MATILDA")

If Corelle can survive a journey halfway around the world...

Imagine how many trips it can make to your table.

356

357

(MUSIC THROUGHOUT)

ANNCR(VO): The bottlers of Tab would like to acknowledge all the athletes and their families for their commitment and their sacrifice on the long, hard road to the Winter Games.

SINGERS: *TAB...*
TAB cola
...what a beautiful drink
...TAB, TAB COLA
for beautiful people.
TAB...
You're beautiful to me.

ANNCR(VO): (Over singers) You are the best and we salute you.

VO: Television should be more than an electronic tranquilizer...
At its best as an art form television should involve you, touch you, move you...
The art of television. Experience it on the one television that is itself a work of art. The Emmy award winning Sony Trinitron.
Sony. The One and Only.

Consumer Television
60 Seconds Single

358
Art Director:
Roger Mosconi
Writers:
Roger Mosconi
Scott Miller
J.C. Kaufman
Client:
Coca-Cola
Director:
Joe Pytka
Production Co.:
Levine Pytka/Los Angeles
Agency Producer:
J.C. Kaufman
Agency:
McCann-Erickson

359
Art Director:
Ron Travisano
Writer:
Jerry Della Femina
Client:
New York Mets
Director:
Werner Hlinka
Production Co.:
THT Productions
Agency Producer:
Linda Tesa
Agency:
Della Femina, Travisano
& Partners

360
Art Director:
Tom Heck
Writer:
Marcia Grace
Client:
N.Y. State Dept. of Commerce
Director:
Steve Horn
Production Co.:
Steve Horn Productions
Agency Producer:
Jack Curtis
Agency:
Wells, Rich, Greene

361
Art Director:
Dennis D'Amico
Writer:
Tom Messner
Client:
Travelers
Director:
George Gomes
Production Co.:
Gomes-Loew
Agency Producer:
Janine Marjollet
Agency:
Ally & Gargano

358

359

MAN: Hey, Slim? Tell it again.

SLIM: Ahhh...O.K.
I'm walking into the kitchen see.
This little breeze is easin' through the curtains.
I open up the refrigerator door...
It's like January in there.
And I look way in the back, back behind the
   mayonnaise.
I spy me an icy bottle of Coke. And I reach in...
it's cold to the touch—almost frozen.
And I pop the top.
And when that ice-cold Coke...
hits the back of my throat...

SINGERS: *A Coke and a Smile—two of a kind.*
   So refreshing
   Makes me feel nice.
   Have a Coke and a Smile.
   Coca-Cola adds life
   Have a Coke and a...

SLIM: Now that's the real thing.

SINGERS: *Smile!*

ALL: gibberish.

(MUSIC "TAKE ME OUT TO THE BALLGAME"
THROUGHOUT)

(SFX: WIND/CROWD)

PLAY BY PLAY EXCERPTS: The New York Mets, for the
first time in their history have gone into first place in
the National League race.

(SFX: BAT CRACKS)

Ron Swaboda with a line drive home run over the left
field wall. And the Mets are the National League
Champions.

ANNCR: This is the sound of Shea Stadium. It's filled
with memories of the past and promise of the future.
Shea Stadium. Where you can show your kids what
real heros are all about. There's a magic coming back
to Shea in the 1980 Mets. Mazzilli. Flynn.
Henderson. Zachery. Sterns. Swan. They're all gonna
play their hearts out for you. Shea Stadium in 1980.
The Magic is back.

(MUSIC FADES OUT)

360

361

(MUSIC "I LOVE NEW YORK" UNDER)

SILLS: At night in New York...all the stars come out.

SILLS AND PERFORMERS: (Singing) I love New York.

ROCKETTES: (Singing) I love New York.

ROBERTS AND ARNAZ: (Singing) I love New York.

EVITA CAST: (Singing) I love New York.

LANSBURY & CARIOU: (Singing) I love New York.

AIN'T MISBEHAVIN' CAST: (Singing) I love New York.

VO: I love New York at Night Show Tours. 23 packages at special prices. For a free brochure, call toll-free 800-241-8444.

SANDY DUNCAN: (Speaking) I love New York at Night. There's something...in the air.

(MUSIC THROUGHOUT)

ANNCR(VO): Before there was a Ford or a Chrysler or a Chevrolet, The Travelers had issued the first automobile insurance.

Before anyone else did it, The Travelers had its claims experts

(SFX: CONVERSATION)

manning 24-hour hot-lines.

Before consumer advocates asked for it, The Travelers founded an office of consumer information to answer questions about insurance. Before the women's movement started to make front page news, The Travelers was offering lower rates for women's life insurance.

Before it was certain that a man could walk on the moon and come back, The Travelers became the first company to issue accident policies for space travel.

Whether your insurance needs are personal or business, call an independent Travelers Agent. Considering where we've been and where we are, why would you call anyone else.

**Consumer Television
60 Seconds Single**

362
Art Director:
Arnie Blum
Writers:
**Arnie Blum
Phil Dusenberry**
Client:
Pepsi Cola
Director:
Rick Levine
Production Co.:
Levine Pytka
Agency Producer:
Arnie Blum
Agency:
BBDO

363
Art Director:
Arnie Blum
Writers:
**Arnie Blum
Phil Dusenberry**
Client:
Pepsi Cola
Director:
Rick Levine
Production Co.:
Levine Pytka
Agency Producer:
Arnie Blum
Agency:
BBDO

364
Art Director:
Arnie Blum
Writers:
**Arnie Blum
Elin Jacobson**
Client:
Pepsi Cola
Director:
Rick Levine
Production Co.:
Levine Pytka
Agency Producer:
Arnie Blum
Agency:
BBDO

362

363

SINGERS:
Catch that Pepsi Spirit.

(MUSIC)

Catch that Pepsi Spirit.

(MUSIC)

Catch that Pepsi Spirit.

(MUSIC)

Catch that Pepsi Spirit. Catch that Pepsi Spirit.

Drink it in. Drink it in.
Drink it in.
Catch that Pepsi Spirit.
Drink it in. Drink it in. Drink it in.
It's the love and the laughter.
The taste of life
the world is after.

(MUSIC)

Catch
that Pepsi Spirit.
Drink it in. Drink it in. Drink it in.

SINGERS:
There's a feeling deep inside you, a spirit you just
  can't hide.
And with every taste of life that's new
Well, that Pepsi spirit
shines right through.
Catch that Pepsi Spirit. Drink it in.
Drink it in. Drink it in.
Catch that Pepsi Spirit.
Drink it in. Drink it in. Drink it in.
It's the love and the laughter.
The taste of life the world is after.
Catch that Pepsi Spirit
Drink it in.
Drink it in. Drink it in.

SINGERS: *You're the Pepsi Generation*

COACH: Hamilton! Today!

SINGERS: *with the dreams of a brand new day.*

HAMILTON: Wanna see me, Coach?

COACH: It's about your scholarship.

HAMILTON: You heard?

COACH: There was some concern about your height and they were looking for a little better outside shooter,

SINGERS: *And that Pepsi Spirit*

COACH: but Hamilton, I think your grades changed their minds.

SINGERS: *shines right through.*
   Catch that Pepsi Spirit.
   Catch that Pepsi Spirit.
   Drink it in,
   Drink it in,
   Drink it in.
   Catch that Pepsi Spirit.
   Drink it in,
   Drink it in,
   Drink it in.
   Catch that Pepsi Spirit.
   Drink it in!

Consumer Television
60 Seconds Single

365
Art Director:
Boyd Jacobson
Writer:
John van der Zee
Client:
Wells Fargo Bank
Production Co.:
Wexler-Hall
Agency Producer:
Jim Allen
Agency:
**McCann-Erickson
San Francisco**

366
Art Director:
Robert Tucker
Writer:
Tom Yobbagy
Client:
Porsche + Audi
Director:
Dick Rucker
Production Co.:
Bluebird Productions
Agency Producer:
Cheryl Herman
Agency:
Doyle Dane Bernbach

367
Art Director:
Gerald Andelin
Writer:
Hal Riney
Client:
Blitz-Weinhard Brewing
Director:
Joe Pytka
Production Co.:
Levine Pytka
Agency Producers:
**Gerald Andelin
Hal Riney**
Agency:
**Ogilvy & Mather
San Francisco**

365

BOY: Here comes the stage!

(MUSIC: ORIGINAL SCORE INCLUDING VARIATIONS
ON WELLS FARGO THEME)

(SFX: SOUNDS OF STAGECOACH APPROACHING)

(MUSIC BEGINS TO INCLUDE ELEMENTS OF
CHRISTMAS SONG)

366

(MUSIC UNDER AND THROUGHOUT)

(SFX: CARS REVVING UP)

VO: The Porsche nine twenty-four Turbo. Even more
amazing than how fast it can go . . .

. . . is how far it can go on a single tank of gas.

367

(FADE IN)

TRADER 1: "... for example, what we have here Mr. Oomak, is what are perhaps..

... the finest beads on the market today...

... so what I'm suggesting is that for 2 pounds of beads..."

TRADER 2: "...*and* five yards of bright red ribbon—"

TRADER 1: "—and the ribbon, you and the fellas there should give *us*, let's say, twenty walrus hides, ten sables, six silver foxes—"

TRADER 2: "—and one bale of snowshoe rabbit skins."

VO: Not long ago... some visitors to a remote Alaskan island...

TRADER 1: "Well..."

VO: ... happened on something most unusual...

TRADER 1: "... what do we have there?"

VO: ... a most unusual beer.

ESKIMO: "Henry's"

VO: Brewed in Oregon in the old-fashioned, traditional way.

TRADER 1: "Well, we might accept three silver fox, twenty rabbit skins and ten cases of Henry's."

VO: How did Henry Weinhard's Private Reserve happen to be there?

TRADER 1: "Two rabbit skins and five cases?"

VO: No one really knows.

TRADER 1: "I agree it's not a lot, Willard... and you might be right."

VO: But if it's worth a trip to Alaska...

TRADER 1: "You will admit, it's a mighty fine beer."

VO: ... It's sure worth a trip to the store.

Consumer Television
60 Seconds Campaign

368
Art Directors:
Jim Swan
Henry Holtzman
Nicholas Scordato
Writers:
Phil Peppis
Nicholas Pisacane
Kenneth Schulman
Client:
Sony Corp.
Directors:
Earl Rath
Peter Schuzitsky
Harold Becker
Production Cos.:
Paisley Productions
Los Angeles
N. Lee Lacy/Los Angeles
Agency Producers:
Ray Johnson
Diane Maze
Joan Bennett
Agency:
McCann-Erickson

369
Art Director:
Robert Steigelman
Writers:
Robert Meury
Lou Schere
Barry Lisee
Client:
Miller Brewing
Director:
Conrad Hall
Production Co.:
Wexler-Hall
Agency Producer:
Barry Lisee
Agency:
Backer & Spielvogel

370
Art Director:
Dennis D'Amico
Writers:
Tom Messner
Ron Berger
Client:
Travelers
Directors:
George Gomes
Norman Griner
Production Cos.:
Gomes-Leow
Myers & Griner/Cuesta
Agency Producer:
Janine Marjollet
Agency:
Ally & Gargano

368

(MUSIC UP AND UNDER)

ANNCR: Sony introduces the art of watching
television. The Sony Betamax gives you the power to
record and see what you want, when you want. To
summon into your home a world of wonder.
And Betamax has a remarkable feature called
Betascan, lets you scan fast forward and reverse so
you can quickly find any single image from amongst
any thousands of images on a tape many hours long.
Betamax frees you from the burdens of time and
circumstance and makes you master of them all.

LITTLE GIRL: Now daddy!

ANNCR: And yet this incredible machine was once
only the vision of one company that wished to do a
simple but magical thing. To transform the act of
watching television into the art of watching television.

MAJOR DOMO: Ladies and Gentlemen, your show is
about to begin.

ANNCR: Sony, the One and Only.

369

SINGER: *Got a long day's work
behind me.*

CAPTAIN: That's it. Let's bring 'em home.

SINGER: *Good times on my mind.
With the setting sun to remind me,
I'm going back to a place called Miller Time.
If you've got the time . . .*

ANNCR(VO): Time for the best tasting beer you can
find.

SINGER: *We've got the beer.*

ANNCR(VO): America's quality beer since 1855.

SINGER: *Miller tastes too good
to hurry through.*

ANNCR(VO): Miller High Life.

SINGER: *When it's time to relax,
one beer stands clear,
beer after beer. If you've got the time,
we've got the beer.
Miller beer.*

370

(MUSIC THROUGHOUT)

ANNCR(VO): Before there was a Ford or a Chrysler or a Chevrolet, The Travelers had issued the first automobile insurance.

Before anyone else did it, The Travelers had its claims experts

(SFX: CONVERSATION)

manning 24-hour hot-lines.

Before consumer advocates asked for it, The Travelers founded an office of consumer information to answer questions about insurance. Before the women's movement started to make front page news, The Travelers was offering lower rates for women's life insurance.

Before it was certain that a man could walk on the moon and come back, The Travelers became the first company to issue accident policies for space travel.

Whether your insurance needs are personal or business, call an independent Travelers Agent. Considering where we've been and where we are, why would you call anyone else.

Consumer Television
30 Seconds Single

371
Art Director:
Al Colello
Writer:
Melisse Shapiro
Client:
McDonald's
Director:
Steve Horn
Production Co.:
Steve Horn Productions
Agency Producer:
Sherri Fritzson
Agency:
Rosenfeld, Sirowitz & Lawson

372
Art Director:
John Bailey
Writer:
Nick Salaman
Client:
Michelin Tyre
Director:
Brian Mindel
Production Co.:
James Garrett/London
Agency Producer:
Nick Salaman
Agency:
Connell May & Steavenson London

373
Art Directors:
Ren Wicks
Alan Kupchick
Writers:
Jeff Gelberg
Alan Kupchick
Client:
Taco Bell
Director:
Victor Haboush
Production Co.:
Haboush Co.
Phil Marco Productions
Agency Producer:
Alan Reed
Agency:
Grey/Los Angeles

374
Art Director:
Jon Guliner
Writer:
Monte Ghertler
Client:
The Wine Spectrum
Director:
Ron Finley
Production Co.:
Iris Films
Agency Producer:
Dave Ottey
Agency:
Kenyon & Eckhardt

371

372

SINGERS: *Don't think small*
Go for it all.

YOUNG MAN: Someday I'm gonna be big

SINGERS: *Think big... Big Mac Big.*
Be the best, not like all the rest.
Think big, Big Mac Big.

KID: Today Little League... tomorrow big league.

SINGERS: *Take a Big Mac bite,*
the price is right...
McDonald's Big Mac meal's a really big deal...
so if you wanna be big

HIGH SCHOOL GIRL: I'm gonna be big

SINGERS: *Big Mac Big*

HIGH SCHOOL GIRL: Really Big.

SINGERS: *Yea, if you wanna be big*
Just think big

HIGH SCHOOL GIRL: Big Mac Big

SINGERS: *Big Mac Big*

OLDER MAN: How do you think I got to be this big?

SINGERS: *So if you wanna be big...*

1st KID: We're gonna make it big

SINGERS: *Big Mac Big*

2nd KID: I just know it.

3rd KID: I can feel it.

SINGERS: *Yea if you wanna be big...*
Just think big.

KIDS: (Singing) *Big Mac Big*

SINGERS: *Big Mac Big*

MVO: For years, tales have reached us of the long life enjoyed by villagers in these mountains.

This man is said to be 115 today.
Just what is his secret.

GEORGIOU: (in broken English) Yoghourt... lots of wives... and Michelin radials...

MVO: Well there it is—the secret of long life all of us can enjoy. Michelin.

GEORGIOU: But you should ask my father.

373

374

WILMA: "I'm so tired of burgers and fries. What can we have that's different?"

EDNA: "I have no idea."

(SFX: BELL CRASHES THROUGH GLASS ROOF OF GREENHOUSE.)

EDNA: "I have an idea. Taco Bell."

ANNCR: "At Taco Bell, we have Burrito Supremes, Enchiritos, and Beefy Tostadas. All fresh and specially seasoned to give 'em that Taco Bell taste you can't get anywhere else."

WILMA: "Best idea you've had in fifty-seven years."

ANNCR: "It's deliciously different. It's . . .

SINGERS: *Taca, taca, Taco Bell!*

ANNCR(VO): The world's largest gourmet society, The Chaine des Rostisseurs, is headed in America by the great food and wine authority Roger Yaseen.

(SFX: TALKING UNDER)

ANNCR(VO): Recently he compared two California Rhine wines.

YASEEN(VO): I compared Inglenook Navalle and Taylor California Cellars Rhine wines. And the wine that I preferred was Taylor California Cellars. What impresses me is how well it goes with food. Almost any dish that you would serve with a Rhine wine would taste better with Taylor California Cellars than it would with Inglenook Navalle.

ANNCR(VO): Taylor California Cellars, a better Rhine wine. Judge for yourself.

Consumer Television
30 Seconds Single

375
Art Director:
F. Paul Pracilio
Writers:
Robert Neuman
F. Paul Pracilio
Client:
Smith Barney, Harris Upham
Director:
Norman Griner
Production Co.:
Myers & Griner/Cuesta
Agency Producer:
Nancy Perez
Agency:
Ogilvy & Mather

376
Art Director:
F. Paul Pracilio
Writers:
Robert Neuman
F. Paul Pracilio
Client:
Smith Barney, Harris Upham
Director:
Norman Griner
Production Co.:
Myers & Griner/Cuesta
Agency Producer:
Nancy Perez
Agency:
Ogilvy & Mather

377
Art Director:
John Armistead
Writer:
Linda Chandler Frohman
Client:
Brentwood Savings
& Loan Association
Director:
Reid Miles
Production Co.:
Reid Miles
Agency Producers:
John Armistead
Linda Chandler Frohman
Agency:
Abert, Newhoff & Burr
Los Angeles

378
Art Director:
Nicholas Gisonde
Writer:
Charlie Breen
Client:
Miller Brewing
Director:
Steve Horn
Production Co.:
Steve Horn Productions
Agency Producer:
Marc Mayhew
Agency:
Backer & Spielvogel

375

376

ANNCR(VO): John Houseman for the investment firm of Smith Barney.

JOHN HOUSEMAN: Old-fashioned Smith Barney. Not something out of Dickens. No green eyeshades and long ledgers here. Today, computers do the paper work. The old-fashioned part—the real work of creating a sound investment program—is still done up here. Smith Barney. They make money the old-fashioned way. They earn it.

ANNCR(VO): John Houseman for the investment firm of Smith Barney.

JOHN HOUSEMAN: Smith Barney executives continually learn about the art of investing. Precious little about selling. You don't sell clients. You work for them. You work very hard researching the right investments. And when they're right, no one has to be sold. Smith Barney. They make money the old-fashioned way. They earn it.

Brentwood Savings
It's a nice place to visit your money.

377

378

ANNCR(VO): While George is relaxing, Brentwood Savings is transferring money from his interest-earning savings account to his checking account, mailing him his quarterly interest check, sending him a low-interest Visa card, and mailing photocopies George forgot when he used our copy machine last week.

GEORGE BURNS: They treat me like I was...

(SFX: CLAP OF THUNDER, HEAVENLY CHOIR)

My backup singers.

ANNCR(VO): Brentwood Savings. It's a nice place to visit your money.

MARSH: I'll tell you, I was a born soccer player. I did everything with my feet—took out the rubbish with my feet, made the bed with my feet—drove my mom crazy. But I finally found something I enjoy doing with my hands. Drinking Lite Beer from Miller.

Lite has one third less calories than their regular beer. It's less filling. But what really makes me happy is the taste. It's terrific. Now my mom should be happy too.

Look mom, no feet!

(SFX: LAUGHTER AND BOOS)

ANNCR(VO): Lite Beer from Miller. Everything you always wanted in a beer. And less.

Lite Beer from Miller. Everything you always wanted in a beer. And less.

Consumer Television
30 Seconds Single

379
Writer:
Don White
Client:
Sunday Times
Director:
Piers Haggard
Production Co.:
Haggard & Phillips
Agency Producer:
Don White
Agency:
Benton & Bowles/London

380
Art Director:
Michael Tesch
Writer:
Patrick Kelly
Client:
Federal Express
Director:
Joe Sedelmaier
Production Co.:
Sedelmaier Films/Chicago
Agency Producer:
Maureen Kearns
Agency:
Ally & Gargano

381
Art Director:
Michael Tesch
Writer:
Patrick Kelly
Client:
Federal Express
Director:
Joe Sedelmaier
Production Co.:
Sedelmaier Films/Chicago
Agency Producer:
Maureen Kearns
Agency:
Ally & Gargano

382
Art Director:
Michael Tesch
Writer:
Patrick Kelly
Client:
Federal Express
Director:
Joe Sedelmaier
Production Co.:
Sedelmaier Films/Chicago
Agency Producer:
Maureen Kearns
Agency:
Ally & Gargano

379

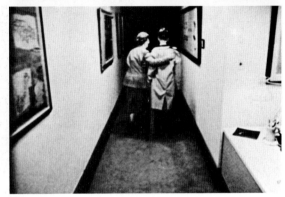

380

TEACHER: Pens down, girls. Now... who's going to read their composition to the class...
...Jill

JILL: "My Form Mistress, Miss Watkins has a secret lover. Last night I saw them holding hands in the biology lab. He tried to kiss her, but..." (Fades under)

VO: Even when she was very small, Jilly Cooper loved to write about the things she saw...Naturally, she grew up to write for the Sunday Times. Jilly Cooper—she's one of the reasons Sunday isn't Sunday without the Sunday Times.

EXEC: Yes, sir, the package will be on your desk tomorrow.
and I say that with the utmost confidence. I will take care of it!!

(SFX: CLICK OF RECEIVER)

EXEC: How will I take care of it? I don't know how I'm gonna take care of it. If I knew how to take care of it...

ANNCR(VO): When it comes to sending a package somewhere overnight, most forceful executives become as helpless as a 2-year old.

EXEC: You'll take care of it?

SECRETARY: I'll take care of it.

ANNCR(VO): And as a secretary you have to take care of him.

EXEC: How will you take care of it?

SECRETARY: I'll just call Federal Express.

EXEC: Oh.

(SFX: JET)

ANNCR(VO): Federal Express, when it absolutely, positively has to be there overnight.

381

382

BOSS 1: Dorsal, you did remember to send that document to Denver?

DORSAL: Denver?

BOSS 1: You know the deadline's tomorrow.

DORSAL: Tomorrow...

BOSS 2: Spigot, I assume you sent the slides to Seattle for the sales meeting tomorrow.

(SFX: GLUG, GLUG, GLUG)

BOSS 3: Fortunately, Bingham here sent the blueprints to Birmingham for the big meeting tomorrow, isn't that right, Bingham?

ANNCR(VO): Next time you blow it, remember there's always Federal Express.

(SFX: JET)

when it absolutely, positively has to be there overnight.

(MUSIC UNDER)

ANNCR(VO): When some people send a package by Federal Express for the first time, they never expect it to work. They're so used to getting chewed out for not getting a package there the next day, they expect it to happen with Federal, too.
So they wait,
and they wait,
and they wait,
and they wait,
for the complaint
that never comes.
Federal Express,
when it absolutely, positively has to be there overnight.

383
Art Director:
Michael Tesch
Writer:
Patrick Kelly
Client:
Federal Express
Director:
Joe Sedelmaier
Production Co.:
Sedelmaier Films/Chicago
Agency Producer:
Maureen Kearns
Agency:
Ally & Gargano

384
Art Director:
Michael Tesch
Writer:
Ron Berger
Client:
Male Jeans
Director:
Bob Giraldi
Production Co.:
Giraldi Productions
Agency Producer:
Janine Marjollet
Agency:
Ally & Gargano

385
Art Director:
Michael Tesch
Writer:
Tom Messner
Client:
Barney's
Director:
Sarah Moon
Production Co.:
Melody Movies/France
Agency Producer:
Janine Marjollet
Agency:
Ally & Gargano

386
Art Director:
Barry Vetere
Writer:
Tom Messner
Client:
Pentax
Director:
Phil Marco
Production Co.:
Phil Marco Productions
Agency Producer:
Jerry Haynes
Agency:
Ally & Gargano

383

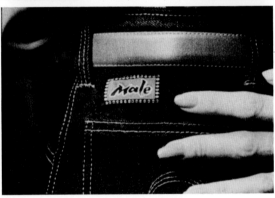

384

(MUSIC UNDER AND THROUGHOUT)
ANNCR(VO): It's coming.
It's taking over in offices coast to coast.
It's...
THE PAPER BLOB
It's packed with important papers
that should move out of your office fast,
but can't get loose.
This is a job for Federal Express.
For as little as $19.00 we'll pick up
your important papers
and deliver them clear across the country overnight.
So you'll never have to worry
about the paper blob again.
Federal Express. When it absolutely positively
has to be there overnight.

(MUSIC THROUGHOUT)
ANNCR(VO): We've got a pair of jeans that are made
for men. But they're really made for women. They're
called Male Jeans. Now a look and fit jeans never had
before. You see, at Male, we think it's time women do
to you what you've been doing to them for years.

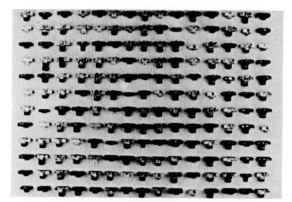

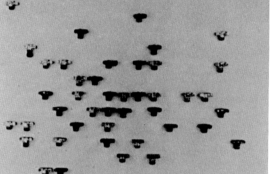

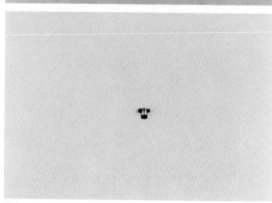

385

386

(MUSIC AND VOICES UNDER)

MAN: Juliette, où avez-vous achetez cette robe?

WOMAN: Barney's

MAN: Chez Barney's?

WOMAN: Oui.

(MUSIC OUT)

(MUSIC UNDER)

ANNCR(VO): Here are all the 35mm cameras in the world.
Here's how many offer interchangeable lenses.
Here's how many are fully automatic.
Here's how many can stop action at 1/2000ths
of a second.
And now here's how many also have push-button
manual override.
Only one.
The Pentax Super Camera.
Maybe the best way to choose a 35mm is by the
process of elimination.

Consumer Television
30 Seconds Single

387
Art Director:
Tom Higgins
Writer:
Rick Meyer
Client:
Breakstone
Director:
Dick Loew
Production Co.:
Gomes-Loew
Agency Producer:
Jean Muchmore
Agency:
Geers Gross

388
Art Director:
George Tweddle
Writer:
Glenn Miller
Client:
Pepsi International
Director:
Don Tortoriello
Production Co.:
Tortoriello/Till
Agency Producer:
Jeff Fischgrund
Agency:
BBDO

389
Art Director:
Arnie Blum
Writer:
Arnie Blum
Client:
Pepsi Cola
Director:
Rick Levine
Production Co.:
Levine Pytka
Agency Producer:
Arnie Blum
Agency:
BBDO

390
Art Director:
John Eding
Writer:
Diane Rothschild
Client:
Volkswagen
Director:
Rick Levine
Production Co.:
Levine Pytka
Agency Producer:
Sheldon Levy
Agency:
Doyle Dane Bernbach

387

388

VO: When Sam Breakstone set out to introduce a cottage cheese that was smooth and creamy, he was demanding!

SAM: And, it's not smooth enough!
You call that creamy? It's got to be the smoothest, the creamiest, the tastiest natural small curd cottage cheese we've ever made! And I don't care if it takes fifty years.

VO: Fifty years later, we proudly introduce Breakstone's Smooth and Creamy Style cottage cheese. Some things even Sam couldn't rush.

SAM: I'm waiting!

(MUSIC UNDER AND THROUGHOUT)

ANNCR(VO):
Introducing Pepsi Cola's tough light 2 liter plastic bottle.
Pepsi's new 2 liter plastic bottle is lighter than glass.
And it pours more Pepsi than ever.
It's resealable.
And disposable.
But the best thing is, it's light.

(MUSIC UP)

And tough.

(ENDS WITH MUSICAL STING)

389

390

SINGERS:
Catch that Pepsi Spirit.
Drink it in.
Drink it in.
Drink it in.
Catch it!
You're the Pepsi Generation.
Catch that Pepsi Spirit.
Drink it in.
Drink it in.
Drink it in.

INTERVIEWER: What kind of station wagon is that?

WOMAN: A Volkswagen Dasher.

INTERVIEWER: That's a nice looking wagon.

WOMAN: It's a diesel wagon.

INTERVIEWER: Oh, it must get good mileage.

WOMAN: It gets better mileage than any other wagon. In fact, it gets better mileage than most cars.

INTERVIEWER: No kidding.

WOMAN: It costs us next to nothing to run.

INTERVIEWER: Gee, what are you buying with all the money you're saving?

WOMAN: Food.

SINGERS: *Volkswagen does it again.*

Consumer Television
30 Seconds Single

391
Art Director:
Robert Gage
Writer:
Jack Dillon
Client:
Polaroid
Director:
Robert Gage
Production Co.:
Directors' Studio
Agency Producer:
Jane Liepshutz
Agency:
Doyle Dane Bernbach

392
Art Director:
Robert Gage
Writer:
Jack Dillon
Client:
Polaroid
Director:
Robert Gage
Production Co.:
Directors' Studio
Agency Producer:
Jane Liepshutz
Agency:
Doyle Dane Bernbach

393
Art Director:
Robert Tucker
Writer:
David Reider
Client:
Porsche + Audi
Director:
Tibor Hirsch
Production Co.:
THT Productions
Agency Producer:
Cheryl Herman
Agency:
Doyle Dane Bernbach

394
Art Director:
John Piccolo
Writer:
Marvin Honig
Client:
Citicorp
Director:
Bob Giraldi
Production Co.:
Bob Giraldi Productions
Agency Producer:
Steven Brind
Agency:
Doyle Dane Bernbach

391

392

MARI: What's the matter with you?

JIM: This is the big one and I'm not in on it.

MARI: What is?

JIM: Polaroid's SX-70 Sonar.

MARI: A camera's a camera. You're doing the OneStep.

JIM: I know, but this is the finest instant camera in the world. It's a motor-driven single-lens reflex, it will even focus itself.

MARI: Of course it will.

JIM: Look, you can't help getting great pictures even in close. You can even count the whiskers.

MARI: Amazing! That's a fine camera. Maybe they're looking for somebody classier!

JIM: I'll wear a tie.

MARI: How about socks?

JIM: No socks!

MARI: If you buy a OneStep, Pronto Sonar or SX-70 Sonar by January 31st Polaroid will send you five dollars.

They're such dears.

And, they'll send you coupons to help you buy time-zero film and flashes.

Isn't that nice?

They're worth a dollar when you buy a OneStep; a Pronto Sonar, five dollars or an SX-70 Sonar, fifteen dollars.

Can you use the coupons to help pay for the camera.

No.

Why not?

They're just nice. They're not stupid!

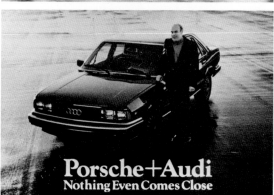

393

394

ANNCR(VO): The new luxurious Audi 5000 Turbo. What happens when you combine Turbo charging with front wheel drive?

Chief engineer Brockhaus will now explain.

Any questions?

HUSBAND: Ahhh.

WIFE: We should have baths like this back home.

HUSBAND: Our money!

WIFE: What?

HUSBAND: It's out in my suit!

MAN: Do you carry travelers checks?

HUSBAND: Yes, Citicorp.

MAN: Hmm, well, refunds are no problem almost anywhere in the world. There's even a large Citibank right near the Imperial Palace.

HUSBAND: Thank you, Mr. ???

MAN: Yama.

HUSBAND: Mr. Yama. My wife Ellen.

WIFE: That's alright, don't get up.

VO: Travel the world with us. Citicorp Travelers Checks.

Consumer Television
30 Seconds Single

395
Art Director:
Robert Gage
Writer:
Jack Dillon
Client:
Polaroid
Director:
Robert Gage
Production Co.:
Directors' Studio
Agency Producer:
Jane Liepshutz
Agency:
Doyle Dane Bernbach

396
Art Director:
Lester Feldman
Writer:
Mike Mangano
Client:
GTE
Director:
Norman Toback
Production Co.:
Toback Associates
Agency Producer:
Phil Bodwell
Agency:
Doyle Dane Bernbach

397
Art Director:
Peter Coutroulis
Writer:
Helen Nolan
Client:
Peugeot
Director:
Nicholas Roeg
Production Co.:
James Garrett/London
Agency Producer:
Marilyn Cook
Agency:
Van Leeuwen

398
Art Director:
Bill Atherton
Writer:
Steve Jenkinson
Client:
Goldenlay Eggs (UK)
Director:
Barry Kinsman
Production Co.:
Kinsman Taylor/London
Agency Producer:
Sandy Watson
Agency:
KMP Partnership/London

395

396

JIM(VO): Please watch closely. This is the fastest developing color film in the world. Polaroid's new Time-Zero Supercolor.

MARI(VO): Aahh!

JIM(VO): You first see the image in ten seconds. And here comes the color.

MARI(VO): It's coming fast.

JIM(VO): Look at that purple come up and the red and yellow—

MARI(VO): And it's so sharp.

JIM(VO): It all happens in just seconds. It's a great new reason to buy a Polaroid camera.

MARI(VO): You know you look a lot better *there* than you really do!

SINGERS: *Time-Zero.*

(VO): You know, most long-distance telephone commercials look more or less like this. They try to get you to call someone by tugging at your heart strings.

Well, we're going to do something a little different. We're going to try to get you to call by tugging at your *purse* strings. You see, right now, because of the time of day it is, if you dial direct it'll cost you a lot less money.

So, why put off that call you've been meaning to make any longer?

397

398

(MUSIC UNDER THROUGHOUT)

VITAS: Hi, Dad.

FATHER: Vitas, *Another* new car?

VITAS: It's a Peugeot.

FATHER: Peugeot. What for do you need *five* cars?

VITAS: This one's for driving, Dad.

ANNCR(VO): The new Peugeot 505 *is* for driving.

From the fine European suspension that protects you from the road's little bumps...

To the responsive engine that lets you adjust to every change that occurs.

VITAS: So what do you think?

FATHER: It's a nice Peugeot, Vitas. When you are going to get a haircut?

GEORGE: Do you know how to tell if it's going to be fine tomorrow?

HAROLD: Aye. Red sky at night.

HAROLD: Do you know how to tell if it's going to rain?

GEORGE: (pleased with himself) Aye, cows lie down.

BOB: Do you know how to tell if your egg has a more golden yolk?

GEORGE: No.

BOB: Make sure it's a Goldenlay egg like from Ted's farm.

GEORGE: Oh ain't that an old wives tale?

BOB: Aye yeah. My old wife told me this morning.

(VO): Goldenlay. The taste of the country.

Consumer Television
30 Seconds Single

399
Art Director:
Bill Atherton
Writer:
Steve Jenkinson
Client:
Goldenlay Eggs (UK)
Director:
Barry Kinsman
Production Co.:
Kinsman Taylor/London
Agency Producer:
Sandy Watson
Agency:
KMP Partnership/London

400
Art Director:
Vince Longo
Writer:
Charlie Robb
Client:
Pittsburgh National Bank
Director:
Carl Norr
Production Co.:
Myers & Griner/Cuesta
Agency Producer:
Jim Calderone
Agency:
**Ketchum MacLeod
& Grove/Pittsburgh**

401
Art Director:
Lars Anderson
Writer:
Peter Levathes
Client:
Maxell
Director:
Steve Steigman
Production Co.:
Steve Steigman
Agency Producer:
Dane Johnson
Agency:
Scali, McCabe, Sloves

402
Art Director:
Lars Anderson
Writer:
Peter Levathes
Client:
Maxell
Director:
Henry Sandbank
Production Co.:
Sandbank Films
Agency:
Dane Johnson
Agency:
Scali, McCabe, Sloves

399

GEORGE: 'Ere, 'arold. Did you 'ave an egg for breakfst?

HAROLD: (distantly) Mmmm.

GEORGE: Were it boiled?

HAROLD: Aye.

GEORGE: Was the yolk more golden?

HAROLD: (Wondering where all this is leading) Aye.

GEORGE: (with satisfaction) It were one of Ted's Goldenlay eggs then?

HAROLD: Aye, 'ow do you know?

GEORGE: You still got some on the front of your shirt.

(VO): Goldenlay. The taste of the country.

400

(MAN MUMBLING WHILE GOING THROUGH CANCELLED CHECKS)

ANNCR: Ever stop to think how much goes through your checking every month.

MAN: Every day.

WOMAN: Yes.

ANNCR: At Pittsburgh National, we think you should get more than just cancelled checks.

MAN: So do I.

(WOMAN GRUNTS AGREEMENT)

ANNCR: Then get Check & Save. You'll get 5¼% interest.

WOMAN: You're kidding.

ANNCR: Nope. With our Check & Save service you'll have more to work with. 5¼% more.

MAN: (Mumbling) Five...

WOMAN: and a quarter.

ANNCR: Right!
Check & Save from Pittsburgh National.
We're a bank that believes in performance.

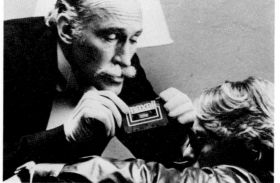

401

402

(SFX: WIND)

(MUSIC THROUGHOUT)

ANNCR(VO): If there's a Maxell cassette tape in this car, and it doesn't work, we'll replace it. Maxell. It's worth it.

(SFX: FOOTSTEPS)

BUTLER: The usual sir?

COOL GUY: Plese.

ANNCR(VO): Even after 500 plays our high fidelity tape...

(SFX: CLICK)

still delivers high fidelity.

(SFX: WAGNERIAN MUSIC BUILDS AND EXPLODES)

Maxell. It's worth it.

Consumer Television
30 Seconds Single

403
Art Director:
Rochelle Udell
Writer:
Doon Arbus
Client:
Calvin Klein Jeans
Director:
Richard Avedon
Production Co.:
Iris Films
Agency:
CRK Advertising

404
Art Director:
Rochelle Udell
Writer:
Doon Arbus
Client:
Calvin Klein Jeans
Director:
Richard Avedon
Production Co.:
Iris Films
Agency:
CRK Advertising

405
Art Director:
Rochelle Udell
Writer:
Doon Arbus
Client:
Calvin Klein Jeans
Director:
Richard Avedon
Production Co.:
Iris Films
Agency:
CRK Advertising

406
Art Director:
Rochelle Udell
Writer:
Doon Arbus
Client:
Calvin Klein Jeans
Director:
Richard Avedon
Production Co.:
Iris Films
Agency:
CRK Advertising

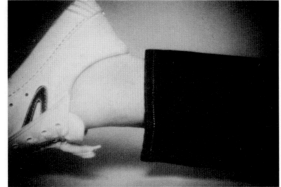 

403

404

BROOKE SHIELDS: (Singing) *Many a heart is aching, if you could read them all, many the hopes that have vanished after the ball...*
I've got 7 Calvin's in my closet and if they could talk, I'd be ruined.

ANNCR(VO): Calvin Klein Jeans

BROOKE SHIELDS: (Whistling "My Darling Clementine")
You wanna know what comes between me and my Calvins?
Nothing.

ANNCR(VO): Calvin Klein Jeans

405

406

BROOKE SHIELDS: (Reading) I took her hand in mine and went out of the ruined place and as the morning mist had risen long ago when I left the forge, the evening mist is rising now, and in all the broad expanse of tranquil light they showed to me, I saw no shadow of another parting from her.
Reading is to the mind...what Calvin's are to the body.

ANNCR(VO): Calvin Klein Jeans

BROOKE SHIELDS: (Counting on fingers) 8% of 38...is 8 × 30 move over 3...OK...38, 39, 40, 41...97 minus 30 is...40 × 46...5...50...56 Whenever I get some money, I buy Calvin's, and if there's any left, I pay the rent.

ANNCR(VO): Calvin Klein Jeans

Consumer Television
30 Seconds Campaign

407
Art Director:
John Triolo
Writer:
Bill Appelman
Client:
Merrill Lynch
Director:
Dick Miller
Production Co.:
Dick Miller
Agency Producer:
Mootsy Elliot
Agency:
Young & Rubicam

408
Art Directors:
M. Susser
J. Perez
Writers:
S. Regenbogen
W. Forys
L. Scholnick
Client:
General Foods/Jell-O Pudding
Directors:
M. Ross
E. Bianchi
Production Co.:
Mark Ross
Stage One
Agency Producers:
E. Pollack
S. Breakstone
Agency:
Young & Rubicam

409
Art Directors:
Matt Basile
Howard Brody
Writer:
Sue Read
Client:
Eastman Kodak
Directors:
Dick Loew
Michael Ulick
Norman Griner
Production Cos.:
Gomes-Loew
Michael Ulick Productions
Myers & Griner/Cuesta
Agency Producers:
Mootsy Elliott
Erin Ragan
Agency:
Young & Rubicam

410
Art Director:
Felix Burgos
Writer:
Marcia Lusk
Client:
Ralston Purina
Director:
Steve Gluck
Production Co.:
Gluck Durham
Agency Producer:
Susan Scherl
Agency:
Drossman Yustein Clowes

407

408

(MUSIC UNDER)

ANNCR(VO): Reaching your financial goal is never as simple as some people would have you believe. You have to know exactly where you're going and make the right decisions at the right time.

At Merrill Lynch, it's our skill at guiding you through the intricacies of investing, that makes us what we are.

Merrill Lynch, a breed apart.

(MUSIC OUT)

COSBY: This is new improved Jell-o Chocolate Pudding, they say it's even smoother than good old Jell-o Chocolate Pudding so let's give it the old...

COSBY & KIDS: smoothometer test.

COSBY: That's right.

COSBY & KIDS: Um...Um...Um...

COSBY: It's so much smoother, I think our smootherometers are going crazy.

COSBY & KIDS: Um...Um...Um...

ANNCR(VO): Introducing New Improved Jell-o Brand Chocolate Pudding. It's so much smoother, you'll love it even more.

COSBY: Smoother, right gang.

KIDS: Um...Um...Um...

COSBY: I think their smoothometers are stuck.

409

410

(MUSIC THROUGHOUT)

ANNCR(VO): Instant photography by Kodak and "The Big Audition".

1st KID: The cornucopia. It is a horn of plenty.

TEACHER: Hold it! Got the flash Marvin?

MARVIN: Sure, it's built right in!

(SFX: FLASH)

TEACHER: Very good. Okay, next!

2nd KID: Fine crops of grain and fruit.

TEACHER: You're on Louise!

(SFX: TOM TOM DRUMMING)

3rd KID: Hi . . . Awatha!

TEACHER: Well, Marvin, what do you think?

MARVIN: I think all my pictures are great.

ANNCR(VO): The Kodak Colorburst 250 . . .
the instant camera with built-in flash and brilliant
color by Kodak.

MAN: A four letter word for great taste . . .

CAT: Meow.

MAN: Starts with an "M" . . . mmmmm . . .

CAT: Meow.

MAN: MMMM . . . mlach . . . no, that's 5 letters.

CAT: Meow, meow.

VO: Any cat will tell you, the word for great taste is
"meow", as in Meow Mix cat food.

Only Meow Mix gives cats the three flavors they like
best in one package.

So Meow Mix is the only cat food cats ask for by
name.

MAN: Mrwl . . . mrak . . . mrok . . .

CAT: Meow

CAT: Meow.

MAN: Meow! Why didn't you say so?

VO: Only Meow Mix tastes so good cats ask for it by
name.

Consumer Television
30 Seconds Campaign

411
Art Directors:
Ren Wicks
Alan Kupchick
Writers:
Jeff Gelberg
Alan Kupchick
Client:
Taco Bell
Director:
Victor Haboush
Production Co.:
Haboush Co.
Phil Marco Productions
Agency:
Grey/Los Angeles

412
Art Directors:
Ted Shaine
Ron Arnold
Writers:
Jay Taub
John Russo
Client:
Chemical Bank
Director:
Steve Horn
Production Co.:
Steve Horn Productions
Agency Producer:
Linda Tesa
Agency:
Della Femina, Travisano & Partners

413
Art Director:
Lee Clow
Writer:
Dave Butler
Client:
Olympia Brewing
Director:
Bob Hulme
Production Co.:
Raintree Productions Los Angeles
Agency Producer:
Richard O'Neill
Agency:
Chiat/Day-Los Angeles

414
Art Director:
Mark Shap
Writers:
Harvey Gabor
Brendan Kelley
Laurie Solomon
Client:
F&M Schaefer Brewing
Director:
Dominic Rossetti
Production Co.:
Rossetti Films
Agency Producer:
Geoffrey Mayo
Agency:
Ogilvy & Mather

411

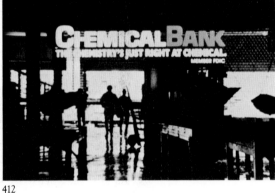

412

LORRIE: (Whispering) "Where can we get a great delicious taco?"

MARVIN: (Whispering) "I have no idea."

(SFX: BELL CRASHES THROUGH BOOK CASES)

MARVIN: "I have an idea: Taco Bell!"

LIBRARIAN: "Shhhh!"

(MUSIC: TACO BELL THEME UNDER)

ANNCR: "The Taco Supreme, Quality ground beef cooked in Taco Bell's own famous sauce, sour cream, lettuce, cheddar cheese and tomatoes. Fresh and specially seasoned to give it that Taco Bell taste you can't get anywhere else."

MARVIN: (Whispers) "Great idea, huh?"

LIBRARIAN: "Shhhh!"

ANNCR: "It's deliciously different. It's..."

SINGERS: *taca, taca, Taco Bell!*

(FADE UP CHEMICAL'S MUSIC THEME)

VO: The ocean, it has a chemistry all its own.

Snappers like the warm waters around Mexico.

Tuna the Pacific.

Lobsters the icy waters of Maine.

And they all wind up at the Fulton Fish Market where we have a Chemical Bank Branch nearby.

And a manager who'll stop by at 5:00 a.m.—just to say hello.

Or bend a few of the rules just to help out a little.

From Long Island Sound to the sounds of the Fulton Fish Market...
the chemistry's just right at Chemical.

(MUSIC FADES)

413

414

NIGHT MAN: Evenin'. I'm the night vatmaster here at the Olympia Brewery. I expect you've heard about the Artesian brewing water we use. Well...I seen 'em...the Artesians. They come up late at night. Little wet footprints all over. I let 'em be though. I figure...what those Artesians do for the taste of Oly...don't want to make 'em mad.

TICKET TAKER: All tickets...tickets

TONY: Ray, those tickets are *orange!*

RAY: Yeah.

TONY: Your Uncle Frank gave you orange tickets?

RAY: Yeah.

TONY: Orange...is ringside!

SINGERS: *Ah, ah sitting pretty*
Altogether in Schaefer City

(THEY BOTH REALIZE THEY ARE SITTING NEXT TO ROSEY GRIER)

TONY: Peanut, Rosey?

SINGERS: *Altogether in Schaefer City.*

TONY AND RAY: We are in Schaefer City!

Consumer Television
30 Seconds Campaign

415
Art Directors:
Paul Walter
Richard Crispo
Writers:
Richard Kelley
Laurie Brandalise
Client:
American Honda
Director:
Henry Sandbank
Production Co.:
Sandbank Films
Agency Producer:
Carolyn Roughsedge
Agency:
Needham, Harper & Steers
West

416
Art Director:
Michael Tesch
Writer:
Patrick Kelly
Client:
Federal Express
Director:
Joe Sedelmaier
Production Co.:
Sedelmaier Films/Chicago
Agency Producer:
Maureen Kearns
Agency:
Ally & Gargano

417
Art Directors:
Paul Jervis
Ron Becker
Writers:
Rick Meyer
Ken Baron
Harold Karp
Client:
Breakstone
Director:
Dick Leow
Production Co.:
Gomes-Loew
Agency Producer:
Jean Muchmore
Agency:
Geers Gross

418
Art Director:
Robert Reitzfeld
Writer:
David Altschiller
Client:
WYNY FM
Director:
Judd Maze
Production Co.:
Flickers
Agency Producers:
Robert Reitzfeld
David Altschiller
Agency:
Altschiller, Reitzfeld,
Jackson, Solin/NCK

415

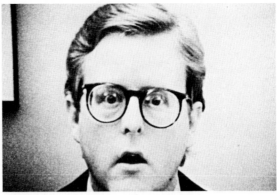

416

VO: Just imagine. If everyone drove a car like the Honda Civic DX, there'd be more room on the freeways.

There'd be more space to park.

And we'd probably all use less gas.

The Honda Civic DX. It could make life a lot simpler.

SINGERS: *Honda. We make it simple.*

(MUSIC UNDER AND THROUGHOUT)

ANNCR(VO): It's coming.
It's taking over in offices coast to coast.
It's...
THE PAPER BLOB
It's packed with important papers
that should move out of your office fast,
but can't get loose.
This is a job for Federal Express.
For as little as $19.00 we'll pick up
your important papers
and deliver them clear across the country overnight.
So you'll never have to worry
about the paper blob again.
Federal Express. When it absolutely positively
has to be there overnight.

417

418

VO: When it came to making great sour cream
only one person was as demanding as Sam Breakstone.

SAM: Mother!

MOM: Sam!

MOM: It's not thick enough, Sam.

SAM: Mm.

MOM: It needs more cream, Sam.

SAM: Mm.

VO: But if Sam and his mother hadn't been
so demanding...

MOM: I've done it again!

VO: ...Breakstone Sour Cream wouldn't be so good.

MOM: What a cute little doggie.

SAM: What a cute little doggie

(SFX: RADIO TUNER)

ANNCR: Everyday New York sings to WYNY.

(SFX: STEVIE WONDER'S "SUNSHINE" THROUGHOUT)

ANNCR: With WYNY radio you can sing to Fleetwood
Mac, Neil Diamond, The Commodores and Kenny
Rogers.

WYNY New York 97 FM, the radio station you can
sing to.

Consumer Television
30 Seconds Campaign

419
Art Director:
John Piccolo
Writer:
Marvin Honig
Client:
Citicorp
Director:
Bob Giraldi
Production Co.:
Bob Giraldi Productions
Agency Producer:
Steven Brind
Agency:
Doyle Dane Bernbach

420
Art Directors:
Roy Grace
Jack Mariucci
Writers:
Tom Yobbagy
Patty Volk
Client:
IBM Office Products Division
Directors:
Henry Sandbank
Michael Ulick
Production Cos.:
Sandbank Films
Michael Ulick Productions
Agency Producer:
Rosemary Barre
Agency:
Doyle Dane Bernbach

421
Art Director:
Steve Singer
Writer:
Nat Russo
Client:
Subaru
Director:
Tibor Hirsch
Production Co.:
THT Productions
Agency Producer:
Bob Nelson
Agency:
Levine, Huntley, Schmidt, Plapler & Beaver

422
Art Director:
Bert Steinhauser
Writer:
Diane Rothschild
Client:
Volkswagen
Director:
Bert Steinhauser
Production Co.:
Directors' Studio
Agency Producer:
Jim Debaros
Agency:
Doyle Dane Bernbach

419

420

HUSBAND: Where in the world are we? Now what's this place?

SHOPKEEPER: Welcome . . . to the last place on earth.

WIFE: Look at all this.

SHOPKEEPER: Like my Boutique? Cute.

HUSBAND: Yeah, we just have Travelers Checks.

SHOPKEEPER: Citicorp?

WIFE: Yes!

SHOPKEEPER: Love them!

WIFE: Imagine . . . Citicorp Travelers Checks are even accepted in the last place on earth.

HUSBAND: Our lucky day.

VO: Travel the world with us. Citicorp Travelers Checks.

(MUSIC UNDER AND THROUGHOUT)

VO: This is the idea behind the IBM Electronic 75 Typewriter . . .

to help secretaries be more productive automatically.

It has automatic retyping and revision.

Automatic centering and underlining.

Automatic erasing and column layout.

The IBM Electronic 75 Typewriter. It saves time. And whatever saves time is more productive— automatically.

BOY: Miss Jones, are these your gloves?

421

422

(MUSIC UNDER)

ANNCR(VO): In most commercials, the cars start up here. With some help from a helicopter.
But these babies from Subaru don't *need* help.
They can switch from front to four-wheel drive.
And for tougher going, they *keep* going...
...with a dual-range gear box.
Any cars would look good up there.
But America's largest choice of four-wheel drives...
...even look good *getting* up there.

(MUSIC UNDER AND THROUGHOUT)

INTERVIEWER: Ahh, a Volkswagen Rabbit Diesel

MAN: Aye, laddie. The best selling diesel in Europe.

INTERVIEWER: Why'd you buy yours?

MAN: Because I make twenty trips between Glasgow and Edinburgh every year.

And you have to think of economy.

INTERVIEWER: Twenty trips across Scotland! Even a rabbit must use a lot of fuel.

MAN: Aye, ... last year I had to buy two full tankfuls.

SINGERS: *Volkswagen does it again.*

Consumer Television
30 Seconds Campaign

423
Art Director:
Neil Leinwohl
Writer:
Stephen Fenton
Client:
Amtrak
Directors:
Dominick Rossetti
Jim Johnston
Production Cos.:
Rossetti Films
Jim Johnston Films
Agency Producer:
Gloria Gengo
Agency:
Needham, Harper & Steers

424
Art Director:
Lars Anderson
Writer:
Peter Levathes
Client:
Maxell
Directors:
Henry Sandbank
Steve Steigman
George Gomes
Production Cos.:
Sandbank Films
Steve Steigman
Gomes-Loew
Agency Producer:
Dane Johnson
Agency:
Scali, McCabe, Sloves

425
Art Director:
David Mitchell
Writers:
Mike Pettle
John Cleese
Client:
Sony
Director:
Robert Young
Production Co.:
Directors Precinct
Agency Producer:
Anne Alexander
Agency:
Benton & Bowles/London

426
Art Directors:
Anthony Angotti
Priscilla Croft
Allen Kay
Writers:
Tom Thomas
Debby Mattison
Allen Kay
Client:
Xerox
Directors:
Jeff Metzner
Dick Stone
Production Cos.:
Jeffrey Metzner
Stone/Clark
Perpetual Motion
Agency Producer:
Sydelle Rangell
Agency:
Needham, Harper & Steers

423

(MUSIC UNDER)

SINGERS:
There's something about a train that's magic
traveling near or far.
Seein' it all and havin' such fun
no matter who you are.
America is getting into training
more and more everyday.
America is getting into training,
training the Amtrak way.

424

(SFX: FOOTSTEPS)
BUTLER: The usual sir?
COOL GUY: Please.
ANNCR(VO): Even after 500 plays our high fidelity
tape...
(SFX: CLICK)
still delivers high fidelity.
(SFX: WAGNERIAN MUSIC BUILDS AND EXPLODES)
Maxell. It's worth it.

425

426

JOHN CLEESE: Look, those awfully nice Sony people have asked me to demonstrate the features of their amazing home video. Can't see why they think I can do it better than the machine, but here goes. It leaps from one programme you've recorded, to the next, at a touch.

(SFX: HOWLING WIND)

JOHN CLEESE(VO): And on to the next.

(SFX: FOOTBALL CROWD)

And the next. You can whizz through a recording without losing picture, so you can find your favourite bits, and savour them.

JOHN CLEESE: And here is a summary. Full remote control. 14 day timer lets you record when you're away...

MVO: Everything you want in home video. From those awfully nice Sony people.

JOHN CLEESE(VO): Who's a clever little Sony then?

JOHN CLEESE: (Ventriloquist) I am.

(SFX: MUSIC)

VO: Business has discovered a whole new problem.

(SFX: WOOSH)

MAN: (Under) Oh my.

VO: ... The flood of information.

MAN: Help! How do you use information instead of being inundated by it?

VO: You get the Xerox 860 information processor. It helps you manage words *and* numbers.

And, if you plug it into the Xerox information outlet, the 860 can share huge amounts of information with other office machines... through the Ethernet network. Giving every organization what it needs most. Better organization.

Consumer Television
30 Seconds Campaign

427
Art Director & Writer:
Gail Shaw
Client:
Planters CSR
Director:
David Smith
Production Co.:
Film Business/Australia
Agency Producer:
Helene Nicol
Agency:
**Schofield Sherbon
Baker Pty./Australia**

Consumer Television
10 Seconds Single

428
Art Director:
Bert Steinhauser
Writer:
Diane Rothschild
Client:
Volkswagen
Director:
Bert Steinhauser
Production Co.:
Directors' Studio
Agency Producer:
Jim Debaros
Agency:
Doyle Dane Bernbach

429
Art Director:
Jim Perretti
Writer:
Larry Cadman
Client:
Volvo
Directors:
**Jim Perretti
Richard Berke**
Production Co.:
The Movie House
Agency Producer:
Richard Berke
Agency:
Scali, McCabe, Sloves

427

JOHN CLEESE: Hello... third time lucky—well we
hope so anyway because Planters the Pretzel people
have threatened to disassociate themselves from these
commercials unless there's a dramatic improvement...
So I've written just the sort of commercial I'm pretty
sure Planters the pretzel people will really go
for—and here it is...

Take it away girls...

CHORUS: *Planters pretzels, Planters pretzels,*
Planters pretzels, Planters pretzels,
Planters pretzels, Planters pretzels,
Planters pretzels, Planters pretzels,

JOHN CLEESE: Amazing isn't it?—the simplest ideas
are nearly always the best.

428

429

(MUSIC UNDER AND THROUGHOUT)

INTERVIEWER: Wilt Chamberlain, what do you see in a Volkswagen Rabbit?

WILT: Me.

SINGERS: *Volkswagen does it again.*

VO: If you're thinking of buying a Mercedes wagon, buy a Volvo Diesel wagon and have enough left over for a Diesel sedan.

Consumer Television
10 Seconds Single

430
Art Director:
Jim Perretti
Writer:
Frank Fleizach
Client:
Volvo
Directors:
Jim Perretti
Richard Berke
Production Co.:
The Movie House
Agency Producer:
Richard Berke
Agency:
Scali, McCabe, Sloves

431
Art Director:
Jim Handloser
Writer:
Sharon Hartwick
Client:
Dribeck Importers
Director:
Tibor Hirsch
Production Co.:
THT Productions
Agency Producer:
Linda Tesa
Agency:
Della Femina, Travisano
& Partners

432
Art Director:
John Armistead
Writer:
Linda Chandler Frohman
Client:
Brentwood Savings
& Loan Association
Director:
Reid Miles
Production Co.:
Reid Miles Productions
Agency Producers:
John Armistead
Linda Chandler Frohman
Agency:
Abert, Newhoff & Burr
Los Angeles

433
Art Director:
Barry Vetere
Writer:
Patrick Kelly
Client:
Pentax
Director:
Tibor Hirsch
Production Co.:
THT Productions
Agency Producer:
Bertelle Selig
Agency:
Ally & Gargano

430

VO: Ever wonder why you're not seeing rebate ads from Volvo? Simple. When you build the right kind of car, you don't have to pay people to buy it.

431

VO: To get the best beer in the world, you have to speak German.

MAN: Beck's

VO: Beck's ·
The number one imported German beer.

Brentwood Savings
It's a nice place to visit your money.

PENTAX®

**FIRST WHERE IT MEANS
SOMETHING TO BE FIRST.**

432

433

GEORGE BURNS: With all the free sevices they give
me at Brentwood Savings you'd think I was...

(SFX: CLAP OF THUNDER, HEAVENLY CHOIR)

GEORGE BURNS: Brentwood Savings.
It's a nice place to visit your money.

(SFX: "HARPS" MUSIC FINALE)

(MUSIC UNDER)

ANNCR(VO): In Japan,
land of cameras...
one company has consistently made some of
the biggest innovations...

(SFX: CLICK)

and some of the smallest.
Pentax.

434
Art Director:
Michael Tesch
Writer:
Patrick Kelly
Client:
Federal Express
Director:
Joe Sedelmaier
Production Co.:
Sedelmaier Films/Chicago
Agency Producer:
Maureen Kearns
Agency:
Ally & Gargano

435
Art Director:
Dennis D'Amico
Writer:
Tom Messner
Client:
Pentax
Director:
Henry Sandbank
Production Co.:
Sandbank Films
Agency Producer:
Jerry Haynes
Agency:
Ally & Gargano

436
Art Director:
Robert Gage
Writer:
Jack Dillon
Client:
Polaroid
Director:
Robert Gage
Production Co.:
Directors' Studio
Agency Producer:
Jane Liepshutz
Agency:
Doyle Dane Bernbach

437
Art Director:
Roy Grace
Writer:
Tom Yobbagy
Client:
IBM Office Products Division
Director:
Henry Sandbank
Production Co.:
Sandbank Films
Agency Producer:
Rosemary Barre
Agency:
Doyle Dane Bernbach

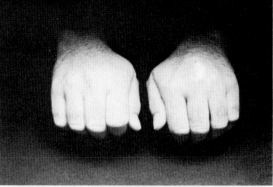

434

(SFX: SNORING)

ANNCR(VO): Federal Express is so easy to use, you can do it in your sleep.

GUY(OC): Helloooooooooo Federal.

435

ANNCR(VO): Which hand has the Pentax camera?

This one, of course.

This one has the lenses.

436

437

JIM: Time-Zero Supercolor film is a great new reason to buy a OneStep.

MARI: So is helping us starving actors.

JIM: That's embarrassing.

(FADE IN ON TWO GEORGE BURNS)

GEORGES: This is the original.
That's the copy.
With the IBM Series III Copier,
it's hard to tell which is which.
He's right.

Consumer Television
10 Seconds Single

438
Art Director:
Robert Gage
Writer:
Jack Dillon
Client:
Polaroid
Director:
Robert Gage
Production Co.:
Directors' Studio
Agency Producer:
Jane Liepshutz
Agency:
Doyle Dane Bernbach

439
Art Director:
James Scalfone
Writer:
Cynthia Beck
Client:
Blue Bonnet
Director:
Michael Ulick
Production Co.:
Michael Ulick Productions
Agency Producer:
Tom Dakin
Agency:
Doyle Dane Bernbach

440
Art Director:
Robert Gage
Writer:
Jack Dillon
Client:
Polaroid
Director:
Robert Gage
Production Co.:
Directors' Studio
Agency:
Jane Liepshutz
Agency:
Doyle Dane Bernbach

441
Art Director:
Priscilla Croft
Writer:
Debby Mattison
Client:
Frigidaire
Director:
Mark Story
Production Co.:
Bean/Kahn Films
Agency Producer:
Peter Cascone
Agency:
Needham, Harper & Steers

438

JIM: All Polaroid Prontos, OneSteps and SX-70's use new Time-Zero Supercolor.

MARI: Won't there be a shortage?

JIM: There better be!

439

VO: Whatever foods you love, Everything's better with creamy, delicious Blue Bonnet.

MICKEY & WILLIE: (Singing) *Everything's better with Blue Bonnet on it!*

440

441

JIM: It's more blessed to give than to receive the
Polaroid OneStep and Time-Zero Supercolor.

MARI: Somebody has to receive.

JIM: We make our living on the givers.

(SFX: MUSIC)

HE: In the past 15 years, I've had 3 cars...

SHE: 6 transmissions...

BOTH: And one refrigerator. A Frigidaire.

VO: Frigidaire.
Here today, here tomorrow.

Consumer Television
10 Seconds Single

442
Art Director:
Priscilla Croft
Writer:
Debby Mattison
Client:
Frigidaire
Director:
Mark Story
Production Co.:
Bean/Kahn Films
Agency Producer:
Peter Cascone
Agency:
Needham, Harper & Steers

443
Art Director:
Lars Anderson
Writer:
Peter Levathes
Client:
Maxell
Director:
Steve Steigman
Production Co.:
Steve Steigman
Agency Producer:
Dane Johnson
Agency:
Scali, McCabe, Sloves

444
Art Director:
Priscilla Croft
Writer:
Debby Mattison
Client:
Frigidaire
Director:
Mark Story
Production Co.:
Bean/Kahn Films
Agency Producer:
Peter Cascone
Agency:
Needham, Harper & Steers

445
Art Directors:
Stavros Cosmopulos
Tom Davis
Tom Simons
Writer:
Dan Brown
Client:
McDonalds
Director:
David Pool
Production Co.:
Mass Casting/Boston
Agency Producer:
David Pool
Agency:
Arnold & Company/Boston

442

(SFX: MUSIC)

MAN: In the past 15 years, I've had 7 sports cars, 14 sports car mechanics... and one refrigerator.
A Frigidaire.

VO: A Frigidaire.
Here today, here tomorrow.

443

VO: If there's a Maxell cassette tape in this car,

(SFX: WIND BLOWING)

and it doesn't work, we'll replace it.
Maxell. It's worth it.

444

445

(SFX: MUSIC)

WOMAN: In the past 15 years, I've had four or five husbands, 104 alimony checks... and one refrigerator. A Frigidaire.

VO: Frigidaire.
Here today, here tomorrow.

(SFX: CHICKENS CLUCKING AND MUSIC)

ANNCR: McDonald's new McChicken Sandwich. Watch for it.

Consumer Television
10 Seconds Campaign

446
Art Director:
Jim Handloser
Writer:
Sharon Hartwick
Client:
Dribeck Importers
Director:
Tibor Hirsch
Production Co.:
THT Productions
Agency Producer:
Linda Tesa
Agency:
Della Femina, Travisano & Partners

447
Art Director:
Priscilla Croft
Writer:
Debby Mattison
Client:
Frigidaire
Director:
Mark Story
Production Co.:
Bean/Kahn Films
Agency Producer:
Peter Cascone
Agency:
Needham, Harper & Steers

Public Service Television
60 Seconds Single

448
Art Director:
John Chepelsky
Writer:
Lindy Kravec
Client:
National Cambodia Crisis
Director:
John Pytka
Production Co.:
John Pytka Productions
Agency Producers:
Lindy Kravec
John Chepelsky
Walter Burek
Agency:
Ketchum MacLeod & Grove Pittsburgh

449
Art Director:
Ross Richins
Writers:
James Gartner
Nedra Sprouls
Ron Anderson
Client:
The Church of Jesus Christ of Latter-day Saints
Director:
Norman Griner
Production Co.:
Myers & Griner/Cuesta
Agency Producer:
James Gartner
Agency:
Bonneville Productions/Utah

446

VO: To get the best beer in the world, you have to speak German.

MAN: Beck's

VO: Beck's
The number one imported German beer.

447

(SFX: MUSIC)

WOMAN: In the past 15 years, I've had four or five husbands, 104 alimony checks... and one refrigerator. A Frigidaire.

VO: Frigidaire.
Here today, here tomorrow.

448

449

(MUSIC UNDER)

(CAMBODIAN WOMAN'S VOICE SPEAKING NATIVE LANGUAGE—FADES UNDER AS TRANSLATOR INTERPRETS)

ANNCR(VO): I have seen grown men too weak to walk. And nursing mothers with no milk for their babies. In Cambodia, the people have been broken by war, famine and disease.

CAMBODIAN BOY: I was 9 years old when they took my parents away...

ANNCR(VO): Children have been separated from their parents. Husbands from their wives. Some wait helplessly in refugee camps in Thailand... all in need of food and medicine.
Right now a nationwide effort is underway to help keep Cambodia from dying. Plese give. Just one dollar from you will buy 6 pounds of rice. Enough for 13 people for one day. Your dollar has never been worth so much.

CAMBODIAN MAN: A single cup of rice a day. It will help a man grow strong again...

ANNCR(VO): Please give today. In Cambodia, your dollar is priceless.

ANNCR: It isn't fair.

WOMAN: You're ugly. You're fat. And that's what I think in bed at night and I hate myself. That's when I'm loneliest. And being single, I really want to belong to someone. Sometimes I just whisper, "I love you" when there's no one there to say it to. Sometimes I just pretend there's someone else saying it to me too.

ANNCR: It just isn't fair.

WOMAN: But being lonely doesn't make me bad. Being lonely doesn't mean I have to hate myself. I'm learning to like myself more and more all the time. And I like me. I really do. But maybe that's why I feel lonely, because I am important.

ANNCR: It isn't fair. It's life. And sometimes it hurts. But it's not what life does to you, it's what you do with life.

From the Mormons. The Church of Jesus Christ of Latter-day Saints.

Public Service
Television
60 Seconds Single

450
Art Director:
John Byrnes
Writers:
Lou Di Joseph
Jim Murphy
Client:
United States Army
Director:
Neil Tardio
Production Co.:
Lovinger/Tardio/Melsky
Agency Producer:
Jim McMenemy
Agency:
N W Ayer

451
Art Director:
Joel Levinson
Writer:
Gary Barnum
Client:
United States Army
Director:
Lear Levin
Production Co.:
Lear Levin Productions
Agency Producer:
Jim McMenemy
Agency:
N W Ayer

452
Art Director:
Jon Fisher
Writer:
Jay Taub
Client:
American Heart Association
Director:
Jon Fisher
Production Co.:
George Gage Productions

453
Art Director & Writer:
Gail Shaw
Client:
Australian Govt. Advertising
Director:
John Clark
Production Co.:
Angela Cherry Prods.
Australia
Agency Producer:
Helene Nicol
Agency:
Schofield Sherbon
Baker Pty./Australia

450

451

ANNCR: Right now the one thing you want most is an opportunity.

SINGERS: *Be all that you can be*
Keep on reachin'
Keep on growin'
Be all that you can be
'Cause we need you in the
Army
There are feelings deep
Inside you
Feelings there's so much
More...

ANNCR: In today's Army, you'll grow, you'll learn, and you'll work with the technology of tomorrow.

SINGERS: *Be all that you can be*
'Cause we need you in the
Army.

(MUSIC UP)

SINGERS: *There's a hungry kind of*
Feeling
And every day it grows.

SERGEANT: Go. go...

SINGERS: *You know there's so much more*
To you than anybody knows
The world outside keeps
Changing and you can't fall behind.
You're stretchin' out now day
By day.
'Cause you've got a future to find.
Be all that you can be
Keep on reachin'
Keep on growin'

ANNCR: In the Army we do more before nine a.m. than most pepole do all day.

SINGERS: *Be all that you can be.*

SOLDIER: Hey, First Sergeant, Good Morning.

SINGERS: *'Cause we need you in the Army.*

452 453

BUSINESSMAN: (On telephone) Honey, I can't help it . . . No, no, I won't be home late . . . Probably about 10. I dunno. Uh, wait, hold on, hold on . . .

SECRETARY: Would you sign this please?

BUSINESSMAN: I'll sign it later. Look, Virginia, it's getting late. Why don't you go home. I'll lock up.

SECRETARY: Thanks, Mr. C, see ya tomorrow.

BUSINESSMAN: Yeah, see ya in the morning. (Back to the phone) Honey, it's the only way I can survive in this business. OK OK look I'll talk to you later. Alright. OK Bye. (Hangs up)
(Heart attack begins)

VO: Every year, 4,000 American businessmen suddenly realize they're in no shape to climb the corporate ladder. Your Heart Association urges you to stop smoking and see your doctor for a sensible diet and exercise program. We want you to be as concerned about staying alive as you are about earning a living.

(SFX: RESTAURANT SOUNDS AND FADE UNDER)

TREVOR: I thought Graham was joining us?

MAX: No, he decided to go for a run instead . . . (Chortling)

TREVOR: Hahaha . . . kill himself if he's not careful . . .

MAX: Decided what you're having?

TREVOR: Ah . . . tossing up between the obesity and the high blood pressure . . .

MAX: What about the coronary?

TREVOR: No . . . I think not . . . Bill had that last week and he didn't like it at all.

MAX: Of course there's always the chronic indigestion . . . or the flatulence . . .

TREVOR: Mmmm . . . I was thinking of saving that for later . . .

(FADE VOICES UNDER)

VO: If you could try eating a little less and drinking a little less your body . . . and you . . . would feel a whole lot better. Test your health and fitness in this Commonwealth Department of Health booklet called "Help yourself". It's at your local chemist's now.

TREVOR: We can stop off on the way back to the office and I'll shout you an ulcer.

Public Service Television 30 Seconds Single

454
Art Director:
Fred Hindel
Writer:
Robert Aurin
Client:
U.S. Dept. of Health & Human Services
Production Co.:
Cooper, Dennis & Hirsch
Agency:
Grey-North/Chicago

455
Art Director:
Allen Kay
Writer:
Lois Korey
Client:
Ad Council
Director:
Mark Story
Production Co.:
Bean/Kahn Films
Agency Producer:
Sydelle Rangell
Agency:
Needham, Harper & Steers

456
Art Director:
Anthony Angotti
Writer:
Tom Thomas
Client:
U.S.D.A.
Director:
Tony Petrocelli
Production Co.:
Petrocelli Associates
Agency Producer:
Gloria Gengo
Agency:
Needham, Harper & Steers

457
Art Director:
Chuck Clemens
Writer:
Tom Overman
Client:
Southern Cooperative for Fire Prevention
Director:
Chuck Clemens
Agency Producer:
Chuck Clemens
Agency:
Liller Neal Weltin/Atlanta

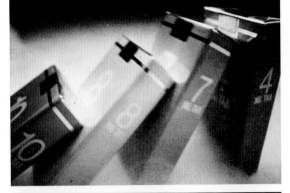

454

ANNCR(VO): You may be among the millions of smokers who have decided to knock down some of the dangers of smoking by knocking down the amounts of tar and nicotine you take in. You're choosing cigarettes by the numbers—not the name. But be careful playing the numbers game—don't start smoking more cigarettes. Smoke the same number—or less. After a while, you may find smoking is something you can—live without.

We'd like to help.
Write: Smoker's Health Book
Public Health Service
Rockville, Maryland.

455

(SFX: BRASSY MUSIC)

VO: We're at the Victory Celebration. It was a close election but the results are now final.

MAN: They didn't win. I don't believe it. They didn't win. I thought for sure they were going to win. All my friends said *they* were going to vote for them. So I didn't bother to vote. Maybe my friends didn't bother to vote either.

VO: Vote. It might be worth the bother.

456

457

WOMAN: Kids. You try to get them to eat the right things, but what can you do? When it comes to snacks, they don't listen. I *tell* them to eat fruit. But look, I can't be with them 24 hours a day. Once they go out that door, forget it. I mean, I didn't listen when I was a kid, and you can't expect...
(Under)

ANNCR: Kids *do* listen. But they pay much closer attention to what you *do* than what you *say*. Please, watch how you snack. Because our kids are watching too.

(MUSIC UNDER)

ANNCR: A most dangerous weapon. Last year it accounted for millions of dollars of damage in the rural South alone. With careless use, it can even backfire on you.

(SFX: MATCH STRIKES)

Controlling a weapon like this makes sense. That's why we ask you to give.

(SFX: MATCH BLOWN OUT)

Not money—give a *call* to your local forestry agent before you burn anything outside. The Southern forest...will you give to save it?

Corporate Television
60 Seconds Single

458
Art Director:
Bob Cox
Writer:
Paul Margulies
Client:
Ford
Director:
Bob Gaffney
Production Co.:
Bob Gaffney Productions
Agency Producer:
Robin Dobson
Agency:
Wells, Rich, Greene

459
Art Director:
Robert Tucker
Writer:
David Reider
Client:
IBM Corporate
Director:
Tibor Hirsch
Production Co.:
THT Productions
Agency Producer:
Ellyn Epstein
Agency:
Doyle Dane Bernbach

460
Art Director:
Bob Gula
Writer:
Bob Montell
Client:
General Electric
Director:
Peter Miranda
Production Co.:
May Day Productions
Agency Producer:
George Bragg
Agency:
BBDO

Corporate Television
30 Seconds Single

461
Art Directors:
Richard Paynter
John Clapps
Writers:
Leland Rosemond
Sueanne Peacock
Client:
First National State Bank
Director:
R.O. Blechman
Production Co.:
The Ink Tank
Agency Producer:
Knight Russell
Agency:
Bozell & Jacobs/New Jersey

458

VO: In Ireland, where the roads are small and the price of gas is large, Ford is number one in sales.

We're also number one in Britain.

And in Norway.

And in Germany—where high-technology and crafts-manship are a matter of pride, our smallest Ford sells more than any other car in its class.

Today, when America needs high-quality fuel-efficient cars, the Incredible World of Ford is working to meet that need.

Building a new generation of small cars with World Class Technology—right here in America.

CHORUS: *If you could see tomorrow...*

VO: It's happening right now...

CHORUS: *The way it looks to us today...*

VO: Building cars right here.

CHORUS: *You'd say incredible...*

VO: Competing with anything in their class.

CHORUS: *Ford that's incredible...*

VO: You'll see them this fall.

CHORUS: *Ford that's incredible.*

459

(MUSIC THROUGHOUT AND UNDER)

VO: This is Kanji. An important part of the Japanese written language. There are thousands of Kanji characters, compared with the 26 in our alphabet. You can imagine how difficult it must be to type, or to print computer data, in Kanji. After many years of work, IBM successfully created a computer system, that can use Kanji, as well as other symbols, and print them with a remarkable ink-jet printer that sprays tiny droplets of ink. IBM developed the basic technology for the ink-jet printer here in the United States.

And—with this special keyboard, information can be entered into a computer, to be processed entirely in Japanese. IBM innovations like these not only help us compete overseas: they help improve productivity right here at home.

IBM. Helping put information to work for people.

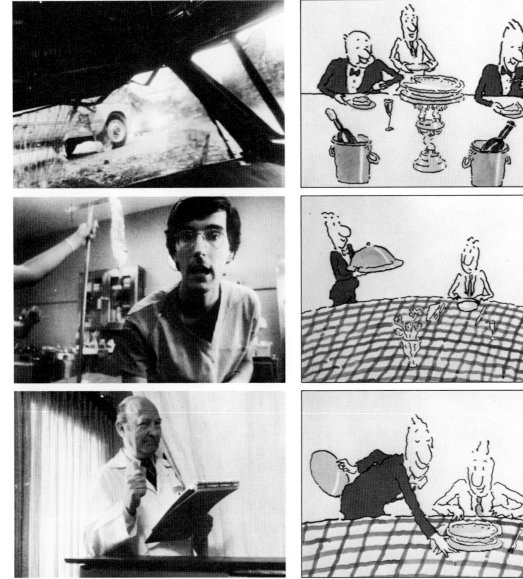

460

461

ANNCR(VO): It can happen without warning.

Suddenly, your very life is in the hands of strangers.

But every year, your chances of surviving an accident get better.

One of the reasons is modern GE technology.

Special General Electric radio equipment not only transmits voice, but makes it possible for the hospital to read your vital signs. Right from the ambulance.

GE has three different ways to take pictures inside the body. With sound waves. With computer scanning. And with modern X-ray machines that take incredibly sharp, clear pictures.

And GE micro-electronics makes possible advanced patient monitoring systems so the staff can closely watch you till you're out of danger.

Today, more and more people are going home from the hospital. And that's no accident.

Progress for people from General Electric.

VO: Some New Jersey businesses like to sit at the table with big New York banks.

When times get tough, these banks just might save the biggest piece of the pie for their big N.Y. customers.

If *you* do business in New Jersey, sit down with the bank whose first concern *is* New Jersey.

First National State.

We'll never leave you eating humble pie.

First National State. Our first concern is New Jersey. And those who do business here.

Corporate Television
30 Seconds Single

462
Art Director:
Mike Withers
Writer:
Barry Greenspon
Client:
Getty Refining & Marketing
Director:
Joe Sedelmaier
Production Co.:
Sedelmaier Films/Chicago
Agency Producer:
Frank DiSalvo
Agency:
**Calet, Hirsch, Kurnit
& Spector**

463
Art Director:
Paul Singer
Writer:
Ken Majka
Client:
King-Seeley Thermos
Director:
Bob Giraldi
Production Co.:
Bob Giraldi Productions
Agency Producer:
Frank DiSalvo
Agency:
**Calet, Hirsch, Kurnit
& Spector**

Corporate Television
Any Length Campaign

464
Art Director:
Bob Cox
Writer:
Paul Margulies
Client:
Ford
Director:
Bob Gaffney
Production Co.:
Bob Gaffney Productions
Agency Producer:
Robin Dobson
Agency:
Wells, Rich, Greene

465
Art Directors:
**John Clapps
Richard Paynter**
Writers:
**Leland Rosemond
Sueanne Peacock**
Client:
First National State Bank
Director:
R.O. Blechman
Production Co.:
The Ink Tank
Agency Producer:
Knight Russell
Agency:
Bozell & Jacobs/New Jersey

462

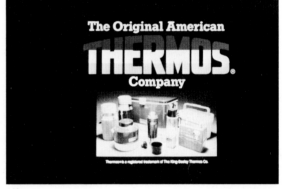

463

ANNCR(VO): People are saving gasoline by car pooling. But not the Gas Guzzler. While others do all their shopping in one trip, he doesn't.

DEALER: Sir, tires are low. I'll put some air in and you'll get better gas mileage.

MR. GUZZLER: Next time.

ANNCR(VO): Excessive air conditioning wastes gasoline, too.

(MUSIC UP)

If we saved a gallon of gasoline a week per car, we'd reduce oil imports over 10%. That's why Getty Oil wishes the Gas Guzzler would reform. We'd all get more miles for our money.

ANNCR(VO): The year is 1909. The place: the icy wastes of the North Pole. Admiral Robert Peary has brought with him only what he needs for survival. Food, a compass...

and a Thermos brand vacuum bottle.

Peary knew that in cold so cruel it snapped metal like matchsticks, there was no better way to keep hot things hot. And there still isn't.

The Original American Thermos Company.

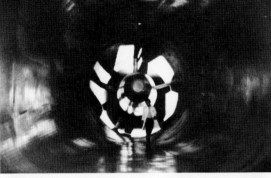

464

465

VO: When Ford started building a new generation of small, fuel-efficient cars we called on the World. The Incredible World of Ford.

BRITISH OPERATOR: Ford Motor Company, Good Morning...Mr. Howard...

GERMAN OPERATOR: Ford, Koeln, Good Day... Mr. Jung...

AMERICAN OPERATOR: Mr. Dobson, we have Italy on the line...

VO: For over 50 years Ford has been building small fuel-efficient cars in Europe. Today, when America needs high quality fuel-efficient cars, the Incredible World of Ford is working to meet that need. Building a new generation of small cars, with World Class Technology—right here in America.

CHORUS: *If you could see tomorrow...*

VO: It's happening right now.

CHORUS: *The way it looks to us today...*

VO: Building cars right here
Competing with anything in their class.

CHORUS: *Ford that's incredible...*

VO: You'll see them this fall.

CHORUS: *Ford that's incredible*

VO: Some New Jersey businesses like to sit at the table with big New York banks.

When times get tough, these banks just might save the biggest piece of the pie for their big N.Y. customers.

If *you* do business in New Jersey, sit down with the bank whose first concern *is* New Jersey.

First National State.

We'll never leave you eating humble pie.

First National State. Our first concern is New Jersey. And those who do business here.

One Club Members

Donald Aaronson
Michael Abadi
Ron Alberty
Robin Albin
Richard Allen
Eileen Alleyne
David Altschiller
Jim D. Anderson
Jack Anesh
Kathy Angotti
Leon Antman
Arnie Arlow
Deborah Armstrong
George Armstrong
Bernard Aronson
Jeffrey L. Atlas
Neal Avener
Ellen Azorin
Cathy Bangel
Mel Barlin
Cheryl Baron
Leo Baron
Janeann Bean
Allan Beaver
Bonni Benstock
William Bernbach
Raymond Bethea
Paul Blade
Laurie Bleier
Shelley Sara Block
Richard K. Bloom
Francesca Blumenthal
George R. Bonner
Virginia Bonofiglio
James Bosha
Kendall J. Bradley
Ed Brodsky
Scott Bronfman
Devaughn Brown
Lonnie Brown
Richard Brown
Gina Bruce
Melinda Bruno
John Bucalo
Felix Burgos
Nelsena Burt
Ed Butler
Larry Cadman
Neil Calet
Cathie Campbell
David Cantor
John Caples
Bob Carducci
David Carlin
Scott Carlton
Earl Carter
R. Michael Chapell

David Chapman
Elaine Charney
Steven Chazanow
Lauren Cherry
Thomas Chiarello
Marcia Christ
Lisa L. Chu
Jo-ann Cirrincione
Joseph A. Civisca
Dave Clark
Peter Clarke
Andrew Cohen
Ilene A. Cohn
Roger Colatorti
Kay A. Colmar
Maria Compton
Uriah Franklin Corkrum
Bob Costanza
Mindy Costanza
Constantin Cotzias
George Courides
Robert Cramer
Marilyn Cull
Sharon Curcio
Elizabeth Cutler
James M. Dale
Boris Damast
Rebecca Dancour
Elizabeth L. Daniell
Russell D'Anna
Wesley Davidson
Glenn Davis
Beth DeFuria
Barbara Del Sorbo
Jerry Della Femina
Gregory Dellamonica
David Demarest
Deyna Detroit
Robert V. Devol
Brian Dillon
Bob Dion
Neil Drossman
Michael R. Duclos
Lorraine C. Duffy
Paula Dunn
Laurence Dunst
Arthur Einstein
Bernadette F. Elias
Patricia A. Ellis
David C. Essertier
Sherie Fas
Leo Fassler
Oksana Fedorenko
Fritz Feik
Steve Feldman
Ralph Fernandez
Richard Ferrante

Jerry Fields
Stan Fields
Lilly Filipow
Carole Anne Fine
Len Fink
Toby Finneman
Camille Focarino
Mel Freedman
Kent Freitag
Jeffrey Frey
Susan Friedman
Jeff Furman
Michael D. Gaffney
Karen Gallo
Lorraine Garnett
Judith Gee
Rose Geller
Joe Genova
Frank Ginsburg
Sharon Glazer
Irwin Goldberg
Linda E. Goldman
Debbie Goldstein
Milt Gossett
Alison Gragnano
Betty Green
Steve Green
Irma Greenfeld
Barbara Greer
Peggy Gregerson
Dick Grider
Maria Grieco
John J. Griffin
Jim Hallowes
Alan Halpern
Maxine Hamburg
Jerome A. Handman
Carla Hardaway
Russ Harris
Sharon Hartwick
Nancy Hauptman
Roy Herbert
Sharon Hewitt
Joan Orlian Hillman
Peter Hirsch
Seth Hochberg
Bruce Hopman
William Horvath
Douglas W. Houston
Graham Hubbel
Mike Hughes
Linda Huss
Patricia Hutt
Stuart Hyatt
Robert Imbrosci, Jr.
Bennett Inkeles
Dorie Iwata

Craig R. Jackson
Richard Jackson
Wendy Jackson
Fifi Jacobs
Corrin Jacobsen
Steven Janovici
Roberta Jaret
Bob Jefferson
JoEllen Johns
Jean Wesche Johnson
Caroline Jones
Jean R. Joslin
Barnaby Kalan
Despina Kaminis
Marshall Karp
Martin Kaufman
Kay Kavanagh
Louise Kittel
M. Helen Klein
Murray Klein
Gene Kong
Lois Korey
Haruo Koriyama
Michael Kosewilt
Tom Kostro
Judy Kozuch
Steven Krammer
Sheldon J. Kravitz
George Kurten
Perrin Lam
Lucille Landini
Andrew J. Langer
Anthony E. LaPetri
Mary Wells Lawrence
Robert Leonard
Paul Lepelletier
Robert Levenson
Barry Z. Levine
Evelyn Lief
Sondra Lifschitz
Jeff Linder
Claire O. Lissance
Tom Little
Angela Locascio
David Lowenbein
Cecile T. Lozano
Peter Lubalin
Ted Luciani
Chuck Lustig
Janet R. Lyons
Tony Macchia
Georgia Macris
Elisabeth Mansfield
Andy Marber
Celeste Mari
Jack Mariucci
Joyce P. Marshall

David Martin

Arthur Cerf Mayer

Mary Means

Mario G. Messina

Lou Miano

Spencer Michlin

S. Michael Minard

Jonathan L. Mindell

Ivy Mindlin

Mary E. Moore

Rafael Morales

Linda Morgenstern

James R. Morrissey

Syl M. Morrone

Yonathan Dov Mozeson

Norman Muchnick

Jill Murray

Kent L. Murray

Ed McCabe

Ruth L. McCarthy

George McCathern

Michael McCray

Mary K. McMahon

Susan McTichecchia

Barbara Najarian

Veronica Nash

Thomas Nathan

Irwin Novick

Bill Oberlander

Dick O'Brien

David Ogilvy

Steve Ohman

Robert M. Oksner

Curvin O'Rielly

Rowan O'Riley

Maxine Paetro

Gerard Pampalone

Thomas Pastore

Don Patla

Stanley Pearlman

Richard Pels

Ellen Perless

Bob Phillips

Peter Phillips

Constantine Pitsikoulis

Ann Wright Pitts

Michael Pitts

Larry Plapler

Amy Harris Pollack

Mindy Pollack

Shirley Polykoff

Joseph Pompeo

Faith Popcorn

Peggy Pulcini

Elissa Querzé

Richard Raboy

June Rachelson

Richard Radke

Bob Ralske

Jim Raniere

Neil Raphan

Richard Rathbun

Ted Regan, Jr.

Michael T. Reid

Anne Reilly

Bob Reitzfeld

Robert Resnick

Ruthann M. Richert

Jean Robaire

Eric Robespierre

Phyllis Robinson

Geoffrey B. Roche

Peter Rodgers

Karen L. Rogers

Leland Rosemond

Michael Rosen

Ron Rosenfeld

Susan Rossiello

Janet Rothstein

John Russo

Antoinette Sacchetti

Harry Sandler

David Saslaw

Nina Scerbo

Susan Schermer

Jennifer Schiffman

Loretta M. Schurr

Mike Schwabenland

Aron J. Schwartz

Ron Seichrist

Ray Seide

Joan Seidman

Charles Sforza

Lorraine Shachnow

Ted Shaine

Marylin Shakofsky

William Shea

Ivan Sherman

Charlotte Sherwood

Brett Shevack

Jamie Shevell

Paul Shields

Virgil Cox Shutze

John Siddall

John Richard Sigler

Don Silberstein

Jonathan Sills

Marjorie Silver

Karen L. Simon

Leonard Sirowitz

Jo Smith

Raymond Smith

Darrol Solin

Martin Solow

Ron Spiegel

Helayne Spivak

Leon Sterling

Lynn Stiles

Debora L. Stone

Scott Stooker

Richard Story

Ira Sturtevant

Martin Suarez

Abie Sussman

Milton Sutton

Daniel Swanson

Leslie Sweet

Katalin Szule

Norman Tanen

Donna Tedesco

Judith Teller

Douglas Thompson

Jessie Tirsch

Cynthia Tocman

Peggy F. Tomarkin

Holly Tooker

David Tourin

Ron Travisano

Anthony Tsang Yee

Matthew Twomey

Ben Urman

Rudolph Valenti

Mary Vanderwoude

Angel Vasquez

Larry Vine

Gloria Viseltear

Ned Viseltear

Larry Volpi

Tom Wai-Shek

Judy Wald

Marvin Waldman

Don Walley

Pam Walters

Jessica Warren

John Warriner

Thomas Weber

Riva B. Weinstein

Kelly Welles

Jenny Wetmore

David S. Wheeler

Diane Whitehead

Bob Whitworth

Richard Wilde

C. Richard Williams

Kurt Willinger

Bruce Wilmoth

Lloyd Wolfe

Ed Wrenn

Elizabeth Wynn

Mark Yustein

Index

Art Directors & Designers

Writers

Artists

Photographers

Agencies

Clients

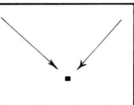
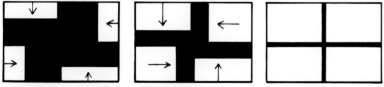

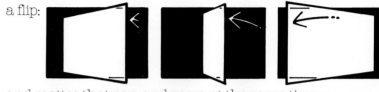
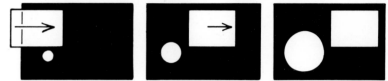
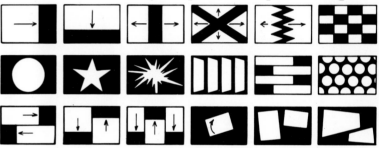

Some people have said to me
that Authenticolor is too big.
They prefer to use a lot of small labs.
One for this, one for that.
This from guys at little places like JWT!
Jeez!

DYE TRANSFERS-
12 day men, 8 night owls

DUPES & PHOTO-COMPS-
4 men, 2 ladies

CHROME RETOUCHERS & STRIPPERS-
19

PRINT RETOUCHING-
(Studio One) 20

"C" PRINTS & CIBA-
16 day men, 7 night owls

SLIDES & PHOTOGRAPHY-
6 day, 2 night

Each client has his own lab-trained Rep. That's big? That's bad?
You can get the whole shootin' match with one phone number.
What's the decision, JUDGE?

AUTHENTICOLOR

227 East 45th Street, New York, New York 10017 Telephone 212-867-7905

THE RETOUCHER'S

AFTER 500 PLAYS OUR HIGH FIDELITY TAPE STILL DELIVERS HIGH FIDELITY.

If your old favorites don't sound as good as they used to, the problem could be your recording tape.

Some tapes show their age more than others. And when a tape ages prematurely, the music on it does too.

What can happen is, the oxide particles that are bound onto tape loosen and fall off, taking some of your music with them.

At Maxell, we've developed a binding process that helps to prevent this. When oxide particles are bound onto our tape, they stay put. And so does your music.

So even after a Maxell recording is 500 plays old, you'll swear it's not a play over five.

maxell

IT'S WORTH IT.

SPANO/ROCCANOVA. THE QUALITY OF OUR WORK IS
SPANO/ROCCANOVA RETOUCHING, INC.   16 WEST

ONE SHOW AWARDS.

RETOUCHING OTHER STUDIOS OUT OF THE PICTURE.

46 STREET   NEW YORK, N.Y. 10036   212 840-7450

PUSH PIN STUDIOS
DESIGNED THIS BOOK.

IN ADDITION TO
PUBLICATION DESIGN
WE OFFER:

ADVERTISING DESIGN
ILLUSTRATION
FILM GRAPHICS & ANIMATION
ENVIRONMENTAL DESIGN
PHOTOGRAPHY FOR PRINT & TV
GRAPHIC DESIGN
CORPORATE COMMUNICATIONS
AUDIO VISUAL PRESENTATIONS
PACKAGING

CHRISTOPH BLUMRICH
SEYMOUR CHWAST
BILL AND STEVE DOLCE
ROGER FERRITER
RICHARD MANTEL
SARAH MOON
EMANUEL SCHONGUT
ELWOOD H. SMITH
STANISLAW ZAGORSKI
ROCHELLE ZABARKES

PHYLLIS RICH FLOOD
ILSE LEBRECHT
REPRESENTATIVES
NEW YORK

EVELYNE MENASCE
TEL: 624.17.27 OR 624.71.55
REPRESENTATIVE
PARIS

PUSH PIN STUDIOS
67 IRVING PLACE
NEW YORK, NY 10003
(212) 674-8080

PUSH PIN
MADE ME.

HF
5816
.05
1982

The One show

Harry A. B.
Gertrude C. **SHAPIRO LIBRARY**

New Hampshire College

2500 North River Road

Manchester, NH 03104

DEMCO

Harry A. B.
Gertrude C. **SHAPIRO LIBRARY**

New Hampshire College
2500 North River Road
Manchester, NH   03104